says who?

says who?

A Kinder, *Funner*
Usage Guide for Everyone
Who Cares About Words

Anne Curzan, Ph.D.

crown
new york

Published in the United States by Crown, an imprint of the Crown
Publishing Group, a division of Penguin Random House LLC, New York.

CROWN and the Crown colophon are registered trademarks of
Penguin Random House LLC.

LIBRARY OF CONGRESS CATALOGING-IN-PUBLICATION DATA
Names: Curzan, Anne, author.
Title: Says who? : a kinder, funner usage guide for everyone
who cares about words / by Anne Curzan.
Description: New York : Crown, 2024. |
Includes bibliographical references and index. |
Identifiers: LCCN 2023048686 (print) | LCCN 2023048687 (ebook) |
ISBN 9780593444092 (hardcover ; acid-free paper) |
ISBN 9780593444108 (ebook)
Subjects: LCSH: English language—Usage | English language—Grammar.
Classification: LCC PE1460 .C87 2024 (print) | LCC PE1460 (ebook) |
DDC 428—dc23/eng/20231204
LC record available at https://lccn.loc.gov/2023048686
LC ebook record available at https://lccn.loc.gov/2023048687

Printed in the United States of America on acid-free paper

crownpublishing.com

2 4 6 8 9 7 5 3

Editor: Madhulika Sikka · Editorial assistant: Fariza Hawke ·
Production editor: Loren Noveck · Production manager: Erin Korenko ·
Managing editors: Allison Fox and Sally Franklin · Copy editor: Michelle
Daniel · Proofreader: Deborah Bader · Indexer: Ina Gravitz ·
Publicist: Jack Meyer · Marketer: Melissa Esner

contents

introduction

The wedding was at a swanky hotel in Boston, and I was early. I picked up my table card and was milling about before the ceremony in a little black dress and higher heels than I can mill about in comfortably. Unable to find anyone I knew nearby, I introduced myself to a friendly-looking couple about my age with a ten-year-old boy who was not-so-subtly trying to loosen his necktie. After exchanging pleasantries, the mother and I turned to questions about what we each did professionally. She worked as an editor, and when she learned that I study the history of the English language and that I was writing a usage guide, her face lit up. "Oh, you're my new best friend!" she exclaimed. "I have so many questions for you. We could talk for hours!"

It's a well-kept secret that being a grammar geek can occasionally be good for your social life.

My new best friend went on, "Okay, let's start with *impact* as a verb. I can't stand that! What do you think?"

I paused, knowing that the conversation was about to get dicey. "Listen," I replied, "I get it. My pet peeve is the adjective *impactful*—it sounds like nails on a chalkboard to me. But, honestly, I think we're both going to have to stand down. *Impact is* a verb and there's nothing grammatically wrong with *impactful*. And, clearly, lots of other people think these words are useful."

I tell this story to highlight that almost all of us notice things in the English language that we wish, well, *weren't* in the English language. There are some peeves that are widely shared, such as *impact* as a verb to mean 'affect,' and there are others that seem to be idiosyncratic: For example, I regularly get emails from an astute language observer who is concerned about the spread of the preposition *toward* into expressions such as *dismissive toward* and *express gratitude toward*. I hadn't noticed this linguistic phenomenon until he pointed it out—and, for what it's worth, I have no strong feelings about it.

As far as I can tell, it is human nature to notice language, both consciously and unconsciously. We make a mental note of some of the new words and new bits of grammar that we hear and see around us, exactly because they are novel. And when we travel to new regions and/or meet new people, we can't help but observe some of the differences we hear in the language. Some of us may notice when speakers don't follow a so-called rule that we learned from a trusted language authority. I'm all for this kind of noticing: It shows our fundamental curiosity about how language works—how it varies from speaker to speaker and how it changes over time.

A key question for all of us then to consider is what we do with our observations. Do we feel compelled to judge that new word or usage as illegitimate? Or do we congratulate ourselves on spotting a new word or bit of grammar? Should we jump in and correct someone when we think they made a grammatical mistake? Or should we stand back and admire how language changes and evolves right before our eyes?

If you care about words—like I do and, as someone who picked up this book, you do—you probably have an inner grammando. The new word *grammando* was introduced in March 2012 in Lizzie Skurnick's feature "That Should Be a Word" in *The New York Times Magazine*. Here's her definition:

Grammando: (Gruh-MAN-doh), n., adj. 1. One who constantly corrects others' linguistic mistakes. "Cowed by his grammando wife, Arthur finally ceased saying 'irregardless.'"

Clever and evocative, the word *grammando* strikes me as an excellent alternative to both *grammar stickler* and *grammar Nazi*. If we're going to talk about Nazis, let's talk about Nazis. If we're going to talk about people who correct other people's grammar, let's talk about grammandos (even though the word is not yet accepted by the spellchecker that is checking my spelling as I write this).

There's another new word—*wordie*—that captures the alternative to being a grammando. Added to the *Merriam-Webster Dictionary* in 2018, *wordie* describes someone who delights in language's shifting landscape. Wordies know the language rules and where they come from, and then they make informed calls about whether or not to follow the rule in a given context. Wordies are the skilled bird-watchers of language, taking pleasure in observing how different speakers creatively deploy the language and how language is changing.

Given that you've chosen to read a usage book with the word *funner* in the title, you almost certainly have an inner wordie who lives alongside your inner grammando. Welcome to my world! When I notice a new species in the language out in the wild (metaphorically speaking) and have an urge to stamp it out—that's my inner grammando talking. When I delight in learning from young people about the rules of texting and new slang, my inner wordie has the upper hand.

We all have our language peeves—those bits of language that grate on our nerves and that make us want to pull out a red pen while reading or stop someone midsentence to go grammando on them. (Yes, *them*—see chapter 18 for an explanation of how *they* can be singular.) And the question at any one of these peevey moments is whether to let our inner grammando say anything or let our inner wordie carry the day. This book will help you sort out when your inner grammando might have useful guidance and when your inner wordie should override concerns that something's "wrong." Believe me, I have had lots of practice.

My mother was a grammando when I was growing up. I was taught to say "This is she speaking" on the phone when someone called for me, and it was certainly "He is shorter than I," not "He is shorter than me." You are well, not good, and you drive slowly, not slow. I spent many an evening at the kitchen table nervously watching my mother, a trained editor, poring over my school papers and marking up grammatical missteps. I am to this day a meticulous copy editor, noticing every comma and inconsistency in usage.

As my sisters and I got older, this attention to grammar became more endearing than frightening, and one of our favorite family stories involves a moment when my mother's inner grammando got the better of her at, of all places, a wedding. My older sister's wedding, in fact. It was the rehearsal dinner, and, in the middle of her toast, my younger sister let slip out of her mouth the phrase "for my husband and I." From the back of the room, my mother interjected, "And me!"

We all laughed, and I've gotten a lot of mileage out of this story in my career as a linguist. But this kind of public grammar policing can be cringeworthy. And silencing. Think about a moment when you had your language corrected in front of other people and how that felt. Or even a moment when someone pointed out something about your language such that you became self-conscious about it. In my second year of graduate school, I was studying regional variation in American dialects, and I learned about what linguists call "positive *anymore*": the use of *anymore* in a positive declarative to mean 'nowadays.' As an East Coaster, I don't do this; I use *anymore* only in a negative declarative such as "I don't eat red meat anymore." Shortly after reading about this largely Midwestern construction, I was talking to a triathlete friend about how he could find everything he needed at the local superstore, and he said, "They sell energy bars there anymore."

I perked right up and exclaimed, "You're a positive *anymore* speaker!"

He looked like a deer caught in the headlights, suddenly unsure how to continue talking with a person who seemed to be listening more to his word choice than to what he was saying. Despite my obvious enthusiasm for how he spoke, the conversation ended quickly and awkwardly.

I learned an important lesson about the power of grammatical knowledge from that conversation. And I wasn't even going grammando on him! I was excited to hear this novel dialect feature (that is, novel to me) out "in the wild," and I didn't mean to make him feel uncomfortable about his language. But I had. Language is deeply personal and fundamentally social. We use it to express ourselves and connect with others—and to push them away. Our language says a lot about who we are and where we come from, so when we point out something about other people's language, it is almost impossible for the comment not to feel personal.

It's not that we should never alert someone to a potential misstep in English usage. But compare a teacher correcting a student in front of the entire class to what a graduate school colleague did for me. This is embarrassing to remember now, but my first semester in grad school, I had the stress in the word *rhetoric* in the wrong place. I'm not sure how I got through college without becoming aware of how this word was pronounced. But what I do remember is my friend saying to me as a brief aside in the library, a day after we had had a long discussion of rhetoric in our required seminar, "You know, Anne, I think the stress is on the first syllable." It was an act of kindness, both to give me the standard pronunciation and to do so in private, quickly, with time for me to get over my embarrassment before the next seminar meeting.

How do we decide which language missteps—or what we perceive as missteps—should be corrected? This is a more complicated question than some style and grammar books suggest when they label some bits of usage "correct" and others "incorrect," simplifying issues of usage into lists of do's and don'ts.* In many ways, this entire book is an answer to the question of how we decide: When

---

* Oy, what an apostrophe conundrum the expression *do's and don'ts* is. Some style guides recommend *dos and don'ts,* following the general principle that the plural *-s* doesn't take an apostrophe. Others recommend *do's and don'ts* to help avoid confusion (people might mistake *dos* for a word that they have just never seen before). No one seems to recommend *do's and don't's*! But two apostrophes in one word is not impossible—consider the wonderful contracted form *I'd've.*

confronted with contested points of usage, how do we balance the perspectives of our inner grammando and our inner wordie, as they both whisper to us about how to address the issue as speakers and writers, listeners and readers, as well as perhaps editors and teachers?

This is where my expertise as a historian of the English language, an experienced English professor, a language radio show host, a frequent public speaker on grammar peeves, and a copy editor becomes invaluable. Over the years, I have honed my skills at helping students, professional writers, radio listeners, and general audiences navigate the rules that govern formal English usage by explaining their backstories, their strengths, and their foibles. As a professor, I have my ear to the ground, learning from undergraduates about the changes happening in the language (e.g., *on accident* is on the rise, potentially replacing *by accident* in the long run). With the radio show on a local National Public Radio affiliate and through public talks around the country, I hear from audience members about the usage issues that are keeping them up at night. As a linguist, I have devoted my career to studying how the English language has changed over time and to digging through old usage guides to uncover the history of complaints about how the English language has been changing over time. With this perspective, I can help us sleep better. Seeing how our worries about usage have shifted over the centuries can provide a helpful perspective on the language changes that may feel linguistically catastrophic today.

I'm using the word *usage* a lot, in addition to *grammar,* because usage is about how we *use* the language in a wide range of contexts, from the most black-tie-dinner formal to backyard-barbecue informal. Broadly defined, *usage* encompasses how words and phrases are used in speech and writing: As such, usage can include pronunciation, word meaning and word choice, morphology (the structure and form of words, including inflectional endings—e.g., is *funner* okay in any way?), syntax (how words combine into sentences), and punctuation. In the field of linguistics, *grammar* is typically used more narrowly to cover morphology and syntax, but not pronunciation, word choice, and punctuation. That said, you can certainly find popular "grammar books" that cover pronunciation, word choice and meaning, and punctuation. Both *grammar* and *usage* can be used descriptively to refer to what speakers and writers actually do with the language, and more prescriptively to refer to what they should do to demonstrate "good usage" or "good grammar." In this book, we'll be comparing what speakers and writers actually do and what we're told we're "supposed to do" in formal contexts, in order to come up with our own, informed decisions about what effective usage is, based on context. As I'll return to again and again in this book, context matters.

We can and should have smart, critical conversations with one another about usage—about, for instance, clarity and rhetorical effectiveness, about our personal preferences and evidence showing what speakers and writers do in real-life speech and writing. This book is designed to jump-start the conversations between your inner grammando and your inner wordie—and equip you with information and a critical perspective on usage that will make you a savvier and more flexible speaker, writer, and editor. I often employ the verb *weigh* when talking about usage because I think it is a helpful metaphor for how we can approach usage questions. As the examples in every chapter will show, there are rarely cut-and-dried "right" and "wrong" answers about usage. Instead, we are asked, as speakers and writers, to weigh the benefits and drawbacks of our language choices, given what we know about the usage rules, the judgments others may make based on our adherence to those rules, our own preferences and purposes, our knowledge of our audience, and our understanding of how the language may be changing. We should also recognize that we, as readers and listeners, have the power to make more informed and generous judgments when we encounter language that surprises us or even jars us. If we can do that, we can call ourselves astute caretakers of the language. And we will be more effective writers and editors as a result.

Advice about usage is like any other kind of advice. Some of it is really good. Good advice about usage helps us create aesthetically pleasing prose, avoid unhelpful ambiguity, and promote clarity of expression. But like all advice, some "rules" about usage are not so good: They may be idiosyncratic to a few influential grammarians, outdated, or never well-founded to begin with. In this book, I'll provide you with information you need to decide how useful a given rule about usage is and how you want to handle it when you are considering your own or other people's speech or writing. Along the way, you'll get to learn a lot of fun facts about the history of words, about how English grammar works, and about how the English language varies across speakers and has changed over time. In other words, there will be a lot of word nerdery (especially in the footnotes!).

Each chapter is organized around a well-known and often contested point of usage, from whether you can use *they* as a singular generic pronoun to what the difference between *less* and *fewer* is—and whether you even need to worry about it. At the end of each chapter, after you've had a chance to learn about the history of the usage rule(s) and what real speakers and writers are actually doing, you will find a short section called "The Bottom Line," which provides pragmatic, tested advice for how to handle the usage issue in your own speaking and writing.

And with that, let's turn to the word *impact,* which my new best friend at the wedding put on the table as her peeve, to see how our inner grammandos and inner wordies might hash this one out. Feel free to jump ahead to chapter 30 if you're already feeling concerned or curious about whether it was okay for me to start that sentence with *And.*

part I

who's in charge here?

1

. . . .

inner grammando vs. inner wordie showdown

"Only teeth can be impacted," a newspaper editor earnestly explained to me a few years ago. "If we're talking about the economy, for example, things can affect the economy or influence it or stimulate it or inhibit it—any of those verbs. But they can't impact it."

Really? Your inner grammando may be shouting, "AMEN! *Impact* is unacceptable here." My new best friend from the wedding I described in the introduction would be nodding in agreement. At the same time, your inner wordie may be wondering, "Don't I regularly read newspaper articles in which journalists write about various factors impacting the economy?" The answer: Absolutely, it's easy to find the verb *impact* in newspaper articles. So, is there anything fundamentally wrong with using *impact* as a verb to mean 'affect'?

According to many standard usage guides, the answer is yes. Consider, for instance, Bryan Garner's entry for *impact* in the fifth edition of his influential book *Garner's Modern English Usage* (published in 2022), in which he explains what "careful" writers do:

> *Impact* was traditionally only a noun. In the mid-20th century, however, it underwent a semantic shift that allows it to act as a transitive or intransitive verb. . . . These uses of the word would be perfectly acceptable if *impact* were performing any function not as

ably performed by *affect* or *influence*. If *affect* as a verb is not suf-
ficiently straightforward in context, then the careful writer might
use *have an impact on*, which, though more verbose, was long
thought better than the jarring impact of *impacted*. Traditionalists
still reserve *impact* for noun uses and *impacted* for wisdom teeth.

Here Garner describes a recent shift that allows *impact* to function
as a verb with the figurative meaning 'to have a significant effect
on,' and he recognizes elsewhere in the passage that the use is widespread. But he then steers careful writers away from it. Why? Garner suggests that it's not because the usage is new (although this is
a reason many grammarians will use) but instead because: (a) there
are adequate synonyms already in the language; and (b) it is "jarring." Let's put on our wordie hats and examine these two reasons.

The synonym argument is a relatively weak one. In fact, many
writers laud English for how prolific its synonyms are, which means
as writers and speakers, we don't have to repeat words often and
can strive for the word with just the right connotation. In this case,
given that English already has the two synonyms *affect* and *influence,* why not three? And for me, at least, the verb *impact* is stronger than *affect*: It suggests a more powerful consequence.

With the issue of jarringness, the question should be: Jarring to
whom? (Or to who—we'll talk about that in chapter 19.) This use
of *impact* as a verb is clearly jarring to many "traditionalists," but
it is clearly not jarring to the many writers who use it, including the
ones Garner quotes in the entry.

Then while we're here, let's talk about the issue of wordiness. If,
as "careful" writers and speakers, we're not supposed to use *impact*
as a verb, then we're left with the wordy (or "verbose") phrase *have
an impact on*. But in many other instances, authors of style guides
point to wordiness as a rationale to condemn a construction as incorrect or unacceptable (e.g., *in regard to*). I'd make the argument
that *impact* as a verb enhances concision.

Let's also briefly revisit the history of the word *impact,* which
surfaces another peeve you may find surprising. While some usage

guides assert that *impact* has traditionally been only a noun as a way to criticize the verb, it's actually been a verb in English longer than it's been a noun. Historically the verb, which appears in written English by the early seventeenth century, had the more concrete meaning of 'to press closely into something'; to this day, your impacted teeth are pressed closely into your gum tissue. By the 1930s, the verb *impact* had come to be used figuratively for things that exuded a force on other things or had an effect of some kind, first primarily in literary works and then in a much wider range of genres. And as the figurative use spread, criticism increased. Grammandos noticed and didn't like it. Here in the 2020s, the Modern Language Association—the largest, most influential professional association in the humanities—still restricts the verb *impact* to describing physical collisions or physical pressing (as in the teeth).

The noun *impact* didn't come on the scene in English until the late eighteenth century, and at first it also had a more concrete meaning, referring to bodies colliding: the impact of an asteroid on a planet, or later two cars on each other. Within a few decades, though, the noun also came to be used figuratively to talk about effects or influences, not just physical collisions. Grammandos once again noticed and didn't like it. The figurative use of the noun *impact* was criticized as "pointless hyperbole" in the 1960s, according to a usage note in the *American Heritage Dictionary of the English Language,* but it is now standard, accepted by 97 percent of the dictionary's Usage Panel in 2015. This same Usage Panel, however, still expresses serious concerns about the use of the verb *impact* to mean 'to have an effect,' although it is getting less cranky over time. In the 2001 survey, 80 percent of the panel rejected the sentence "The court ruling will impact the education of minority students"; in 2015, only 50 percent disapproved.

Wait a minute! (you might be thinking). Who are the people on this so-called Usage Panel and why do they get to make these decisions about acceptability? That is a very good question. If you look at the opening pages of the *American Heritage Dictionary*—although I realize almost no one other than me reads the preface of a dictionary—or follow the Usage Panel link on the dictionary homepage, you can find a list of all the members of the Usage Panel. The panel comprised about two hundred people (or I could say "was comprised of"—but I know that usage probably makes some readers cringe), including academicians from a range of disciplines (e.g., Harold Bloom, Henry Louis Gates, Jr.), journalists (e.g., Frank Rich, Susan Stamberg), creative writers (e.g., Maxine Hong Kingston, David Sedaris, Barbara Kingsolver, Junot Díaz, Jonathan Franzen), a world-class puzzler (Will Shortz), and until 2016 a Supreme Court justice (Antonin Scalia). Also on the Usage Panel were about a dozen linguists, including Steven Pinker, who chaired the panel—and, beginning in 2005, me.

Sadly, we never met in person as a full panel, although *The New Yorker* reported on just such a gathering in 1977. I can't tell you how much I would have relished the opportunity to gather in a room with this eclectic group of illustrious people and discuss in nitpicking detail the finer points of English usage. What a fascinating grammatical argle-bargle (to quote Justice Scalia) that could have been! Instead, all of us on the panel received an online usage survey about once a year, with anywhere from twenty-five to fifty questions about a range of usage issues, from pronunciation (e.g., Where is the stress in the word *hegemony*?) to word meaning (e.g., Is it acceptable to use *anxious* to mean 'eager'?) to syntax (e.g., Is it acceptable to advocate for things as well as to advocate things?). For most questions, we were asked to rate examples of usage (be that a pronunciation or a sentence) as completely acceptable, somewhat acceptable, somewhat unacceptable, or completely unacceptable. Those were the four choices. We could take as much or as little time filling out the survey as we desired. We clicked submit, and our answers went into the tally that then appeared in the dictionary's usage notes as a percentage (e.g., 80 percent of the panel rejected this sentence).

The people on the panel represented not only a range of professions but also a range of attitudes about language. Some of us had strong inner grammandos and were more conservative about language variation and change when we filled out the survey; some of us had vocal, well-informed inner wordies and were more accepting of new or nonstandard usage. Some of us relied on gut feelings about acceptability and what "sounds right"; some of us sought out data on actual usage. I haven't done a systematic survey, but I would guess most of the linguists on the panel were on the data-driven, more-accepting-of-language-change end of things. It's inherent in our training and profession. Historically, though, the panel as a whole tended to be fairly conservative, and it was sometimes critiqued as an overly male, white, older-than-hip group.

The Usage Panel was discontinued in 2018, although our names still appear on the website. The publisher, Houghton Mifflin, cited the decline in print dictionaries as a cause, and it is certainly true that in our digital world, dictionaries are not the profitable enterprise they once were. When I went to college, most of us arrived with clothes, bedding, perhaps a lamp or a beanbag chair, and a good collegiate dictionary in hand. No longer. That said, the Usage Panel's ratings about acceptability live on, both in print and online.

If you go into an *American Heritage Dictionary* and see the judgment of the Usage Panel, then, you should keep in mind the makeup of the panel and voting process that I have just described. Clearly the outcome of our voting does not determine what is "right" and what is "wrong" in any objective or universal way. Our vote instead can give you a sense of how a particular usage may have been received in academic and/or more formal contexts, at least up until 2018. The Usage Panel can be a helpful reference point because it gives you, as a writer or speaker, more information to decide how you would like to use a given word in any given context.

The adjective *impactful* never showed up on the usage survey, although I suggested its inclusion. If I were asked to rate new words on a scale from 1 to 10 based on their aesthetic appeal (of course, this is the word's aesthetic appeal in *my* opinion—this scale cannot possibly be objective), with 10 being the most appealing and 1 being the least, I would give *impactful* about a 3. In other words, I notice the word, and I don't like it. There is no particularly good reason for my displeasure with this word. There are plenty of similar adjectives in the language, formed by a noun + -*ful* to mean 'full of or having a lot of or being characterized by [the noun]': for example, *playful, joyful, meaningful, eventful*. The adjective *impactful* is relatively new to the language, but that's not a good reason for my distaste either—there are lots of other new words that I like (e.g., the wonderfully playful verb *recombobulate**). The meaning of *impactful* is a bit vague (e.g., is the impact good or bad?), but the same critique could be made of well-accepted adjectives like *influential*.

So what would I have done had *impactful* appeared on the survey to judge acceptability in formal prose? I would lean into my inner wordie and listen to the data, rather than listening to my own personal preferences and idiosyncratic likes and dislikes—that is, my inner grammando.

What data? This is a remarkable moment in the history of technology to be studying usage, both contemporary and historical. There are massive online databases of texts freely available that we can search to see where and how speakers and writers are using the English language. In other words, every single one of us can gather real evidence of usage in order to make informed decisions as speakers, writers, and editors. For example, the Corpus of Contemporary American English, which is designed specifically for linguistic research, contains more than one billion words and encompasses speech (from the transcripts of unscripted radio and television programs), fiction, magazines, newspapers, and academic prose from 1990 to 2019. If we search this database for *impactful*, we learn

---

* Every January, the American Dialect Society votes on the Word of the Year, as well as a few other winning word categories. In 2008, *recombobulation area* won Most Creative Word of the Year. The original recombobulation area appeared at the Milwaukee Mitchell International Airport: a place right after the security checkpoint for passengers to put their coats and belts back on, repack their laptops and toiletries, retrieve keys, etc.—in other words, to recombobulate. I have been trying to help this new verb catch on ever since!

that the adjective seems to be trending: It occurred fifty times more frequently in the period 2015 to 2019 than it did from 1990 to 1994. Looking for even more data? Try searching the millions of books that Google has digitized with the Google Books Ngram Viewer. A search of *impactful* in this ginormous database (my inner wordie *loves* the word *ginormous*) shows the dramatic rise in the popularity of *impactful*.

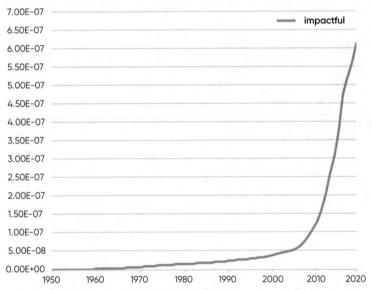

A Google Books Ngram Viewer search showing the relative frequency (with a smoothing of 3) of the word *impactful* from 1950 to 2019

Bryan Garner, in the 2022 edition of *Garner's Modern English Usage*, describes the word as originating in jargon (in the previous edition he described it as "barbarous jargon") and "a word to be scorned," but you can find it regularly in newspapers from around the United States, magazines, academic journal articles, and literature. It's not barbarous or jargony. My inner grammando doesn't especially like the word, but that is neither here nor there. My inner wordie embraces language change as a natural and inevitable part of living languages. Part of being human is being creative with language, which means that we are forever changing the language in subtle and sometimes not-so-subtle ways. That said, there may be a few changes that strike us, even those of us who are professional linguists, as less aesthetically pleasing than others. That's natural too. There are plenty of times when I find my inner grammando saying, "Really? The language is really going to change that way?"

But my personal opinion on the aesthetics of *impactful* should not justify my telling other people not to use it. The word is now in general use in a range of formal, edited genres of written English (or written "registers," as linguists would call these different ways of using language dependent on context). I can choose not to use *impactful*, but even that will probably be short-lived; give me another couple of years and I will probably have gotten the hang of *impactful* and may not even notice it anymore.* Either way, had I ever been asked on the usage survey about whether *impactful* is acceptable in formal written usage, I would have let my inner wordie prevail and say yes. The data shows it is, and I would bow to the data and the inevitability of language change, not to my inner grammando. (Can *data* be singular, the way I used it right there? Check out chapter 13.)

I also, always, look to lessons from the past. In the eighteenth century, Benjamin Franklin didn't like the verb *colonize*. Henry Alford, Dean of Canterbury, despaired over the newish word *reliable* in his 1864 book, *The Queen's English*. And even though, in 2024, Anne Curzan thought *impactful* was not very pretty, I also know from historical example that in the inner grammando versus inner wordie showdown, time is on the inner wordie's side.

---

* If you've been told "gotten is rotten," I hope this footnote will help you leave that worry behind. The verb *get* has long had two past participles: *got* and *gotten*. While British English speakers now primarily use *got*, North American speakers use both, and the only thing "wrong" with *gotten* is that a few usage commentators, starting in the late eighteenth century, mistakenly said *gotten* was obsolete, which inspired later commentators to claim there is something wrong with it.

the bottom line

Given the Usage Panel's overwhelming rejection of *impact* as a verb synonymous with 'affect,' do you want to use it that way in your writing? Clearly there are a significant number of highly educated readers who may feel cranky about it. At the same time, if you look at published academic writing, newspapers, magazines, and the like, you can consistently find the verb; editors are letting it through, if they're noticing it at all. I am not convinced by any of the objections to the verb—in fact, it seems quite useful to me—and I use it in my formal writing precisely because of the censure I know is out there. How else do we overwhelm the grammandos who are clinging to this ill-informed judgment against *impact*?

As a reader, I also would never mark the verb *impact* in students' work as a problem or change it in a piece I am copyediting—simply because writers *are* using it as a verb. Together, we can lower the gate that the gatekeepers have been propping up to keep out of formal writing this perfectly logical and usefully concise verb.

2

. . . .

ain't: what gets into dictionaries, and how

David is now a dear friend, but we got off to a rocky start over one word—or nonword, he would argue. I had invited David and his wife over for dinner, and as we got to know each other, they were asking questions about my field and what I teach. At some point David said, "The next thing I know, you'll tell me *irregardless* is a real word." I am not sure exactly what expression crossed my face, but it clearly indicated that I was about to tell him precisely that. He immediately responded, "My respect for you just went down three notches!"

I have told this story many times over the years, and at least half the people who hear it side squarely with David. *Irregardless* taps into some deep-seated feelings about what is not allowed to be counted as a word, undoubtedly fueled by parents and teachers and other authority figures who had also learned that *irregardless* is "not a word." The fact that generations of authorities have handed down this lore suggests that *irregardless* is not new, and, in fact, the first known instance of the word comes from 1795, in the *Charleston (South Carolina) City Gazette*: "But death, irregardless of tenderest ties, Resolv'd the good Betty, at length, to bereave." In the nineteenth century, the word shows up in congressional documents, magazines, law journals, and the like. And yes, I did just describe *irregardless* as a word. It meets all the criteria. Let me explain.

A word is a set of sounds (or the written representation of those sounds) that functions independently to communicate a meaning that is shared within a community. If I decide that the string of sounds *gaballfry* refers to the wheel on a shopping cart that spins out in a different direction from the others, but no one else knows that *gaballfry* is meant to be meaningful and they do not understand me when I describe my frustration at the gaballfry making my shopping cart go careening down the supermarket aisle, then *gaballfry* is not a word. It does not have a shared meaning within a speech community. But *irregardless,* like it or not, does have a shared meaning, and even the folks who go grammando on it and say it isn't a word know what it means: It means 'regardless.' And it's formed through the regular word formation process of blending: *Irrespective* and *regardless* got smushed together ("smushed" being my very technical term), in the same way that *breakfast* and *lunch* make *brunch,* or *bro* and *romance* create *bromance.*

When people say that a word like *irregardless* isn't a "real" word, I think they mean that it hasn't been legitimized by language authorities and perhaps specifically by dictionaries. And this belief raises a host of questions, such as: Who writes dictionaries? How does a word get included in a dictionary? How different are different dictionaries?

I wish more people asked these questions more often.

Even the most critically thoughtful people out there tend not to distinguish among dictionaries or ask who edited them. Just think about the phrase "look it up in the dictionary," as if they were all the same. Or consider a university library: When you go into the reading room, you can walk up to a big unabridged dictionary, there on its pedestal, in a place of honor and respect. We go stand before it to get answers. Not to say it's not a fantastic resource (it is), but it's still produced by humans, and it is not timeless. As a teacher myself, I am struck that we teach students to question pretty much every text they read, every website they visit—except dictionaries. As if dictionaries are unauthored works, like they appeared from nowhere and just tell us what words "really mean."

Here's the thing: If you ask dictionary editors, they'll say that they are just trying to keep up with *us* as we change the language. They're tracking our speech and our writing, trying to see which new words or word meanings will stick and which won't—and record it. They have to gamble: They want to include new words that are going to make it (e.g., *lol*) but not include words that will later appear faddish. And different dictionaries have different aims.

Despite my best efforts, I still catch myself using the phrase "the dictionary," but it's important to remember that there is no such thing as *the* dictionary. There are widely known dictionaries (e.g., those published by Merriam-Webster, American Heritage, Random House, Oxford). There are unabridged dictionaries and collegiate dictionaries. There are bilingual dictionaries and slang dictionaries and historical dictionaries and a whole host of other specialized dictionaries (dictionaries of regional words, scientific terms, computer jargon, and much more). There are print dictionaries and online dictionaries (some of which correspond to print dictionaries and some of which are wholly independent). When we use the phrase "the dictionary," I think we usually have in mind a "standard" dictionary published by an established publishing house like Merriam-Webster; many of us may not have thought about which version (unabridged, collegiate, etc.) or which edition. But different publishers and editors have different philosophies about selecting and defining words, applying usage labels, handling etymologies, and more. How a given word is defined can depend on which dictionary you use. And a dictionary is only as up-to-date as its year of publication—although no teacher at any moment in my K–12 or college education asked me to consider the publication date of any dictionary I referred to. (See chapter 29 if you're concerned about the preposition at the end of that sentence.)

Usage labels attached to words in dictionaries are an especially powerful tool. Dictionary editors typically use them descriptively, trying to capture what they are observing about how a word is used. For example, the label *slang* is trying to suggest a specific kind of irreverent informality, compared with a label like *informal* or *colloquial* (more characteristic of spoken language). And the decisions are hard! Should *cool,* in the sense of "it's cool if you don't want to talk about it," still be labeled slang, or is it now just informal? Not all dictionary editors agree. And we can imagine why it feels only responsible to include labels like *offensive* or *highly offensive* or *vulgar,* so that anyone unfamiliar with a word will know what it could mean to use it. But even that is really hard. As just one example: When I was growing up, my mother made it clear that it was vulgar and unacceptable to say "That sucks" to mean that something isn't good. Some dictionaries warn readers about attitudes like my mother's, and others describe this meaning of *suck* just as slang, with no *vulgar* or *offensive* label.

The usage label *nonstandard* is a tricky one. *The American Heritage Dictionary of the English Language* defines it as "forms and usages that educated speakers and writers consider unacceptable in standard contexts." What becomes immediately apparent is that this is a subjective judgment—and one with real-world implications. If a word is labeled as *nonstandard* because it has typically not been used in, say, formal prose, then people may assume that it has always been that way and will always be that way. But if "educated speakers and writers" (whoever gets to count in that group) all started to allow a form to be used in more formal contexts, then it would become standard. In other words, nonstandard is not an inherent characteristic of a word; it is a collective decision that a community makes about what contexts a word can be used in. And we could, at least in theory, change our minds.

And sometimes the language authorities we have decided to empower to make decisions about "educated usage" do change their minds, in a way that changes the labels in dictionaries. Consider the verb *finalize.* Do you have any concerns? When I poll audiences, most people have no strong feelings about *finalize*—and are surprised to learn how strong the feelings used to be. This verb shows up in the early twentieth century, and when American Heritage polled the Usage Panel in the late 1960s, 90 percent of the panel judged it unacceptable; it was seen as bureaucratic jargon. In 1988, the disapproval range was 71 percent, but just nine years later, in 1997, there had been a dramatic shift: Now only 28 percent called *finalize* unacceptable. By 2014, only 15 percent of the panel was still clinging to this negative judgment. (See chapter 18 on singular *they* to read about another example of shifting opinions on acceptable "standard" usage.)

The word *irregardless* is labeled *nonstandard* in many dictionaries, including Merriam-Webster and American Heritage. So, the dictionaries are recognizing the word's use and trying to alert readers that they would likely be judged for using the word in formal contexts. Again, let's just be clear that it is a decision to be judgy about this word—it's not inherent in the word.* Sure, we could argue that the word *irregardless* is illogical in its redundancy: The *ir-* prefix is unnecessary because of the suffix *-less*. But a word like *debone* is also redundant (the verb *bone* already means you are taking the bones out, and you can't take them out twice!), yet it is deemed standard. Why? Because language judgments are subjective and often inconsistent. For some speakers, the *ir-* also isn't redundant: *irregardless* is an emphatic way to push something to the side, and the *ir-* doubles down on the *-less*. *Irregardless* has the power to end the discussion.

It would be irresponsible, given that we're talking about subjective and inconsistent language judgments captured in dictionary usage labels, not to talk about the word *ain't*. And, of course, *ain't* is in the title of the chapter, which would make it even weirder not to discuss the word in the chapter itself. I grew up hearing the ridiculous saying "*Ain't* ain't in the dictionary"—ridiculous because *ain't* has been in dictionaries for decades. And when I give lectures around the country, I hear lots of reasons why people think there is something fundamentally wrong with *ain't*. It's not transparent:

---

* Not all dictionaries yet recognize the informal word *judgy,* but it is, of course, a word. And while I could have used the word *judgmental* here, *judgy* seemed to better capture the shaky foundation on which this judgment sits.

You can't tell what it is a contraction of. The sound of it "grates." It sounds uneducated. It has too many uses. It is illogical.

Let's take each of those reasons in turn. It is true that *ain't* is not fully transparent. It appears in written English by the 1700s and probably originates in the contraction *amn't* (*am* + *not*), and may also have roots in *isn't* and *aren't*, with pronunciation changes over time. We know, for example, that *haven't* sometimes became *haint*. But a contraction like *won't* (from *will* + *not*) is also not transparent, yet it gets to be standard.

As to whether the sound of *ain't* is "grating," I rarely hear people complain about words like *paint* or *faint*—and, obviously, they all rhyme. People do often judge *ain't* as uneducated. For example, the former University of Michigan football coach Rich Rodriguez was criticized as not living up to the university's premier academic reputation for using the word *ain't* in press conferences. Yet it is worth noting that the word is dropped into more formal prose to create emphasis on a regular basis—for example, when it ain't over yet.

It is certainly true that *ain't* has a lot of uses: It can be used in place of *am not, is not, are not, has not,* and *have not,* and for some speakers, *does not* and *do not.* In plenty of other contexts, versatility would be seen as a positive attribute for a word. And *ain't* does important work. Compare "That isn't right" and "That ain't right." For speakers who can use the latter, it often suggests a stronger moral or ethical infraction. Word choice matters, and *ain't* carries specific rhetorical power.

Finally, some argue *ain't* is illogical. Where even to start with this criticism? First, the logic of language is different from the logic of math or philosophy, as I'll return to in the next chapter. And second, we accept as standard the hard-to-defend-as-logical construction "aren't I?" The phrasing "I aren't" is not grammatical in most people's speech—that is, it doesn't happen out there in real speech—as opposed to "I ain't," which is a regular part of many people's speech. And yet it is seen as standard to use the question "aren't I?" rather than "ain't I?"

While *ain't* is labeled as *nonstandard* in the *American Heritage Dictionary of the English Language* (fifth edition) and *informal* in the *New Oxford American Dictionary* (third edition), it has no usage label in Merriam-Webster. That lack of a usage label has a controversial history, described in wonderful detail in David Skinner's book *The Story of Ain't: America, Its Language, and the Most Controversial Dictionary Ever Published.* That controversial dictionary was *Webster's Third New International Dictionary of the English Language,* published in 1961, whose editor Philip Gove decided to include thousands of new words and eliminate many usage labels, which enforced or reinforced particular, subjective notions of correctness. When the dictionary was published, it was condemned as radically permissive and irresponsible (and that is the kind version) by numerous newspapers and magazines, including *The New York Times,* the Toronto *Globe and Mail,* the *Chicago Tribune,* and *Life* magazine, which claimed, to quote just one line, that *Webster's Third* "has now all but abandoned any effort to distinguish between good and bad usage—between the King's English, say, and the fishwife's." The fact that judgments about language are wrapped up in judgments about speakers—their class, gender, race, and ethnicity—is sometimes subtle, but goodness, not in that quote.

At the center of the criticism was the dictionary's treatment of the word *ain't,* which had become entirely confused by a confusing press release. *Webster's Third* was not the first dictionary to include *ain't,* although you'll sometimes hear that it was. The dictionary includes no usage label for the meanings 'am not, is not, are not'; but the meanings 'has not, have not' are labeled as *substandard.* There is also a descriptive usage note for the first set of meanings, which reads: "though disapproved by many and more common in less educated speech, used orally in most parts of the U.S. by many cultivated speakers esp. in the phrase *ain't I.*" The original press release quoted only the second part ("used orally . . ."), without the first part recognizing judgments, and the controversy over *ain't* spun out from there.

It didn't have to be that way. In 1781, the Reverend John Witherspoon, one of the Founding Fathers of the United States and the sixth president of Princeton University, condemned a whole list of "vulgar abbreviations," including "an't, can't, han't, don't, should'nt, would'nt, could'nt, &c." As you can see, most of these contractions (with the apostrophe occasionally in a different place—for that story, see chapter 26) have been allowed to enter the realm of informal and sometimes even more formal prose, even if not everyone would invite them to the written "black-tie" event. Except for *ain't*. And here we need to remember the lesson of the fishwife: that stigmas become attached to words that are often used by historically marginalized speakers, including in this case many speakers of African American English and southern varieties of American English. This is part of why debates about words are so important: They are almost never just about words—they're about people and prejudice, about social and political issues, and about power.

the bottom line

One key point for everyone who uses dictionaries is that dictionary editors are trying to walk a fine line between capturing words as they are used and providing guidance about the contexts in which some words are generally accepted or not accepted. While the editors of today's dictionaries are usually trying to describe actual usage, we as dictionary users often erroneously assume that they are prescribing correct usage. Your inner grammando would do well to accept that dictionaries are actually built to educate and delight your inner wordie. At the same time, usage notes can provide useful information for navigating judgments we may encounter.

So the next time you read a usage label or usage note, remember that fellow humans decided on that usage label, and human hands wrote that usage note—as well as the definition of the word. Attitudes change over time, along with the language itself. Dictionaries will never be able to fully keep up (note the split infinitive). Irregardless (yes, I really did just go there!), it is the job of dictionary editors to track our usage, from the slangy to the technical, and to try to include all the words and the new meanings of words that seem to have legs.

3

....

double negatives: how rules become rules

t's 1965. Mick Jagger and the Rolling Stones release the song "(I Can't Get No) Satisfaction." There is a double negative. No one is confused.

I start with this anecdote to counter some of the nonsensical notions that circulate about "double negation," or what linguists often call "negative concord" (I'll come back to the reason for that). The most nonsensical is that the two negatives in a statement like "I can't get no satisfaction" automatically cancel each other out to create a positive. Let's get real: This simply isn't true. Mick Jagger is not saying that he *can* find satisfaction because he tries and he tries and he tries. As we listen to the song, whether or not we ourselves use double negation in our speech, we know that all of Mick Jagger's trying is not leading to satisfaction. He can't get none of that.

So where did this idea come from, that two negatives cancel each other in English grammar and become a positive? It's everywhere! For example, it's embedded in this joke that people send to me every few weeks, with the lecture taking place at a range of elite universities in the United States and England:

An MIT linguistics professor was lecturing his class the other day. "In English," he said, "a double negative forms a positive. However, in some languages, such as Russian, a double negative remains a negative. But there isn't a single language, not one, in which a double positive can express a negative." A voice from the back of the room piped up, "Yeah, right."

The joke perpetuates the myth that this is how English grammar works. And there's another myth out there: that double negation in English is wrong or ungrammatical. This chapter will address these myths and use the case study of double negation as a way to show how grammar rules can become "rules" and how grammatical constructions that used to be acceptable can come to be seen as "wrong."

We'll turn back the clock to look at the history of double negatives in English. But first: a little terminology. When we talk about double negation, we're referring to two negative grammatical elements or markers being used in one clause to convey negation.[*] For example, using *not* along with *nothing* (e.g., "I can't do nothing about it") or with *never* (e.g., "I haven't never doubted her") or with *no* (e.g., "I can't get no love from her"). I'm using the shorthand "double negatives" given how common the phrase is, but in the history of English, varieties of English actually allowed multiple negation, and many varieties around the world still do—for example, "I haven't never doubted nothing she's said."

As I typed that sentence, the grammar checker running in the background of this document became unhappy and started putting

---

[*] I grew up watching *Schoolhouse Rock!*, educational short films that aired between the Saturday morning cartoons my sisters and I were actually trying to watch, including the grammar-focused short "Conjunction Junction." The lyrics of the short film's catchy song begin: "Conjunction Junction, what's your function? Hooking up words and phrases and clauses." I sang this for years without knowing the exact difference between a phrase and a clause. You might be in the same boat. Syntactically, a phrase is a group of words functioning together like a familiar part of speech—e.g., a noun, verb, adverb. A clause has a subject and a predicate (a verb and its "accoutrements," as a student once put it). A clause can be a sentence, but a sentence can also have more than one clause (this sentence, for example, has two clauses).

squiggly lines under words, specifically *never* and *nothing*. "Stop with all this negation in one clause," it seemed to be whining. "That should be *ever* not *never*, *anything* not *nothing*." But a grammar checker one thousand years ago would not have flagged the multiple negatives in that sentence, had the *Beowulf* poet been typing out the poem and happened to include that sentence in Old English (okay, I know that is a stretch, but you see what I'm after). Multiple negation was standard in Old English. And in Middle English. And into Renaissance English.

If you're finding it hard to believe that multiple negation really used to be standard in speech and formal writing, let me give you some examples. The first comes from the *Peterborough Chronicle,* a history of England compiled over multiple decades. Here the scribe, writing in 1137 CE, is describing the awful consequences of the civil war under King Stephen, with double negation:

> *þe erthe ne bar nan corn*
> The earth not bore no corn ('The earth bore no corn')

Jumping forward a couple hundred years to the late 1300s, here's Chaucer, in his description of the knight in the General Prologue of *The Canterbury Tales,* using not two but three negative markers in one clause:

> *He nevere yet no vileynye ne sayde*
> He never yet no villany not said ('He never ever said anything vile')

And then a little Shakespeare, in *As You Like It,* when Celia asserts:

> *I cannot go no further* ('I cannot go any further')

Linguists call examples like these "negative concord" because all the negative markers are working together in the grammar of the clause to make it negative. They are not working against each other grammatically and canceling each other out. If anything, adding more negative markers makes the negation stronger. Many languages around the world express negation with negative concord, such as French. In French, to say "I don't know" would typically take two negative markers: "Je ne sais pas" ('I not know not').

In English, multiple negation or negative concord has lived alongside single negation for centuries, and one wasn't considered more standard or better than the other. But starting in the Renaissance, single negation came to be standardized. In other words, the variety of English that was standardized through the printing process and education during this period used single negation. But the speakers and writers of many other varieties of English happily continued to employ multiple negation—to this day.

And at least some commentators were sad to see standardized English leave multiple negation in the rearview mirror. Let me share one of my favorite quotes—and when I present this one at talks, audiences often express disbelief. In his book *Modern English* (1873), Fitzedward Hall includes a great quote from *The London Review,* from October 1, 1864, that laments the loss of double negation as one of many lamentable changes in the English language. The quote sets up the King James Bible of 1611 as the high point of English usage, after which, the author asserts, many changes have been for the worse. The author goes on to specify one of those changes: "The double negative has been abandoned, to the great injury of strength of expression." Wait, really? Yes, double negatives can be and have been seen as a powerful grammatical asset. Of course, double negation wasn't exactly abandoned: It was relegated to a nonstandard construction.

But double or multiple negation is now considered not just nonstandard but often "ungrammatical" or "illogical" or "wrong." Sound familiar? You may be thinking about what a teacher or a parent told you about double negation, or perhaps your own inner grammando–fueled judgment you have conveyed to others.

Once you know this history, though, you can see that multiple negation is fully grammatical as a way to express negation, in English and many other languages around the world. It just didn't happen to be the version of negation that was standardized in standardized English in the Renaissance.

So where did the idea that the two negatives in English cancel each other out come from? Bishop Robert Lowth. Yes, we can pinpoint this one. Bishop Lowth published a highly influential text called *A Short Introduction to English Grammar* in 1762. He states in the text: "Two negatives in English destroy one another, or are equivalent to a positive." This statement got picked up in his student Lindley Murray's best-selling grammar called, wait for it, *English Grammar,* first published in 1795 and going through almost fifty editions. And with the proliferation of this and other grammars influenced by Lowth, the "rule" that two negatives always make a positive in English grammar was out of the barn. In fact sprinting away from the barn, with grammandos in the saddle. The barn right now is nowhere in sight.

Why would Lowth have said this? Well, there's math, and some people, some of the time, try to argue that the logic of language should work like the logic of math. Of course, language is not math, and it's important to remember that. But let's address the comparison. I started college as a math major before I discovered linguistics, and I love math. There are times in math when two negatives cancel each other out and make a positive—that is, when you multiply them. But you don't have to be a math major to know that when you add two negatives in math, you get a bigger negative. This can happen in language too. And for languages with negative concord, like many varieties of English, those negatives are not the canceling kind.

Now, there are times in English when two negatives can cancel each other out, and intonation is important here. Let's imagine someone says to me, "Anne, I assume you have none of those worries." I consider the question, quickly catalogue all the things I

worry about, and reply, in all honesty: "I don't have *none* of them."
In my answer, the *not* (or contracted *n't* to be completely accurate)
and the *none* cancel each other, to indicate that I have at least some
of those worries. The answer works best if I put some intonational
emphasis on *none*. But in another context, say if someone asked,
"Do you have any concerns?" and I replied, "I don't have none,"
with no pointed intonation to suggest this wasn't straightforward
negative concord, it would be synonymous with "I don't have
any."*

Interestingly, if we go back to Bishop Lowth's grammar, we see
that his example is more along these canceling-out lines. The full
quote reads: "Two negatives, in English, destroy one another, or are
equivalent to an affirmative; as 'Nor did they *not* perceive the evil
plight in which they were.'" Lowth puts into a footnote the caveat
about the times that double negatives do not cancel each other out
because they work together in negative concord. The footnote
seems to have gotten overlooked, and Lowth's "rule" got erroneously generalized to condemn a fully grammatical construction.

Yes, I said "grammatical." This is grammatical in what linguists
would call the descriptive sense of grammatical. In other words, it
is a systematic pattern or rule that describes how people actually
use the language. It is not formal or, in this case, standard, but it is
completely systematic: The negative markers have to appear in specific places (e.g., "We have none not" would not be grammatical),
and the constructions must be widely understood. When Pink Floyd
sings "We don't need no education," we know they are speaking
back against formal education—and we know that as part of the

* It's also worth noting that sometimes in the constructions where two negative
markers are working against each other in meaning, they do not completely cancel
each other. Consider *not* preceding a negated adjective. If I tell you that my mother
is not unhappy in her job, I have not confirmed that she is happy. She could be completely neutral about the job, or maybe even satisfied without rising to the level of
happy. But if I said that my decision is not unprecedented, I am confirming that there
is precedent. These two examples capture differences in how adjectives work (e.g.,
whether they are binary, such as *alive* and *dead*, or work on a continuum, such as
hot and *cold*).

speaking back, they are breaking a prescriptive rule by employing double negation. Prescriptive rules are the formal rules created by grammarians, English teachers, editors, and others to govern what language is seen as "acceptable" or "correct" in often more formal settings—but sometimes all settings. It is prescriptive in the sense of prescribing the do's and don'ts of speaking and writing formal standardized English.

This book both describes the prescriptive rules that many of us have learned—or are worried we haven't learned—over the years and compares those with the descriptive patterns of how speakers use English in a range of varieties. A key point to remember: All varieties of English spoken in speech communities have systematic grammars. Multiple negation, as I have described in this chapter, is as systematic as single negation.

Here are two more examples of grammatical systematicity at work in nonstandard varieties of English. A dialect like African American English that uses *hisself,* not *himself,* and *theirselves* rather than *themselves,* is following a systematic pattern of possessive pronoun + *-self* (*myself, yourself, ourselves, herself, hisself, theirselves*). In this case, it is the standardized variety of English that has more exceptions to the pattern, with *himself* rather than *hisself, themselves* rather than *theirselves.* As a second example, a variety of English that has held on to the final *-s* in *she talks*— a variety like standardized English—is clinging to a relic in its grammatical system; it is a relic that many varieties of English have left behind so that the present tense systematically has no inflectional endings (*I/you/we/he/she/they talk*).

The variety of English that was standardized, which happens to use single negation and *himself* and third-person singular *-s,* is one variety of English. It is not the source of all the other nonstandard varieties. Perhaps that statement catches you off guard. I find this idea is often hard for people to get their head around at first. Standardized English is not the parent with lots of offspring varieties. It is a sibling, with lots of siblings. And it is the sibling that got picked out by speakers with social, political, and economic power to be the one whose habits get recorded as a model for the other siblings. One can imagine that the other siblings can resent this, and that the standardized sibling doesn't always fit in, being seen as too formal or pretentious or many other things.

Okay, the analogy is far from perfect: Language varieties are not people with siblings. But I hope you can see what I'm getting at. A key lesson for us: The standardized variety is not neutral, and it's not better in any linguistic or structural sense. At the same time, it carries a lot of power, and it is the password to jobs and connections with lots of social and economic power. We as speakers, writers, readers, and listeners have the responsibility to decide if and how we want to change that password, which is a key goal of this book.

the bottom line

This chapter has highlighted that there are rules and there are rules. There are the descriptive rules for what a language allows, and there are the prescriptive rules for what grammandos have told us make "better" use of language. With each chapter of this book, you're becoming a savvier consumer of both kinds of rules, so that your inner wordie has more linguistic tools at hand to hash things out with your inner grammando.

What I'm encouraging you to do, as part of this hashing out, is separate out the social judgment from the grammar. It is helpful for us to understand the social judgment and be able to navigate it as speakers and writers; it is also intellectually interesting to see how those judgments can change over time. Imagine a world in which we (re-)accepted double negation as a legitimate option in all spoken and written genres or registers, informal and formal. Speakers who have both single and double (or multiple) negation in their repertoires would have more grammatical and rhetorical options available to them in all contexts, without having to worry they will be judged as "not knowing better" when double negation is exactly the right choice.

This perspective and background knowledge makes us better editors, kinder and more informed teachers, and more inclusive citizens, because we understand the formal, standardized written variety in the context of all the varieties of English out there.

4

······

"pc" language: why emotions run high

The expression *vertically challenged* rather than *short*, or a complete ban on the word *seminal*, given its masculine etymology—it's easy to find examples of "politically correct" language that feel excessive. And sometimes PC language critics will lob these examples into an argument as conclusive proof that these attempts to create more inclusive language are nonsense at best and censorship and an impingement of freedom of speech at worst.

We're not going to fall into that trap here. A trap? Why? It's a trap because the examples are too easy and don't get to the heart of the matter. At the heart of this matter are more fundamental and challenging questions such as:

- What is actually involved in using language that is inclusive and not known to be offensive? What are the benefits and the drawbacks of using this language?

- Do these efforts to promote inclusive language inappropriately curb our freedom of speech and even silence people? Or do these efforts make more people feel like their voices are recognized and included?

There is no question that attempts to create more inclusive language involve prescriptive rules about usage. Are these prescriptive rules—or at least some of these prescriptive rules—better motivated than, say, the prescription against double negatives that I discussed in chapter 3?

In answering these questions, we're tackling what is often called "politically correct" or "PC" language, except that I am going to propose that we don't use those terms. The expression *politically correct* has undergone semantic pejoration—that is, its meaning has become more negative over time. The term has become so charged that it's hard to have reasoned conversations about it, and it turns out we don't all agree what it means. It cannot refer neutrally to efforts to reform language in order to make it more respectful and inclusive of all persons (not that this was its original meaning). Instead, *political correctness* often suggests overly sensitive, or silly and unnecessary, efforts to change language "at the whim" of underrepresented groups and their advocates, if not downright censorship.

I remember watching the term being pulled out on all sides in the lead-up to the 2016 U.S. presidential election. For example, Ben Carson, at the Republican National Convention, stated: "I'm not politically correct. And I hate political correctness because it is antithetical to the founding principles of this country. And the secular progressives use it to make people sit down and shut up while they change everything." In that view, political correctness is severely limiting freedom of speech and not allowing debate about social change.

A few months earlier, Kareem Abdul-Jabbar, famous for his sky-hook and his remarkable basketball career with the Los Angeles Lakers, wrote an editorial for *The Washington Post* arguing that these kinds of accusations about the threat of political correctness are a strategy to maintain the status quo. Abdul-Jabbar defines *political correctness* as "a relatively benign combination of good old-fashioned manners and simple sensitivity toward others." That doesn't sound so threatening. What Abdul-Jabbar and Carson share is their sense that underlying the stated concerns about political correctness are more fundamental concerns about social change.

Because this book is about language, we'll focus on politically correct language—which is a big chunk of the PC pie but not the entire pie (trigger warnings, affirmative action policies, and attention to all kinds of microaggressions are also often seen as part of political correctness). And to avoid the loaded term *politically correct,* we'll focus on what is at stake in using inclusive and/or sensitive language choices. I recognize that when I put it that way, it may sound nonthreatening, but passions run high. For example, when I wrote a column in 2021 for *The Washington Post* on singular *they,* which is the most inclusive third-person singular option (see chapter 18), the column received more than two thousand comments on all sides of the issue, and I received some stunningly angry email directly to my inbox. Over a pronoun! I didn't use the term *political correctness* in the column, but it was about what grammatical choices are respectful of people's identities.

So why the heat? Because, as we've already observed, debates about language are almost always about more than language. This might be one of the most profound things I will say in this book, so let me say it again: Debates about language are almost always about more than language.

In this case, debates about inclusive and sensitive language are about who has the power to call the linguistic shots about what language is and isn't inclusive and sensitive. It's fundamentally a power struggle between groups that have historically held most of the political, economic, and social power—what I'm going to call having the biggest microphone—and historically marginalized groups whose voices are becoming more and more centered in the broader public discourse. It's not that some of the language that today is deemed offensive is newly offensive; it's that the people who have been denigrated by this language have gained more power to call the language out as offensive. They have a bigger microphone than they have had in the past.

This fundamental power struggle about who gets to call the shots is obscured by the argument that it's only in the past few decades that language has been politicized. Many people, understandably, want to believe that throughout its history, language has been a neutral medium and that it recently shifted. In this view, language was a neutral conveyor of a message, not the message itself, and then historically marginalized groups started politicizing the language by asserting what language they found offensive and inoffensive.

But here's the thing: The language has never been neutral.

As speakers, we are always making choices about what language to use, both speaking and writing. Consider, as just one small example, politeness conventions. You might want to say, "Give me that dinner reservation at eight!" But in all likelihood, if you actually want to get a reservation at a busy restaurant, you would go with something more like "Could I get a dinner reservation at eight?" I know it doesn't seem like a big difference, but it is. You are respecting the power of the person booking tables to decide whether or not* to help you by employing what is conventionally seen as more polite language. This example seems mundane because we make these kinds of language choices all the time, every day, as part of navigating our social landscape. And power is part of that social landscape.

Every day we make choices about how to address others, which is also a negotiation of power. When I go to see a medical doctor, do I call them Dr. Patel? Or can I call them by their first name, given that they are calling me Anne, not Dr. Curzan? It is a kindness to tell others what to call us when there is a structural power difference and we have more power, as it can feel loaded and even scary for those with less power in terms of the potential consequences for getting it wrong.

Speakers with less social power, institutionally and/or in a given situation, typically need to be more careful in their language choices. One wrong word and you can lose your job—or your life. Don't

---

* There is absolutely nothing grammatically wrong with the expression *whether or not*, even though my word processing grammar checker doesn't like it. Sure, I could have just used *whether* here, but the added *or not* can function emphatically. So you might disagree with my choice rhetorically, but there is nothing grammatically amiss here.

forget, for example, the horrifying grounds on which African Americans were sometimes lynched in the history of the United States. This is why, when people say, "It's just words" as a way to dismiss the power of language, you should be suspicious. Language is powerful—it's usually not "just words." Words often have consequences. It's not as if all of us in the United States (where we have a constitutional guarantee of freedom of speech) have just been saying whatever we want, whenever we want to, for centuries, with no social consequences. That's not what freedom of speech means or has ever meant, given the social conventions that govern our daily interactions. Certainly, we *can* say whatever we want, but we are aware that there may be social consequences, small or severe, for a given language choice.

But those who have historically enjoyed a lot of social power have had to worry less about consequences—making it seem like freedom of speech is the same as freedom from consequences for getting it wrong. And this is what is so interesting and disruptive about recent movements advocating for more sensitive, inclusive language for and about historically marginalized groups. These movements have empowered the historically less empowered to call the linguistic shots, so to speak. Groups from African Americans to the LGBTQ+ community to women to people with disabilities— and the list goes on—have gotten a bigger, more powerful microphone to say what terms they find offensive and what identity terms they prefer. No one is telling people to "sit down and shut up," as Ben Carson feared. But times are changing—that part is definitely true—and we are all being asked to rethink some of our language choices to be respectful and inclusive of everyone around us. For the more powerful who have not had to be as careful with their choices, they are now getting a taste of how careful everyone around them has been with their language.

I hear four common concerns about these calls for more sensitive, inclusive language: First, "Preferred terms keep changing and I can't keep up, which doesn't seem fair." Second, "Some of the terms people are saying I should and shouldn't use seem ridiculous and over the top." Third, "I can't know everything that people think is offensive, and people should know that I didn't mean to be offensive—there's too much focus on the medium and not enough on the message itself, and it's hard and exhausting." And finally, "When I get it wrong, I risk being 'canceled,'" to use a current term for being publicly shunned.

Let's take each concern in turn.

First, preferred terms for groups do change over time (e.g., *woman* replacing *lady, African American* competing with *Black*), so it's fair to worry that our usage may not be current. At the same time, it's not unreasonable to ask us to be sensitive to changing conventions. We keep track of changing language in many areas of our lives, from evolving jargon in our workplaces to new slang (if we're young enough or cool enough to still be using slang!) to new technological terms. If we care about being part of a group and knowing the "in" language, we don't see it as an unreasonable expectation to know and keep up with the language. So in this case, the question for each of us is whether we're invested in paying attention to what language is seen as inclusive over time, especially from the perspective of the groups who are closest to the identity terms.

Sometimes we may discover there isn't agreement about preferred identity terms, and then we need to navigate the territory carefully. For example, the term *Latinx* originated in the academy and as I finish this book, studies show it is not preferred by most members of the Latina/Latino community, a good number of whom opt for *Latine*. This is an inclusive usage issue still under rigorous discussion within the community, and one of the kind, respectful, inclusive things you can do if you're not a member of the community is ask, in an open-minded and genuine way, what term a person or a group prefers.

Speaking of things still being sorted, let's turn to the second concern. As we work to create more inclusive language, some of the guidance can "swing wide" as I like to say: It can overshoot the mark and feel excessive. *Personhole cover* was not a good contender to replace *manhole cover,* and it's not clear to me how seriously it was ever recommended—but it was certainly out there as a punching bag for critics of PC language. (*Street hole cover* may work better for this essential item.) The *chief* in *CEO* is not historically a case of cultural appropriation and may not merit revision, as linguist John McWhorter has argued in *The New York Times*—although the case is complicated. I would struggle to support a wholesale rejection of the word *seminal*—although I have made the personal choice to use a term like *foundational* instead.

But examples we think may not be well-founded shouldn't be tools to try to dismantle the entire inclusive-language project. It's worthwhile to step back from our language and see what biases and offensive stereotypes have become embedded in the words we use—and do better. This whole book is about being intentional, careful, well-informed speakers, and using sensitive, inclusive language is part of that.

This is when well-intentioned speakers can feel frustrated: "Can't people just see that I'm well-intentioned and hear my message, even if I don't get all the words right?"

This brings us to the question of intention versus reception. Many of us as speakers want to believe that intention trumps reception. The reasoning goes like this: "If I didn't mean for what I said to be offensive, then it shouldn't be offensive. If the listener heard it as offensive, they are being oversensitive and need to understand I didn't mean it that way."

Okay, let's unpack that. Intention matters, but it doesn't trump.[*] That's not how language in real life works. Reception matters too. As speakers, we are responsible for what we intend to say as well as for how our words are received. So even if we didn't mean to offend, we should take seriously any offense our words have caused, seek to understand what happened, and repair what needs to be

---

[*] Multiple standard dictionaries I checked do not include this intransitive use of the verb *trump,* yet it seems clear and rhetorically effective in context. So I have decided to keep it despite editors flagging the use as potentially nonstandard. Would you have noticed without this footnote?

repaired. There may be times when we decide that the response to a language choice we have made does not justify a change in usage or a repair, but we should listen hard and be open to changing our minds.

Let me share a quick story about changing my own mind about what is and isn't inclusive language. I grew up using the second-person plural pronoun *you guys*, as did many speakers around me in the suburbs of Washington, D.C. Early in my academic career, I wrote a book on the history of gendered terms in English, and I argued, in print, that the word *guys* in *you guys* has been "bleached" of gender and functions neutrally as a plural marker. A few years ago, students in my introductory linguistics course persuasively challenged that argument. For them, it was not so easy to divorce the gendered meaning of *guy* from the plural *you guys;* some of them heard *you guys* as implicitly masculine. One student, Jason Dean, wrote an op-ed for *The Michigan Daily,* our university's newspaper, in which he notes, "I can't solve the gender wage gap by personally implementing sweeping policy changes, but I can, for instance, stop using 'you guys' to address my mostly-female physics study group in order to combat attitudes that STEM is a male domain." Since that class, I have been consciously trying to use *you all* as my second-person plural pronoun. (I wish I could pull off *y'all,* but I can't.) I slip sometimes and *you guys* pops out, but it seems worth the effort given what I'm hearing from young people.

These interactional dynamics bring us to the last question: Are we too quick to cancel each other over insensitive language choices? Let me start by saying that sometimes people intentionally use hateful, awful language to do harm, and we need to call that out and condemn it for what it is. But much of the time, in our daily lives, we're managing insensitive language choices by people who may not realize what they have said and its effects. In these cases, I would encourage us to be generous listeners in addition to sensitive speakers. Being a generous listener doesn't mean letting everything roll off your back and not alerting others to insensitive language choices; it does mean giving the speaker the benefit of the doubt and the space to course correct. It can mean saying something like, "This is what I just heard you say, which felt surprising and hurtful to me. I have a feeling you didn't mean for that to happen, so I wanted to say something." When we approach each other this way, it creates grace and space for repair and for learning for everyone in the interaction.

the bottom line

Next time you see a scathing critique in the mainstream press of "outlandish" attempts to help people use more inclusive language, consider thinking of this as (a) part of an ongoing attempt to create kinder, more inclusive language in a diverse society, which may sometimes veer off course on the way to a worthwhile destination; and (b) an easy target that makes fun of an important larger project. The larger project is a worthwhile one.

I hope we can debate questions of inclusive language with an understanding of how language works, recognizing that our language choices are not neutral and never have been, and that sometimes we get to call the linguistic shots, and sometimes we're asked to listen to other people's calls. Sometimes these debates will happen in public, and sometimes they'll be in our own heads, between our inner grammando and inner wordie—or perhaps between our inner wordie and itself. As I reflect on my change of heart on *you guys,* it was my inner wordie taking in new data about the reception of *you guys* to rethink how that pronoun works and then to convince me it was worth the effort to change my usage.

Changing language may not always change hearts and minds, but it does change what people hear and see. And because we can't hear and see one another's thoughts directly, changed language makes for a more inclusive space for everyone. Students in my classroom don't know I still consciously have to remember to say *you all;* they just hear me use that inclusive pronoun.

Let's remember that our language choices matter, even the small and mundane ones. And let's be generous with each other whenever we can, as speakers and listeners, as writers and readers.

part 2

what does that
word mean?

5

···············

the funnest chapter

unner is a cringeworthy word. Did you just groan or stick out your tongue or otherwise express displeasure when you read it? Did you contemplate not buying or reading this book because it has *funner* in the title? I have had audiences literally boo when I have brought up the word. Recently a friend wrinkled his nose at *funner* and said, "I just don't like the way it sounds." I asked how he felt about the word *runner,* and he had no concerns about the sound of *runner.* Never mind that the two words rhyme: People's negative response to *funner* isn't actually about the sound. If enough teachers and parents and other authority figures have told you that a word is wrong, then it comes to sound wrong.

Why people think *funner* is wrong is a more interesting question than you might expect, and part of the answer is that some folks still think that *fun* shouldn't be an adjective at all. Wait, what? Am I saying that there are people who think it is not okay to say that we went to "a fun party" last night? Yes, that is exactly what I am saying. And once you know that, one of the questions on the *American Heritage Dictionary* usage survey will make more sense.

In fall 2015, I opened the usage survey to discover that there were five sentences focused on the word *fun.* As I mentioned in chapter 1, members of the Usage Panel were asked to rate each sentence on a four-point scale: completely acceptable, somewhat acceptable, somewhat unacceptable, completely unacceptable, in a "more formal setting." Here are the first three sentences:

- That party was really fun.
- That party was so fun.
- We went to a fun party.

I voted completely acceptable on all three sentences, given that you can find this use of *fun* all over edited prose, and I would guess many of you concur. In fact, it is hard to see why the sentences were even included in the survey, unless you know that there is lingering concern about *fun* as an adjective. Why?

For the first hundred years or so of its life in English, *fun* was a noun and a verb, but not an adjective. The verb is the earliest form recorded, and you can still hear the verb *fun* in an expression like "I'm just funnin'!" when someone is joking around or teasing. The word first shows up as a noun around 1700, and it could refer to a trick or an act of fraud, as well as enjoyment or amusement, which is the most common meaning today. So we can still have fun or look for fun or make fun of someone; in all of those phrases, *fun* is a noun.

It's hard to know exactly when *fun* took on work as an adjective. The *Oxford English Dictionary* has an example of "rather fun" (which suggests that the writer believes it is an adjective) as early as 1827 and of the phrase "fun jottings" in 1853. But as the editors note, *fun* could still be a noun in "fun jottings" the same way that *leisure* is a noun in "leisure reading." It isn't until the mid-twentieth century that the adjective *fun* starts to occur with any regularity, which helps explain why not everyone accepts it. This is a change that has occurred within the lifetime of folks who are still alive.

It is relatively easy to understand how speakers reinterpreted the noun *fun* as an adjective. Imagine that you are a kid who hears your parent exclaim, "That game was fun!" Your parent may have meant *fun* as a noun, similar to saying "That game was chaos!" But if you're a kid who is just learning the language, you have good reason to think *fun* might be an adjective in the exclamation "That game was fun!" After all, you could also say that the game was funny, great, ridiculous, challenging, goofy—all adjectives. And once you have reinterpreted *fun* as an adjective, then you can refer to a fun game, a very fun game, a game that was so fun.

Given the ubiquity of adjectival *fun,* I think it is fair now to call it standard. But you still may not find it often in *The New York Times.* In 1999, *The New York Times Manual of Style and Usage* had this to say about *fun*: "Though the commercials may someday win respectability for *fun* as an adjective (*a fun vacation*), the gushing sound argues for keeping the word a noun." I'm not sure I would describe the sound of *fun* as "gushing," but in any case, ouch! No respect or respectability for *fun* in 1999. By 2015, the *Manual* has softened its tone and states that *fun,* as an adjective, "remains colloquial." Bryan Garner agrees, describing adjective *fun* as a "casualism" in the 2022 edition of *Garner's Modern English Usage.* Now, obviously, often we are talking about fun things in more casual contexts, but at this point, there isn't good reason to restrict *fun* to colloquial contexts. What did the Usage Panel say? In 2015, 84 percent voted the sentence "We went to a fun party" acceptable—so you're in good company if you feel like you don't want to worry about using *fun* as an adjective.

Now, back to the usage ballot and the last two sentences in the *fun* entry:

- That party was funner than I expected.
- That was the funnest party I've been to this year.

If your inner grammando was fine with the first three sentences but just put its foot down at these two sentences, you are not alone. *Funner* and *funnest* elicit strong reactions, even from folks who accept a lot of changes in the language. *Fun* can be an adjective, fine, but it is still *more fun* and *most fun,* not *funner* and *funnest.* So why do *funner* and *funnest* keep popping up, like an annoying game of Whac-A-Mole? And are they really wrong?

To answer this question, we need to go back to the relative new-ness of *fun* as an adjective. As a noun, if we are comparing how much *fun* we are having, we would use *more* and *most,* just like we would talk about *more chaos* or the *most chaos* we have ever seen. So perhaps you are having *more fun* than your best friends, but I am having the *most fun* of anyone. And because people were used to talking about having more fun and the most fun, even when *fun* became an adjective, it still sounded right to say *more fun* rather than *funner,* and *most fun* rather than *funnest.*

When little kids learn the language, though, they naturally come up with the words *funner* and *funnest*—and odds are that those persistent kids will, eventually, win. Why do they keep doing this? Let's consider other one-syllable adjectives and how they make the comparative and superlative. The adjective *tall* typically becomes *taller* and *tallest;* we have *wide/wider/widest, smart/smarter/smart-est, blue/bluer/bluest.* The pattern is crystal clear. So if you are a kid learning the language, you have good reason to try to make *fun* behave like all these other one-syllable adjectives, which means that you say *funner* and *funnest.*

When kids are then corrected by adults or teachers to say *more fun* and *most fun,* they will learn the exception, just like *brought,* not *bringed,* is the past tense of *bring,* and *oxen,* not *oxes,* is the plural of *ox* (at least for a few more years!). I think we're already seeing some shift in attitudes, though, which means that kids may not always be corrected. When I talk about this issue with under-graduates, they still go full grammando on *funner,* but they have a more mixed, rather "meh"-like reaction to *funnest. Funnest* sounds more okay to them, if not downright fine—and I would guess that the iPod ad about fifteen years ago for the "funnest iPod ever" didn't hurt. My prediction is that *funnest* will be acceptable in more and more contexts first, and then *funner* will scoot in on its coattails. They're both words to be cautious with right now, given the visceral reaction some folks have to hearing or reading them (88 percent of the Usage Panel rejected *funner,* with 80 percent rejecting *funnest*), but this change in acceptability could happen relatively quickly.

MORE UNIQUE

As long as I have your teeth on edge and your inner grammando worked up by using the word *funner* so many times in the first half of this chapter, let's move right on to another peeve: *more unique.* I know, I know: If something is unique, it is one of a kind, which means that it can't be more unique or more one of a kind than something else. And it certainly can't be very unique or quite unique. Unless it can . . .

There are some adjectives that, at least theoretically, can't take comparative and superlative forms because their meanings do not allow for comparison: *unique, equal, perfect, pregnant.* But when you look at actual usage, in fact all four of these adjectives do show up in comparative constructions sometimes. Let's focus on *unique* and *perfect,* as those are the two that make people grumpiest.

In the second edition of the influential usage guide *The King's English* (1908), H. W. Fowler and F. G. Fowler lay down the line: "A thing is *unique,* or not unique; there are no degrees of uniqueness; nothing is ever somewhat or rather unique, though many things are almost or in some respects unique." They then compare *unique* to the historically synonymous *singular,* which has, they believe, been worn down through "slovenly use" to mean just 'remarkable.' The Fowler brothers worry that *unique* "will be worn out in turn, and we shall have to resort to *unexampled* and keep that clear of qualifications as long as we can." Or we could use *one of a kind.* The fact is that we come up with alternatives as needed. The Fowler brothers add a funny note about the "regrettable" uses of *unique* in advertising, with all the offers of "unique opportunities." They conclude: "It may generally be assumed with safety that they are lying; but lying is not in itself a literary offence, so that with these we have nothing to do."

William Zinsser takes on *unique* in his 2012 guide *On Writing Well*, alongside the grammando favorite *-wise*: "Any dolt can rule that the suffix 'wise,' as in 'healthwise,' is doltwise, or that being 'rather unique' is no more possible than being rather pregnant." It's a clever criticism, but *pregnant* is a tricky comparison. The adjective *pregnant* is sometimes used comparatively. A nine-month pregnant woman may well say to a four-month pregnant woman: "Oh, just wait until you get more pregnant!"

Bryan Garner picks up Fowler's language in the most recent edition of *Garner's Modern English Usage* and notes that phrases like *very unique* and *quite unique* have been seen as "slovenly." The fact that the *Oxford English Dictionary* has examples of *unique* meaning 'uncommon, unusual' back to the nineteenth century (and examples go back even further than that) is unpersuasive to him; this is a change in the language "worth resisting." But why?

Semantic changes—or changes in word meaning—often seem interesting if not downright cool to us in retrospect. Who knew that *nice* used to mean 'silly' and that *lollygag* meant to 'fool around,' in the kissing sense of 'fool around'? Well, I knew, obviously, but I wanted to share these fun facts with you. (Did you catch that adjectival *fun* there?) And *decimate* started out meaning 'kill one in every ten'—seriously. If you know some Latin, you can see the root for 'ten' (*deci-*) in the word, in the same way that you can see the root for 'one' (*uni-*) in *unique*. We can trace the word *unique* back to Latin *unicus,* 'single, sole, alone of its kind,' which we can trace back to Latin *unus,* 'one.' The word comes into English via French, and when it appears in the early seventeenth century, it really does seem to mean 'one of a kind,' and only that. But by the mid-eighteenth century there are already examples where it means 're-markable' or 'unusual.'

It's not that surprising that once Latin borrowings like *decimate* and *unique* became integrated into English, their meanings started to drift over the years. *Decimate* shifted its meaning toward 'destroy a large part of,' and *unique* has picked up the meaning 'uncommon,' while retaining the meaning 'one of a kind.' Is this a loss? Sure, at some level. But word meanings drift, and nothing terrible happens. We adapt and find ways to say what we want to say. It's not sloppiness or, as Garner argues, a signal that our culture doesn't believe in absolutes. If we really want to say that something is one of a kind, we can say that: The wording *one of a kind* is unambiguous right now.

When the *American Heritage Dictionary* Usage Panel was asked in 2004 about the sentence "Her designs are quite unique," 66 percent rejected it as unacceptable. That seems pretty damning, and it certainly signals that we still need to watch this usage in formal writing; at the same time, it's worth noting that 80 percent of the panel rejected the same sentence in 1988. And the editors of the dictionary point out some very rhetorically effective uses of comparative *unique*, such as this sentence from Martin Luther King, Jr.: "I am in the rather unique position of being the son, the grandson, and the great-grandson of preachers." The adjective *unique* here is stronger than *unusual;* it doesn't make the claim that Martin Luther King, Jr., was the only man to have been in this position, but it strongly suggests there can't be many.

The expression *more perfect* is perhaps the most famous noncomparable adjective used comparatively, at least in the United States, given that it shows up in the phrasing "a more perfect Union" in the preamble to the Constitution: "We the People of the United States, in Order to form a more perfect Union, establish Justice, insure domestic Tranquility, provide for the common defense, promote the general Welfare . . ." We could argue that the Constitution is wrong (which grammandos have certainly done over the decades about different bits of wording in the document), or we could try to understand what the wording is seeking to express here. I think Patricia O'Conner and Stewart Kellerman, on their blog *Grammarphobia,* provide a compelling defense: They argue that *more perfect* is capturing the process of striving toward perfection, so this is closer to the ideal, not more than the ideal.

Much the same thing happens with *more equal*. Let's imagine we're talking about the ratio of apples to oranges, and while there are still more apples than oranges, you might note, "Well, it's more equal than it used to be." Here again *equal* represents a goal or an ideal, toward which we are working. Part of the message: Word meaning is complicated and dependent on context. Sometimes *equal* is precise and absolute: Things are exactly the same on whatever count they are being measured. But sometimes *equal* is aspirational.

the bottom line
. . . .

Some of these comparatives remain a siren call for grammandos, so your inner grammando isn't wrong if it's counseling you to be careful when you're writing in formal, high-stakes contexts. But know that the changes we're witnessing follow predictable patterns or unsurprising paths in the history of English, and they're not "wrong" in any absolute sense. *Funner* is "wrong" only because we've decided *fun* should be an exception to the rule about how one-syllable adjectives make comparisons. And *more unique* is "slovenly" only if you don't accept that *unique* has broadened its meaning—like hundreds and hundreds of words before it. Our inner wordies have good reasons to overrule our inner grammandos in encouraging us all to be more accepting of the changes here. It's worth quieting the siren call if we can.

verbing

n one of my favorite *Calvin and Hobbes* cartoons, six-year-old Calvin states, "I like to verb words."

"What?" replies his tiger companion, Hobbes.

"I take nouns and adjectives and make them verbs," explains Calvin. "Remember when 'access' was a thing? Now it's something you *do*. It got verbed." Calvin then concludes, "Verbing weirds language."

"Maybe," adds Hobbes, "we can eventually make language a complete impediment to understanding."

Of course, verbing rarely is an impediment to understanding because it is relatively easy for us as listeners or readers to interpret from context what a newly verbed word means. The verb *to verb* is first recorded in the *Oxford English Dictionary* in 1928, and its synonym *verbify* goes back to at least 1828, but concerns about verbing or verbifying go back even further.

Benjamin Franklin, for example, had serious concerns about nouns becoming verbs—so serious, in fact, that in 1789 he wrote to Noah Webster about these rogue nouns. Webster had recently written his book *Dissertation on the English Language*; he had not yet written his famous *American Dictionary of the English Language*. Franklin's letter begins with thanks for receiving a copy of Webster's book, and Franklin then warms up to sharing a few peeves:

I cannot but applaud your Zeal for preserving the Purity of our Language, both in its Expressions and Pronunciation, and in correcting the popular Errors, several of our States are continually falling into with respect to both. Give me leave to mention some of them, tho' possibly they may already have occurr'd to you. I wish however that in some future Publication of your's, you would set a discountenancing Mark upon them.

Franklin clearly relished the idea of helping with the project of correcting the language to preserve its purity. If you feel strongly about standard use of apostrophes, your inner grammando may have grimaced at the *your's* in Franklin's letter, especially given his concern about correct usage; you can read more about the history of apostrophes in chapter 26. Franklin also liked to capitalize nouns, much like German (more about that in chapter 27); he would not have seen his sporadic capital letters, or his apostrophes, as errors. But there were three new verbs—*notice, advocate,* and *progress*—that he thought were errors. Here's his take:

During my late Absence in France I find that several other new Words have been introduced into our parliamentary Language; for Example, I find a Verb formed from the Substantive [noun] *Notice. . . .* Also another Verb, from the Substantive [noun], *Advocate, The Gentleman who* ADVOCATES, or *who has* ADVOCATED that Motion, &c. Another from the Substantive [noun] *Progress,* the most awkward and abominable of the three. . . . If you should happen to be of my Opinion with respect to these Innovations you will use your Authority in reprobating them.

The verb *progress* is not only awkward but abominable? It is hard to imagine now, given how standard it is for things to progress through time (in fact, this chapter is progressing as I write). And no one notices anyone else using the verb *notice* or *advocate* anymore, let alone singling them out for comment and criticism. (The usage question with *advocate* is now whether it is okay to *advocate for a position* in addition to *advocating a position*. When I was asked as part of the usage survey, I voted that both were acceptable.)

I have started with Franklin going grammando on these three verbs as context for concerns about new verbs today, from *impact* (which I covered in chapter 1) to *gift* to *dialogue*. Or at least what people think are new verbs! Both *to gift* and *to dialogue* go back to the 1600s. In any case, Franklin's letter is a helpful reminder that what seemed abominable in the past, often because it was relatively new usage, can become standard and unremarkable. In 1789, *notice* as a verb meaning 'become aware of' would have been around a little over a century, *progress* and *advocate* closer to two centuries—but they had hit Franklin's radar as new and unnecessary.

Linguists refer to the process of words moving from a noun to a verb or a verb to a noun or an adjective to a verb (you get the idea) as "functional shift." Over the past several hundred years, many words in English have jumped categories this way, and we have two choices: We could give in to our inner grammando and lament the jumping, or we could marvel at the way the structure of English facilitates this jumping. Wordies lean toward the latter. How, after all, are these new words born so easily?

The answer lies in the structure of modern English. English grammar now involves very few inflectional endings—suffixes on words that show things like past tense or plural—which makes it relatively easy to use words as new parts of speech. For example, once *gift* becomes a verb, we know how to make it behave like a regular verb by adding *-ed* to make the past tense (*gifted*), *-ed* to make the past participle (*has gifted*), and *-ing* to make the present participle (*gifting*), and voilà! A new verb.

We can just as easily make a new noun because English no longer has grammatical gender, like Spanish, Russian, Latin, and many languages around the world. (You'll notice that I said "no longer"— Old English, back when the poem *Beowulf* was written, did have grammatical gender, so that all inanimate nouns were masculine, feminine, or neuter.) As a result, we can take a verb like *hire* and turn it into a noun, which lets us talk about a new hire. No one has to assign this new noun a grammatical gender—it just gets to be a noun. Multiple new hires? No problem, just add *-s* to make the noun plural. In the seventeenth century, when we took the adjective *clean* and made it a verb, we didn't have to do anything to the form of the word: We could just start cleaning things as a way to make them clean. When you think about it, it's a remarkable attribute of English that the grammar allows this flexibility in category crossing.

English has gained a lot of new verbs through functional shift, in addition to *notice, progress,* and *advocate.* Recently, just to name a few, we have added the verbs *network, trash, friend,* and *google* (which also involved genericization, when a trademarked term starts to be used generically). A listener to my radio program recently wrote to me with concerns about the relatively new verbs *action* and *whiteboard,* which felt like business jargon to him.

Is it fair sometimes to criticize a new word as jargony? Sure. But wordies, with the skills of a good bird-watcher, would note that some jargon escapes its original habitat—such as the business workplace—and comes to feel much less jargony. And so you should be open to listening to your inner wordie and revisiting this criticism. Let me give you an example with a whole set of verbs: new verbs that end with *-ize.*

In chapter 1, I mentioned that Benjamin Franklin didn't like the verb *colonize.* He wrote in a 1760 letter to David Hume: "I give [it] up as bad." The verb had been in English for about 150 years at that point; and now *colonize* is completely unremarkable. About two hundred years later, as I described in chapter 2, the verb *finalize* was causing some consternation as an example of bureaucratic jargon. *Finalize* first appears in written English in the early twentieth century, and in the late 1960s, 90 percent of the *American Heritage Dictionary* Usage Panel rejected it as unacceptable. Ninety percent! By 2014, only 15 percent of the Usage Panel disapproved of *finalize.* That is the sound of a peeve dying.

Concerns about *-ize* verbs proliferate, and they often signal a verb about to take off in usage. The verb *utilize* was borrowed into English from French in the early 1800s, meaning 'to make or render useful.' When *utilize* rose in usage in the mid-twentieth century, commentators started to critique it. Eric Partridge, in his 1954 guide *Usage and Abusage,* notes that *utilize* is "99 times out of 100, much inferior to 'use'; the other one time it is merely inferior." William Strunk and E. B. White, among others, have recommended that *utilize* be eschewed because we already have *use.* But *utilize* has a distinct meaning, a helpful verb when we are describing intentionally making something useful or practical. In the early 2000s, it was the verb *incentivize* that was getting a lot of grammandos' attention: "boorish bureaucratic misspeak," writes Edward Rothstein in *The New York Times* in 2000, and "ungodly" is the term Benjamin Dreyer uses in 2019 in *Dreyer's English.* The verb goes back to at least the 1960s, and it started to rise in usage in the 1990s—hence the going grammando on it.

Let me also share a personal example of my wrestling with business jargon. A few years ago, I had a colleague in the business school who loved the verb *double-click.* Not in reference to double-clicking on a computer icon or application but to diving deeper on a topic. It was his transition between slides during a presentation: "So there are three factors. Let's start by double-clicking on the first factor. Next slide!" My first reaction was fueled by my inner grammando. I thought, "How ridiculously business school-y! We don't need this verb to describe metaphorically digging into something." One day, after listening to one of these presentations, I vented to my partner about this verb, and he looked at me with bemusement. "I think it's rather clever," he responded. And, of course, he is right. It's a good metaphorical extension, almost poetic. Why not enjoy it, as opposed to being cranky about it? I appreciated my partner calling out my inner grammando, so that I could wrestle my initial reaction to *double-click* into acceptance and even a bit of joy.

Before we finish this chapter on verbing and new verbs more

generally, let's return to look seriously at the "we don't need more synonyms" argument, which is often pulled out to criticize a new verb. English has a lot of synonyms. Given the language's history of borrowing, and given humans' pleasure in word creation, synonyms proliferate. For example, think about a few different verbs for asking: *ask, question, interrogate, query, inquire*. They differ in formality, but they generally refer to the action of asking questions. To take a more dramatic example, consider all the words that refer to being drunk: *drunk, intoxicated, inebriated, smashed, trashed, hammered, sloshed, tanked, blitzed, bombed,* and the list goes on and on and on. Students in my classes love the day when we try to generate as long a list as we can of slang words for drunk, and from year to year, there are always new ones. My point is that English has lots of synonyms in many areas of the lexicon, and they demonstrate the remarkable creativity we as humans bring to language, the many languages that have contributed to the English lexicon, the diversity of our linguistic identities, and the nuanced choices we get to make as speakers and writers.

the bottom line

Remember the bird-watcher analogy, and do not try to kill the new birds! And by birds, I mean verbs. I would generally recommend talking down your inner grammando as you hear or see new verbs. If you have been complaining about the verbs *impact* or *gift* or *dialogue* or *incentivize*, know that your concerns will likely look as quaint in fifty years as Benjamin Franklin's complaints about *notice, progress,* and *advocate*. Remember the Usage Panel reversing themselves on *finalize* in a fifty-year span. Often the primary reason to criticize a verb is that it is relatively new or newly popular, but really, that is not a very good reason at all.

As a speaker or writer, it can be helpful to be aware of a new verb's reputation as potentially jargony—that's where the usage labels in standard dictionaries can be a useful guide. That said, it may not seem jargony to you, or it may not be overly jargony in the context in which you're speaking or writing. Or you may want to be part of de-jargonizing the verb by using it in a wider range of contexts. We have the power to open the gates in both how we use and how we respond to new uses of language.

feeling hopeful about *hopefully*

"Hopefully Anne took the neon yellow scooter out for a test ride."

There are two ways to understand that sentence, and it comes down to who is doing the hoping. In one version, Anne is full of hope as she jumps on the scooter and takes it out for a spin. She has always wanted a scooter and loves this neon yellow one (yellow makes it safer, right?).

If that is not how you interpreted the sentence, though, you are far from alone.

In the other version, the speaker or some generalized "we" are all hoping that Anne took the neon yellow scooter out for a test ride. Perhaps we know that Anne can be an impulsive buyer, and we want her to try riding the scooter before she sinks money into it. Or perhaps we know that the neon yellow scooter is not well-built (definitely not safer), even though it looks cool.

In the first version, the adverb *hopefully* modifies the verb in the sentence: *took*. It describes how Anne approached her test scoot. In the second version, the adverb *hopefully* modifies the entire sentence. It describes the stance of the speaker or writer toward the entire proposition of the sentence: that Anne took the neon yellow scooter out for a test scoot.

Can an adverb do that, modify the entire sentence? Or, more to the point, should we let an adverb do that?

WHAT ADVERBS CAN AND CAN'T DO

There's a reason adverbs are sometimes called the "trash can cate-gory" of English grammar. A lot of kinds of words have gotten rammed into this category, which makes it messier than, say, nouns. Adverbs modify verbs, as you undoubtedly learned at some point—and they modify adjectives, other adverbs, and entire clauses or sentences. The one thing they don't modify is nouns: Adjectives al-ready have that covered. So, in general, adverbs are hard to pin down in terms of what they modify.

Many adverbs also are hard to pin down within a sentence: They have the flexibility to move around in a sentence the way few other words do. Consider the sentence: "Anne scooted unsteadily out of the parking lot." (For all her enthusiasm, Anne has never ridden a scooter before.) The adverb *unsteadily,* which modifies the verb *scooted,* has three other spots it could occupy in that sentence: "Unsteadily Anne scooted out of the parking lot," or "Anne un-steadily scooted out of the parking lot," or "Anne scooted out of the parking lot unsteadily." The noun phrase *the parking lot* can't move within the phrase "out of the parking lot," and neither can *of*—or the subject *Anne* for that matter. But the adverb is more rest-less and it doesn't have to sit next to the verb it modifies.

I sometimes tell students that if they're not sure what part of speech a word is, the safest guess is "adverb" as it is such a catchall category. What part of speech is *very* in "very messy"? Adverb. *However*? Adverb. *Not*? Many dictionaries and grammar books call it an adverb. (Some let it be its own part of speech.) What about *yes,* in "Yes, I can"? Adverb.

You can likely already see another issue lurking: These four dif-ferent adverbs do not work the same way. At all. *Very* is an intensi-fier: It modifies an adjective or an adverb and adds emphasis. We have a slew of these in English, from the more formal (e.g., *quite interesting*) to the more colloquial (e.g., *really great, so crazy*) to the downright slangy (*wicked cool, hella pumped, super chill*). They have to occur right before the adverb or adjective, and they can't modify a verb (you wouldn't say "very eat").

However is an adverb that semantically joins one clause to another, expressing a contrastive relationship. The difference between *however* and *but* is complicated enough that it gets its own section in this book (see chapter 24).

The word *not* is a one-off: It is how we create a negative sentence and it follows very specific rules about where it can occur in the verb phrase. In today's usage, it will always be "I will not lie," not "I not will lie" or "I will lie not." And if *not* is going to negate an adjective or adverb, it will come right before it: "not happy" or "not quickly." *Not,* like intensifiers, is not flexible about where it can show up in a sentence; the adverb *however,* however, is more flexible (see, I could have written "however, *however* is more flexible").

Then, *yes,* when it is expressing affirmation or agreement (often in conversation), is an adverb modifying the whole clause or sentence: "Yes to what I am about to say."

So with that description of adverbs behind us, let's return to *hopefully* and whether it can also be one of these adverbs that modifies an entire clause or sentence.

THE "PROBLEM" WITH *HOPEFULLY*

Hopefully started to be used as a sentence adverb meaning 'I/we hope, it is hoped' in the first decades of the twentieth century. And it took off in use because it's useful. Sure, I could say "I hope" or "It is hoped," but *hopefully* does that more efficiently. In addition, *hopefully* can be helpfully ambiguous about exactly who is hoping. Let's imagine I say, "Hopefully the road construction will be finished before the holidays." Clearly I am hoping that this will be the case, but odds are that I am trying to express a more generalized, shared hope that the construction will be finished and not cause terrible traffic delays. As speakers and writers, sometimes we want to leave it open as to exactly who is hoping, and sentence adverb *hopefully* does the trick.

Hopefully is also far from alone in the category of sentence adverbs that express the speaker's or writer's stance toward what they are saying. Consider *mercifully* and *thankfully*: "Mercifully his lecture lasted only an hour," or "Thankfully no one fell asleep and started snoring during the lecture." You can see the ambiguity in those sentences about just how many people might think it was merciful that the lecture was on the shorter side or are feeling thankful there wasn't snoring. *Curiously, notably,* and *interestingly* work much the same way. Another set of sentence adverbs, including *frankly, truthfully,* and *bluntly,* capture the way the speaker is speaking: For example, if I say, "Frankly, I thought the lecture was dreadful," you know that I am speaking candidly. With these sentence adverbs, it's not ambiguous who is being frank, truthful, or blunt.

So, given all that, what is wrong with *hopefully*? Frankly, what's wrong with *hopefully* is that some grammarians in the 1960s noticed what had happened to *hopefully* (that is, that people had started using it as a sentence adverb), and they decided it was bad usage. The idea that it was bad usage took hold, and sentence adverb *hopefully* started to get edited out of formal writing, even though speakers continued to use it. The graph below from *Time* magazine shows the dramatic drop in the use of *hopefully* in the magazine after the 1960s. The numbers are calculated as how many times the word *hopefully* occurs per one million words of text. You can see the use peak at around fifteen occurrences per million words in the middle of the twentieth century and then plummet down to two or three occurrences per million words after prescriptivism against it kicks in. (It doesn't disappear because editors can't edit it out of direct quotes.)

Why is it bad usage? Many commentators have argued that the ambiguity of sentence adverb *hopefully*—that it isn't always clear who is hoping—is the reason to avoid it. Point taken, but *mercifully* hasn't been criticized in the same way, even though the same issue

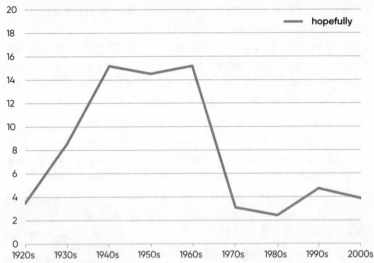

A *Time* Magazine Corpus search showing the relative frequency per million words of the word *hopefully* from the 1920s to the 2000s

of ambiguity applies. And as noted earlier, sometimes that ambiguity is useful and just what you mean. There is a reason that sentence adverb *hopefully* shot up in popularity over the course of the twentieth century—and it indicates that the ambiguity inherent in a sentence adverb is something that we as speakers are able to manage, if we notice it at all. Rather than calling sentence adverb *hopefully* categorically wrong, we could say that writers should minimize any unhelpful ambiguity with *hopefully*.

The opinion of the *American Heritage Dictionary* Usage Panel on *hopefully* is instructive about how judgments shift over time. When the panel was surveyed in 1969, almost half of the group (44 percent) accepted *hopefully* as a sentence adverb. Remember, this would have been when the condemnation of using *hopefully* this way was fairly new. By 1999, the number who accepted sentence adverb *hopefully* had gone down to 34 percent. That is, the panel became crankier about the usage over those thirty years, as the idea that there is something wrong with *hopefully* took hold— even as the panel showed much less concern about sentence adverb *mercifully*. But now the tide seems to have turned. In 2012, 63 percent accepted the sentence "Hopefully, the treaty will be ratified." (I was among those who voted it acceptable, you are probably not surprised to know.)

In the spring of 2012, *The Associated Press Stylebook* changed its treatment of this word and started to allow *hopefully* with the meaning 'it is hoped.' This change made headlines in newspapers such as *The Washington Post* and was featured on National Public Radio, which is fascinating in and of itself. At the end of the day, it's just an adverb. But you wouldn't have known that from the public reception of the change. In the more than six hundred online comments to the article about the decision in *The Washington Post,* commenters used words like *butcher, degeneration,* and *sin.* While some journalists accepted the AP's decision, others fiercely rejected it, arguing that journalistic prose cannot tolerate the ambiguity. The spoken language is one thing; journalistic prose is another.

That is certainly true, but remember what was happening in *Time* magazine before grammarians clamped down on this "unacceptable" ambiguity. And if we're honest about it, how confusing is "Hopefully, the treaty will be ratified"? We know that the speaker or writer feels the hope, and the real question is how many others share it. It doesn't necessarily seem better to try to specify that broader hopeful group: for example, "People around the world, including me, are hoping the treaty will be ratified"? Or we could make clear that it is a general, less specified hope: for example, "There is a general hope that the treaty will be ratified." But that's wordy, and unnecessary wordiness is rarely a virtue.

the bottom line

All indicators point to the decline of this "rule" about not using *hopefully* as a sentence adverb, which wasn't an especially helpful rule to begin with. Hopefully, at some point soon we'll go back to the attitude of the 1950s when everyone was chill about sentence adverb *hopefully,* if they even noticed it at all. That said, a modicum of caution may still be in order. With 63 percent of the Usage Panel accepting the construction, that means one in three panelists still judge this use of *hopefully* as incorrect. But the ground is shaky under their feet.

There is no good reason to single *hopefully* out for censure over *mercifully* or *curiously.* Using *hopefully* does not make your writing inherently imprecise, as some experts have opined. And sometimes the kind of ambiguity or latitude in the circumference of the hopefulness that *hopefully* allows can serve our writerly purposes well.

8

....

quite literally

Before we turn to the question of whether using *literally* to mean something like 'figuratively' is killing the English language (as a Reddit user put it in 2013), I want to start with another wedding story. I promise this is relevant.

It was over fifteen years ago at the wedding of a dear friend, let's call him Michael (because that is his name), who also happens to be a lexicographer and a linguist. After a lovely ceremony, the handful of linguists and lexicographers who had come as guests were all seated together—undoubtedly so we would not annoy the other guests! As the hosts clearly anticipated, the conversation turned to the oddities of language, and Jesse Sheidlower, then the principal North American editor at the *Oxford English Dictionary*, posed a puzzle to our end of the table. Listen to this sentence, he requested, and let me know if you hear anything unusual about it. The sentence went something like this:

> Mary and her partner had just moved in upstairs, and their boxes lay on the kitchen floor, still unpacked.

Are you wondering if *lay* is okay? It's fine. It's a red herring in the sentence. *Partner?* Sure, we don't know if it is a romantic partner or a business partner, and the gender of the person is unspecified—but that is all okay.

I nodded to Jesse: Sounds good—nothing unusual jumps out to me.

So here's the question: In your imagination, is stuff in the boxes or not? In my head, the boxes are still taped up, with stuff in them. But look at the sentence: The boxes are *unpacked*. Unpacked! It seems like that should mean that the boxes are empty, because they have been unpacked. But at least some of the time, especially if *unpacked* appears with *still*, *unpacked* can mean 'un-unpacked'—that is, still packed. Will this meaning of *unpacked* stick? It's hard to know. The verb *unpack* remains unambiguous. But it might stick.

Perhaps you, or your inner grammando, are thinking, "But that's not possible! A word can't *also* mean its opposite." But we have multiple examples already in the language, sometimes called auto-antonyms or contronyms. If we dust a table, we are removing the dust from it; but if we dust a cake with powdered sugar, we're sprinkling the sugar on the cake. If we sanction an action, we might be allowing it or we might be punishing people for doing it. If we cleave to something, we are clinging to it; but if we take a cleaver and cleave a piece of meat in two, we have split it apart (hence a cloven hoof and a cleft chin).

The verb *peruse* now means two opposite things, as you may or may not have noticed. Dictionaries are just catching up on this one, and some are still calling the newer meaning a "usage problem." Historically, *peruse* meant 'to read closely, to pore over,' and some speakers still use it that way. But when I survey a room of undergraduate students, I hear meanings much closer to 'skim' and 'scan,' such as quickly perusing the newspaper headlines to see what has happened in the world or perusing the grocery store shelves to locate an item. And we can imagine how this happened. My mother used the verb *peruse* to mean 'read closely.' Let's imagine that she's perusing the classified ads to find a used bike for one of her grandkids.

"Grandma, what are you doing?"

"Perusing the classifieds for your bike." (Yes, my mother did talk to even her young grandchildren like adults.)

From the child's perspective, Grandma appears to be looking up and down the classifieds in a way that could be described as scanning or skimming, even though Grandma sees herself as poring over those ads. And voilà: That word has been reinterpreted to mean something close to its opposite. Once enough young people have adopted the new meaning, it gets momentum—and then dictionary editors start to pay attention and decide how and when to enter the new meaning into the entry for *peruse*.

The *American Heritage Dictionary of the English Language*, online edition, includes the 'read carefully' definition first and then labels the meaning 'glance over, skim' as a usage problem. The usage note reads:

> *Peruse* has long meant "to read thoroughly." . . . But the word is often used more loosely, to mean simply "to read," as in *The librarians checked to see which titles had been perused in the last month and which ones had been left untouched*. Seventy percent of the Panel rejected this example in 1999, but only 39 percent rejected it in 2011. Further extension of the word to mean "to glance over, skim" has traditionally been considered an error, but our ballot results suggest that it is becoming somewhat more acceptable. When asked about the sentence *I only had a moment to peruse the manual quickly*, 66 percent of the Panel found it unacceptable in 1988, 58 percent in 1999, and 48 percent in 2011.

Here we're seeing a peeve die in the face of an "illogical" change—but one that you may not have noticed.

So now: *literally*. Can it really mean 'in the literal sense' and 'figuratively' at the same time? Well, clearly, yes. Because it does. But I recognize that doesn't mean you have to like it. And, goodness, do I hear from those of you who don't like it!

It's not that I don't want to giggle sometimes over *literally*. My brain can't help but create cartoon-like images of my friend who was "literally climbing the walls" while working from home during the COVID-19 pandemic or of my running partner who "literally ate everything in sight" after a long run (but I know didn't go to the hospital for consuming a fork or a sponge or the cat for that matter). But I keep the giggle inside because I know exactly what these speakers mean and there is no need for me to derail the conversation with an inner-grammando-informed giggle.

So given that there is no literal wall-climbing or omnivorous eating because both speakers are speaking figuratively, why the *literally*?

Because now *literally* doesn't always mean that something happened in the literal sense. It *can* mean that. For example, let's imagine that I am telling you about my university colleague in engineering and say, "She's a rocket scientist." And you respond, "She really is brilliant." And to clarify I say, "No, she is literally a rocket scientist," because she is in aeronautical engineering and, well, that makes her a rocket scientist. There *literally* means: true to the primary, non-metaphorical use of a word.

Or let's imagine that you then decide to go to a talk by my remarkable rocket scientist colleague. But you get the time wrong. You might report back to me, "There was literally no one there" to emphasize that you showed up for a talk, discovered you had the time wrong, and were, truly, literally, nothing figurative about it, the only person in the room.

But *literally* can also mean 'not literally,' and the example of the missed talk helps explain what has happened to the word *literally* over time. Notice how *literally* is creating emphasis in "There was literally no one there." It wasn't a far jump for *literally* to go from that use of emphasizing a statement that was literally true to emphasizing statements that actually weren't literally true. If I'm listening to you tell that story, maybe I understand you to be saying that you were truly the only person in the room—or maybe I understand you to be saying that there was pretty much no one there. It felt like there was no one there because you were expecting lots of people, and there were only a few. In this second scenario, it's not literally true because there were a few people there, but it felt like no one to you, and *literally* helps you express that feeling through a bit of exaggeration.

If your inner grammando is balking at this "new usage," I need to offer a correction: It's not new. The word *literally* came to be used emphatically (in addition to meaning 'word for word') by the late seventeenth century. And by the 1800s we find writers such as Mark Twain and Louisa May Alcott using the word *literally* in that exaggerated way that is equivalent to 'figuratively': Tom Sawyer was described as "literally rolling in wealth" in *The Adventures of Tom Sawyer,* when he was not on the ground rolling around; and near the end of *Little Women,* at an annual apple-picking party where the families gather, Alcott writes: "The land literally flowed with milk and honey on such occasions, for the lads were not required to sit at table, but allowed to partake of refreshment as they liked." But no, the food and drink were not flowing from the ground but had been brought in baskets.

When Twain and Alcott were writing, pundits hadn't yet clamped down on this new use of *literally* as a "misuse." That happened in the early twentieth century, and we haven't yet recovered. The influential grammarian H. W. Fowler, in his 1926 *Dictionary of Modern English Usage,* expressed deep disapproval of the hyperbolic use:

> We have come to such a pass with this emphasizer that where the truth would require us to insert with a strong expression "not literally, of course, but in a manner of speaking," we do not hesitate to insert the very word we ought to be at pains to repudiate.

We can hear the echoes of Ambrose Bierce, who from what we have found was the first to criticize this newer use of *literally.* In 1909, he complained in *Write It Right: A Little Blacklist of Literary Faults* (which was a compilation of Bierce's language peeves):

> It is bad enough to exaggerate, but to affirm the truth of the exaggeration is intolerable.

But exaggeration comes with being human, from all I can tell, and this new meaning of *literally* helps us indicate that we're being hyperbolic. When you think about it, the intensifier *really* has done exactly the same thing: It no longer means that something is necessarily real; it emphasizes or intensifies whatever comes after it. If I said my niece was "really an angel" for coming to help me move, I doubt anybody's inner grammando is shrieking, "But she is not actually, in real life, an angel!" Words change meaning over time, including this kind of weakening into intensifiers (which has also happened to the words *very* and *truly*).

Here's the thing: Semantic change (another way of describing words changing meaning over time) looks interesting in retrospect and yet often causes anxiety and grammando-ing in the present. When I give talks about language peeves, people are fascinated by what some words used to mean. As I mentioned in chapter 5, *decimate* used to mean 'kill one in every ten,' but now has strengthened to mean 'destroy almost entirely.'* Semantic change isn't bound to etymology. In fact, linguists have a term for the erroneous belief that a word has to mean what it meant historically: "the etymological fallacy."

Pretty meant 'cunning, crafty' back in Old English, back when *nice* meant 'silly.' Those two words have taken on more positive meanings over time.

On the flip side, *awful* used to mean 'worthy of awe,' and then its meaning got more negative over time, as opposed to *awesome,* which has become more positive.

The word *wife*'s meaning narrowed over time: Back in Old English, it referred to any woman, and now it is specifically a married woman. The word *aroma* has expanded its meaning, because it

---

* Did you know the word *myriad* also goes back to a number? It is borrowed from Latin and used to be linked specifically to ten thousand and multiples of it, as well as a countless number of things. Now it means only 'a countless number.' And it's fine to use *myriad* as an adjective (e.g., *myriad choices*) and as a noun (e.g., *a myriad of choices*), the latter of which is older but sometimes attracts criticism (for no good reason).

used to refer only to the smell of spices. (I think it retains a pleasant, positive connotation: It seems odd or joking to refer to the aroma of sweaty socks.)

This is just a taste of the thousands of examples of semantic change in the earlier history of the English language. I love sharing these in public talks, and they are consistently crowd-pleasers—until I get to some of the semantic changes that have happened more recently and been singled out by commentators for critique. What do I mean? Remember the commotion over *unique,* which now can mean 'one of a kind' as well as 'unusual,' described in chapter 5.

COULD OR COULDN'T CARE LESS

As long as we're talking about auto-antonyms . . . it seems obvious that if you couldn't care less, then you don't care at all because it is not possible for you to care less than you do. In contrast, if you could care less, then you must care at least a little bit, because it is possible for you to care less than you currently do. And yet, many people say they "could care less" when it is clear that they don't care. At all. Take, for example, this excerpt from a 2017 interview with Steve Bannon, a political strategist who worked in the Trump administration in 2017, quoted on Fox News:

> You know what my super power is? I don't give a damn. I could care less what they say about me. I could care less. It's about action.

If Mr. Bannon doesn't give a damn, then he must not care what people say about him—even though he says he could care less. And while it is much more common to encounter this use of *could care less* to refer to not caring in speech, it pops up in edited writing too. Here's an example from *The Daily Beast* in 2017 trashing the Academy Awards:

Everyone knows that the annual Academy Awards is a slog—
a nearly four-hour-long ceremony that requires sitting through acceptance speeches for technical categories you could care less about
until the very end of the show, at which point you're often too exhausted and annoyed to appreciate the teary tributes and political
rallying cries that accompany the big awards.

The setup clearly suggests that the technical categories are the boring ones that most people don't care about—that is, couldn't care
less about.

In sum, if we parse these two versions of the expression about
whether we care word by word, it is clear that they don't mean the
same thing. But in practice, sometimes they do mean the same thing,
which raises the question of whether we should be parsing these
two versions of the expression word by word. Is it fair to do that to
an idiom? And the answer is no, unless you're comfortable with most
idioms failing the test.

The kind of idiom we are concerned with here is a phrase or
group of words that through usage has taken on a specific, distinctive meaning that cannot be inferred solely from the meanings of
the words in the expression. For example, *a can of worms* often no
longer refers to a can of worms but instead to a complicated issue
or situation that is perhaps best left unexamined or "unopened"
because trouble will ensue if it is opened. You just need to know
this when you hear someone fret, "I may have opened a can of
worms here." The literal meaning of the phrase is not going to help.
(This comes from fishing, as you can likely guess, and appears in the
mid-twentieth century.)

Idioms remind us of the power of usage: Through usage, phrases
can become fixed, at which point they take on a life of their own,
beyond the grammar of their parts. In this way, they can seem illogical, but often their histories reveal a certain logic, as you can see
the human mind extending meanings through metaphor (think of
the worms escaping the can) and the like.

Some argue that "I could care less" originates in a sarcastic remark: I *could* care less, but I don't. Others have suggested that in fast speech, the final consonants in *couldn't* get blurred or elided to the point where the word is hard to distinguish from *could*. I think it may be simple confusion, as the idiom means what it means—and the word *less* is already negative in a way that suggests very little caring because, perhaps, I care about this less than many things.*

the bottom line

Change happening in the language around us can cause some anxiety and bring out our inner grammandos, worried about whether new meanings are wrong or somehow a degrading of the language. I urge you to remind your inner grammando that when we look at semantic change in retrospect, it is often interesting and fun to learn about. We do well to bring that same sense of curiosity to current changes, knowing that our concerns and criticisms will likely look quaint in fifty or one hundred years.

That said, in formal writing, word choices matter. With an auto-antonym, does the context clarify which meaning we intend? In writing especially, we want to avoid unnecessary ambiguity, so your inner grammando can be helpful in flagging potentially ambiguous terms. But don't pull out logic and go grammando on someone who says "I could care less" when they clearly don't care. You knew what they meant, and any logical arguments can't stand up to the nature of idioms.

Beyond its auto-antonymness, *literally* is a word worth watching. Like many intensifiers, it is often unnecessary in formal writing (e.g., if a finding is important, then let it be important—it

---

* Another idiom that is being reinterpreted such that it means opposing things: *sight for sore eyes*. Originally, this idiom referred to a happy or good sight, something that makes sore eyes feel better. For some speakers (I have been polling students and having them poll others for quite a few years now), it is a sight that creates sore eyes—for example, someone who looks bad.

adds little to say it is "very important"). And *literally* can signal a moment when we may be exaggerating or falling into hyperbole. Do we mean *literally* in the literal sense? If so, is it necessary to stress the literalness of the statement? And if not, does it add ambiguity or unnecessary intensification? These are savvy writerly questions that show a wordie at work, not judging whether that word's meaning is "correct" but rather whether that word is working effectively in context.

Then quietly enjoy the humor of a well-placed figurative *literal* if and when you notice it, knowing that some of these instances will likely slip right on by you, as is the nature of language change.

9

·················

because *like*

The word *like* was controversial before Valley Girl culture emerged on the pop culture scene in the 1980s. Noah Webster, the famous lexicographer who also wrote a grammar book in 1790, had thoughts about *like*: He included it in a list of "improper and vulgar expressions." This wasn't about *like* used as a quotative, as in "I was like, you have got to be kidding," or *like* used as a focuser, as in "It was like awesome," or *like* used as a filler, as in "Maybe, like, it will be okay," or *like* used as an approximative or hedge, as in "He is like six feet tall." These uses are more modern (although some are older than you think!). Webster's concern was about *like* as a subordinating conjunction, as in "He thinks like you do." Gasp!

Oh wait, you're not gasping? Subordinating or conjunctive *like* has been the subject of criticism for a couple hundred years. In the 1950s and '60s, the controversy's flames were fanned by a Winston cigarette ad: "Winston tastes good, like a cigarette should." How dare that grammatical mistake be plastered on billboards?

Critics wanted *like* to function only as a preposition, not as a subordinating conjunction or subordinator. On May 26, 1956, the controversy about the Winston cigarette ad made it into "The Talk of the Town" in *The New Yorker* magazine. The note begins:

We hope Sir Winston Churchill, impeccable, old-school grammarian that he is, hasn't chanced to hear American radio or television commercials recently. It would pain him dreadfully, we're sure, to listen to the obnoxious and ubiquitous couplet "Winston tastes good, like a cigarette should." That pesky "like" is a problem for us Americans to solve, we guess, and anyway Sir Winston has his own problems.

But, as a wonderful entry on this construction in *Merriam-Webster's Concise Dictionary of English Usage* points out, Winston Churchill had been known to use *like* this way. Here he is describing special committees in one of his wartime letters: "We are overrun by them, like the Australians were by rabbits."

Like as a conjunction meaning both 'as if' and 'as' predates the Renaissance, and if you want to find it in the works of Chaucer or Shakespeare, you can. Or the works of Charles Dickens, George Eliot, Emily Bronte, T. S. Eliot, Willa Cather, and the list goes on. As this use of *like* rose in popularity in the nineteenth and twentieth centuries, criticism of it increased. It wasn't new. It was useful and regularly deployed by writers and speakers. But, as we've learned can happen, a consensus judgment had emerged that it was incorrect and inappropriate.

In the end, what do we make of the Winston cigarette ad? At the most fundamental level, the grammatical choice was excellent: The ad did its job! It had people talking. And the people who were talking knew exactly what the ad meant. It's not that they were confused by this use of *like*—it is not ambiguous. They had just learned to criticize it, and criticize it they did.

To this day, I sometimes pause before I use *like* as a subordinating conjunction or a preposition because this ill-founded stigma has so permeated writing instruction and editing. Yes, that's right: There are writers and editors who will even avoid *like* as a preposition because it has been criticized as a conjunction. My inner grammando, no matter how often we chat about this one, remains on alert, even though I override it almost every time.

As a preposition, *like* can mean 'similar to' or 'such as.' Some commentators have pointed out possible ambiguity between the two meanings, but the possibilities for serious confusion seem relatively low. Consider a sentence like "The novel will appeal to new parents like my friends Alex and Morgan." New parents such as Alex and Morgan or new parents who are similar to Alex and Morgan? The meaning is different, but not out-of-the-ballpark different. And I'm sure some of you (but likely not all of you because this use of *like* is so standard) caught my unambiguous prepositional use of *like* setting up the example: "Consider a sentence like . . ."

The many other grammatical uses of *like,* some of which I capture in the first paragraph of the chapter, have attracted a lot of attention over the past few decades. Linguists have been fascinated, busily documenting *like*'s expanding uses and discerning patterns in the data. Usage commentators—and, honestly, a remarkable number of people I meet who talk with me about their feelings about language—are going grammando on *like.*

As a fluent quotative *like* speaker myself, I marvel at its versatility in informal speech. It can quote direct speech (e.g., "She was like, 'That's not right' ") or a thought (e.g., "I was like, who does she think she is to say it's not right?"). It can even introduce a gesture (e.g., "My brother was like [hands up in the air]"). Yes, that versatility can create ambiguity if there isn't enough context, and that ambiguity is something to watch for and generally avoid in writing—unless it is stylistically useful. And for all of us who think that quotative *like* is new within our lifetimes, spreading from California, we have fallen prey to what linguists call the "recency illusion": the belief that a usage is new because we have just recently noticed it. Linguist Alexandra D'Arcy, at the University of Victoria, has evidence of quotative *like* from nineteenth-century England. That said, the use of *like* has been increasing over many of our lifetimes.

Many other uses of *like,* such as focuser *like* and approximative *like,* are also informal. And they live alongside filler *like*—*like* used to hold the conversational floor while a speaker prepares to deliver the next part of an utterance—which may account for the strong feelings people have about the whole lot of *like*'s. (I explain that odd plural apostrophe use in chapter 26.)

Some speakers use *like* frequently, especially as a focuser and filler (that is, as a discourse marker—which I talk about in more detail in chapter 30), and any word that is used a lot can become noticeable to listeners and sometimes grating. The same is true of speakers who pepper their speech with *um* or *right* or *look* or *you know*. Remember that what you're likely noticing and reacting to is the word's frequency, not its grammaticality.

BECAUSE

While we're talking about controversial subordinators, I would be remiss not to pay some attention to *because,* because it has raised some hackles over the years. There are two major concerns.

First, can you begin a sentence with *because*?

Yes.

I love it when I can give you that straightforward an answer. The idea that we cannot begin a sentence with *Because* may come from writing instruction at earlier ages, when teachers are trying to help young writers avoid fragments (e.g., "Because the law is confusing"). If we start a sentence with *Because,* we need to remember to add the independent clause after the subordinate *because* clause. But stylistically, there can be good reasons to start a sentence with *because,* and it's all over published prose. It may help us structure the presentation of information in a logical, effective way (see chapter 33).

The second concern about *because* focuses on the redundancy of the phrasing "the reason is because" rather than "the reason is that." Is it redundant? Yes. As Bryan Garner puts it in *Garner's Modern English Usage,* "*reason* implies *because* and vice versa."

But other similarly redundant constructions receive little to no attention, such as "The first time I met her was when we both showed up for the dance class."* The word *time* implies *when* and vice versa. It is also worth noting that redundancy can be helpful. As listeners, we are processing enormous amounts of information in just a few seconds of speech, and having information cued twice can aid in processing. As readers, we can work through the language more slowly, but often we do not. And what some might call redundancy in a construction like "the reason is because," others might call mirroring, where the subordinate clause (starting with *because*) is semantically mirroring the opening noun phrase (*the reason*). There is something aesthetically pleasing about that.

See how easy it was to turn that negative judgment on its head?

If you're wondering about the title of this chapter, "Because *Like*," it is a reference to a relatively new and playful use of *because*: *because* + noun phrase. I ask my college-aged niece, "Why are you so stressed?" She sighs and answers, "Because finals." This construction appears to be less than twenty years old, and it lives alongside the standard compound preposition *because of*. Most of us older speakers wouldn't blink if my niece had answered, "Because of finals." The American Dialect Society voted *because X* the Word of the Year for 2013. There are "Because Science" T-shirts and a website. Your inner wordie should keep an eye on this new construction—it may well stick.

---

* There's redundancy all over English grammar. In standardized English, the third-person singular *-s* on verbs (e.g., *she thinks*) is redundant—and you don't hear complaints about that. We already know the verb is in the third-person singular because the pronoun *she* precedes it. And in the first person, the second person, and the third-person plural, verbs no longer carry any inflectional endings because we don't need them (*I/we/you/they think*). In older varieties of English there were different endings based on person and number, but all the inflectional endings fell off except *-s* in contemporary standardized English. Many nonstandard varieties of English have dropped the redundant *-s* in the third-person singular too (e.g., *she think*), and paradoxically that is sometimes described as "ungrammatical."

the bottom line
· ·

With your wordie hat on, first strive to disentangle and understand the many uses of *like,* so that decisions you might make about one use don't spill over into others. *Like* as both preposition and conjunction is well-established as standard usage, in speech and writing. Many other uses of *like* are more informal, but informal doesn't mean ungrammatical.

If you're someone who worries that you use *like* more than you would like to, it's likely filler and focuser *like* on your radar. Many of us have discourse markers we use frequently enough in speech that listeners may start to notice them. When I discuss this issue with students in my course on how conversations work, they have sometimes noted that I use a lot of "right?" when I teach. Guilty! Is it overuse? There's no clear line between use and overuse—one question to ask ourselves is whether we think a discourse marker is becoming so frequent that it detracts from the message. You can try recording yourself when you're presenting or even just in casual conversation (if the others participating in the conversation agree, I hope!) if you want to become more aware of your own speech patterns. That said, remember that discourse markers such as *like, right, you know, um,* and the like (yet another use of *like*!) do conversational work, and the goal doesn't have to be zero. As listeners, we should beware of judging anyone's intelligence, competence, or worthiness of being listened to based on patterns of discourse marker use.

And finally, when you hear a criticism of usage as redundant, pause for a moment. Redundancy in and of itself doesn't have to be cause for avoidance. The redundancy may be minor, not likely to draw attention, and it may even be stylistically effective.

10

. . . .

gender-neutral chairs

t is now so commonplace for me to refer to the head of a university department as a chair that I forget anyone might mistake a person for a piece of furniture when I say, "I was talking with a chair yesterday. . . ." Um, Anne, talk with furniture often? The word *chair* is fully integrated into my lexicon as a gender-neutral term for a department head—in addition, of course, to being a place to sit. It requires no conscious effort to use or to interpret.

When I was growing up, departments were run by chairmen, even when those people were women. When it came time to find replacements for *-man* words—due to the success of calls for nonsexist language in the 1980s and '90s—it wasn't clear how or how well this was all going to work. *Chairman* and *chairwoman*? *Chairperson*? Here in the United States, we tried on different options for size (too long? too clunky? too weird?), and, interestingly, we often came to different solutions in different cases—except for the general trend of avoiding *-person* words. We don't have *chairpeople, firepeople, mailpeople* (which given the homophones *mail* and *male* is not ideal for many reasons), *policepeople,* or *waitpeople.*

Instead, chairs now run committees and departments, firefighters fight fires, mail carriers deliver our snail mail,* police officers

---

* The term *snail mail* is a retronym. For whatever reason, I love retronyms, which are words (often compounds) newly formed from existing terms in response

make up our police forces, and servers take our orders in restaurants. I couldn't have predicted this (or at least I didn't have the foresight to predict it!), but in each case, we have come up with a tailored generic option. We collectively eschewed the option of pairing -*man* and -*woman* words, which can feel clunky and is not fully inclusive for those who do not identify within the gender binary. And we have largely stayed away from -*person* words, other than *spokesperson* and a handful of others. In some cases, a couple of generic terms competed to see which would catch on, such as *server* competing with and then taking hold at the expense of *waitron* (designed to get around the *waiter/waitress* pairing—and the term that my university was trying out for size when I was an undergraduate).

You could have given me a lot of money to bet on what would replace *stewardess* (and the much rarer *steward*) in the airline industry, and I would not have put any of it on *flight attendant*. What a clunky four-syllable alternative! And yet, and yet. *Flight attendant* is now the coin of the realm, not only in writing but also in speech. And in song! I was struck by flight attendants popping up in the lyrics of the 2010 song "Fly Over States," written by Neil Thrasher and Michael Dulaney and recorded by country singer Jason Aldean, in the line about two men "flirting with the flight attendants." If *flight attendant* helped the rhyme scheme, or the meter for that matter, then it would be less surprising—but it doesn't. There is the alliteration of *flirting* and *flight*. But it seems most likely that either *flight attendant* slid into lyrics because it is now an unremarkable part of everyday speech, or it mattered to the songwriters that they not limit our imagination about who is working in this role.

The speed with which gender-neutral language efforts have succeeded over the past three decades has been striking. When a pow-

---

to technological or other developments. Once we had email, we needed to specify *regular mail*, or *snail mail*, because just saying *mail* was no longer clear. Other retronyms include *acoustic guitar*, *landline*, *independent bookstore*, *hardcover book*, *cloth diaper*.

erful social movement such as second-wave feminism aligns with concerted efforts to change language, it can lead to targeted, conscious changes to the language of public—and then often private—discourse. Changing language consciously is not easy. How do you tell millions of people to stop using this term and start using that one? Well, you don't. But you change the norms of what is accepted language use, including in usage guides, and we adjust our speech patterns to be accepted—whether we believe it is a good change or not. (For more on singular *they* as part of gender-neutral language, see chapter 18.)

There are some odd holdouts in terms of gender-neutral language, such as *freshman*. Students have made the argument to me that they don't think of *freshman* as gendered. "It's 'mun,' not 'man'!" they tell me. And, therefore, the word is gender-neutral—which may be true. There aren't yet convincing studies either way. But similar arguments were made about *chairman* a few decades ago. In the liberal arts college at the University of Michigan, we have changed our style guide to use *first-year student* (as well as *first-year seminar*, etc.). It's not the most streamlined of changes, I agree, but it's no worse than *flight attendant*! I once had someone counter that *first-year student* somehow awkwardly broke up the progression of terms for students as they go through high school and college, and I replied, "What progression?" After the first year, it's *sophomore, junior, senior*: It's not that these terms were beautifully parallel with *freshman* either! Sure, we could change the whole progression to *first-year, second-year*, and so on, rather like law schools with their 1L, 2L, 3L system. Or we could continue to let the system be idiosyncratic, this time with the hyphenated *first-year* rather than a stray *-man* word.

Do any of these language changes matter? It's hard to know for certain—we don't have conclusive evidence about whether, for example, girls who hear *firefighter* rather than *fireman* are more likely to imagine that as a possible career—and there are so many other factors to consider. Are girls also seeing women depicted as firefighters in books, in movies and on TV, in advertisements, etc.? Are they encountering women firefighters in real life? All these factors matter—that we know.

But changing language can affect (or impact!) the framing of people's experience and identity. For example, the shift to talking about *enslaved people,* rather than *slaves,* in the history of the United States is an important one. First, it does not equate enslavement with the African peoples who were enslaved, as a, or the, key part of their identity, as a term like *slave* can do. Second, it reinforces that enslavement was something that was done to Africans—and while the term *enslaved people* does not name the enslavers, it does not completely erase them either. I also appreciate that many style guides now recommend against calling people *aliens* or *illegal.* People are not aliens and they are not illegal. They may have crossed a border illegally and thereby be in a country illegally, but they themselves are not illegal, and our language should reflect that.

I sometimes hear people dismiss the issue of changing the language as the most superficial of factors—superficial to the point of being irrelevant or a waste of time and energy. "It's just language," they say. "It doesn't actually change anything in the real world." As I cautioned in chapter 4, the argument "it's just language" should put you on high alert.

First, language does matter—it is part of the "real world," and changing what people see and hear in language changes their experience of the world. The linguist Deborah Cameron has made the thought-provoking analogy to changing policies about smoking in public. These policies may not cause people to stop smoking (what people do in their homes and yards and cars is their business), but they do stop people from smoking in public places—which means that smoking becomes less visible, with a not-too-subtle message that it's not fully acceptable or at least accepted. Changing the language we use in public works much the same way. People may think about less inclusive language in their heads or use it at home or in their yards or in their cars; but when people use inclusive language in public spaces (spoken and written), it means that more people feel and are included in those spaces.

Second, we can work on changing language and changing discriminatory laws, pay inequities, and other problems in the real world all at the same time. There is nothing mutually exclusive about these efforts, and language is a fundamental part of our identities and how we understand the world.

MARKED AND UNMARKED LANGUAGE

Over the past few pages, I have been talking about what linguists call *marked* and *unmarked* language. Let me explain what we mean by these terms with a well-worn (and awful) riddle:

> A man and his son get into a terrible car accident. The father is killed, and the son is rushed to the hospital. The surgeon comes into the child's operating room and says, "I cannot operate on this child. He is my son." Who is the surgeon?

I first heard this riddle in middle school, and I tried to come up with a plausible scenario in which the surgeon was the stepfather. Perhaps you have concluded that the child has two fathers. Did you come up with the explanation that the surgeon could be the boy's mother?

This riddle has been used to show the pervasiveness of gender bias in our society, which gets embedded in our language. The word *surgeon* isn't explicitly marked as a masculine term (unlike *-man* words), but for decades if not centuries, its connotations have been masculine. One of the results is that you can get compounds like *woman surgeon*—or more generally, *woman doctor.* We call *surgeon* and *doctor* unmarked terms, and then *woman surgeon* and *woman doctor* are marked for gender. *Author* is unmarked, *authoress* is marked. Markedness helps us see what values and identities we as a society see as neutral for a given term or concept. To see what I mean, consider the word *nurse*. Here the marked version is *male nurse*.*

Most style guides now advise avoiding these marked terms, from *-ess* words to *woman doctor* to *male nurse*. And it's good advice. It asks us to check our biases and determine when gender is relevant and why—and if and when it is relevant, how we want to integrate that into our writing, without making assumptions that the default surgeon is a man or the default nurse is a woman.

We should be similarly cautious about when we need to introduce other identity descriptions, for example, for someone's race or ethnicity, sexuality, or religion. First, are these identities relevant and if so, why? Second, are you identifying, for example, everyone's race or ethnicity or only those who are not white? If the latter, then you are falling into a markedness trap, where people are assumed to be white unless identified otherwise. In other words, whiteness is unmarked and everything else is marked. It's not an inclusive or especially nuanced way to write.

the bottom line
....

This kind of thoughtfulness about how we talk about people, their identities, and their histories can make a real difference. With your wordie whispering in your ear, strive to be open to more inclusive language and careful about how commonplace expressions can embed bias into our speech and writing. I know that sometimes the new language may feel stilted (remember my initial reaction to *flight attendant*) or you may wonder whether

---

* Markedness applies to words other than those referring to people and animals (e.g., *lion/lioness*). Consider the pair of adjectives *tall* and *short*. You might think those both seem unmarked. Then consider the question "How tall is she?" versus "How short is she?" We can immediately see that *tall* is the unmarked in the pair: The question about how tall someone is makes no assumptions about height one way or the other. The question about how short someone is, however, embeds a clear assumption that this person is not tall, and it's just a question of how not tall!

we really need to change the language we have (remember my students' reaction to changing *freshman*). Your inner grammando may understandably be reluctant to give up phrases that have seemed neutral or inoffensive to you for much of your life. This is an ongoing conversation, with more and more voices at the table—which is a really good thing—and as long as we listen respectfully to each other, we will continue to sort through various options to make the way we talk and write more respectful and inclusive for more and more people.

part 3

....

what's the difference?

ask, aks, and asterisk

n linguistics, we mark hypothesized historical forms (that is, ancient words for which we have no written evidence) with the symbol *, which means that as a linguist, I need to say the word for this
symbol out loud on a regular basis—in class and at talks. Every
time I say this word, I have to slow down to say it "right." The
word is spelled *asterisk* and historically it has been pronounced like
the spelling. My natural pronunciation, however, is "asteriks." In
my version, the sounds /s/ and /k/ have switched places—a process
linguists call "metathesis." And I am far from alone. For years,
now, I have polled audiences at public talks about their pronunciation of this word, and there are at least four pronunciations: "asterisk" (usually the most common, but often clocking in with not
more than 50 percent of the audience), "asteriks" (my pronunciation, as I affectionately refer to it), "asterik" (with no /s/ at all*),
and "asteris" (with no /k/).

Here's where things get really interesting: When I ask audiences
how many of them have been focused on this pronunciation variation with *, the answer is relatively few. They either haven't noticed

---

* This pronunciation could be the result of straightforward deletion of the
sound /s/. It could also be that speakers reinterpreted "asteriks" as plural and back-
formed the singular "asterik." The singular noun *pea* was similarly back-formed
from the singular mass noun *pease* (which explains "pease porridge hot").

it, or they haven't been bothered by the different pronunciations they hear. But if I ask them about the difference between "ask a question" and "aks a question," much of the audience will audibly respond, some with derisive or nervous laughter and others with groans that the pronunciation "aks" (or "ax") is "bad English."

Now, wait a minute. The pronunciation difference between "ask" and "aks" is exactly the same as the pronunciation difference between "asterisk" and "asteriks": the metathesis of the /s/ and /k/ sounds. Yet the former is highly socially stigmatized, and the latter, at least right now, flies largely under the radar. No one is saying I shouldn't have my job because I say "asteriks." What is going on?

As I pointed out in chapter 4, debates about language are almost always about more than language, and judgments about "bad language" are often about speakers more than any feature of the language itself. In this case, the stigma that has been attached in the United States to the pronunciation "aks" over the past couple of centuries reflects the history of anti-Black racism in the country. There is nothing wrong with the pronunciation "aks." But it provides a way to judge and discriminate against speakers who use it. And "aks" is now a characteristic feature of African American English.

Are you still having trouble wrapping your head around the idea that there is nothing wrong with the pronunciation "aks"? It wouldn't be surprising given the pervasiveness of the bias—so pervasive that many "aks" speakers have also internalized that their pronunciation is wrong. Here's some history to shake up your thinking: In Old English, the verb had two forms: *ascian* and *acsian,* and it may well be that *acsian* (with the /k/ sound before the /s/) is the older of the two—which, yes, means that the original metathesis was the equivalent of "aks" to "ask." The famous Middle English poet Chaucer used both *ask* and *axe* in his writing—it appears there was no stigma attached to either pronunciation. In the subsequent centuries, it so happened that the pronunciation "ask" was in the variety of English that was standardized, but "aks" continued to be spoken throughout Great Britain and the United States (for example, Noah Webster noted that the pronunciation was common in New England in the late eighteenth century). In the U.S., "aks" eventually came to be seen as a Southernism and, with the migration of African Americans out of the South, as a feature of African American English.

The pronunciation "aks" isn't lazy. It isn't ignorant. It isn't uneducated. It is a dialect feature that for many speakers of African American English is important to their identities—a feature they do not wish to leave behind when in school or formal interviews. Part of being a wordie is to recognize that the social stigma that has been ferociously attached to "aks" is socially constructed, rather than linguistically motivated—and that we have the power to stop judging the pronunciation as incorrect. We manage not to judge "asteriks." We can similarly not judge "aks."

Pronunciation differences are chum for the sharks that are our inner grammandos. Some of the harshest criticisms I hear about language are about "ignorant" pronunciations, and people use those pronunciations as the reason not to give someone a job or rent them an apartment or go on a date with them.

A large subset of pronunciation differences in the U.S. reflect dialect differences—the different accents we hear as we travel from region to region, social group to social group. In much of the southern United States, words like *pen* and *pin* sound identical. And while speakers outside the South often notice this pronunciation, less on the radar is the merger of the vowels in *cot* and *caught* in much of the U.S., from western Pennsylvania westward (which linguists creatively call the "cot-caught" merger!). If your only pronunciation of *route* has the same vowel as *boot*—and you couldn't interchange this with a pronunciation that has the vowel of *out*—then you're probably from New England or the Eastern Seaboard.

This is the stuff of dialectology, and it's fascinating. What is important for each of us to remember is that how we talk is an essential part of our identity and our community, and many people want to sound like their community. Linguistic diversity is part of our cultural diversity, and we shouldn't want or expect everyone's accent or dialect to be the same.

Some of the variation in pronunciation in American English (and other world varieties) is not linked to any specific dialect, and it goes unnoticed and unstigmatized. For example, American English speakers have two different vowels in the first syllable of *ideology* ("ay" or "ee"), *economics* ("ee" or "eh"), and *data* ("ey" and "aa"). Some speakers have an /l/ in *almond* and *palm,* and some don't. Right now, all these pronunciations are considered standard.

The sound /t/ is coming back into *often,* and while some people notice it, the newer pronunciation is largely unstigmatized. I am an "offen" speaker, but many of the undergraduates I teach have a /t/ in *often,* either as their only pronunciation or their more formal pronunciation of *often.* Here's the history of this one: The word *often* lost the medial /t/ back in the Renaissance, as did the words *soften, moisten,* and *hasten.* In the very literate society in which we now live, we're seeing a "spelling pronunciation" emerge with *often*: Speakers are putting the /t/ back in because it is in the spelling. For some speakers, the pronunciation "offen" seems sloppy (in other words, the historical pronunciation is becoming stigmatized), because we're not articulating all the letters in the spelling; the pronunciation "often" (with the /t/) is more careful and formal. I am putting my money on the /t/ pronunciation to become dominant in the coming decades.

My bet on *often* raises the question of who gets to decide when a new or alternate pronunciation becomes standard. There isn't a straightforward answer to this question. Dictionary editors determine which pronunciations get recorded as standard and which get labeled as nonstandard—and which don't get included at all. For example, I have two pronunciations of the word *affix,* but only the pronunciation with an initial "aa" (as opposed to "ey") is recorded in most standard dictionaries. The *American Heritage Dictionary* editors would occasionally survey the Usage Panel about the acceptability of specific pronunciations, but these were a small subset of the variant pronunciations out there.

Official judgments about standard pronunciations hit home for me a few years ago when I heard myself say the word *mischievous*. I was previewing a recorded radio program, during which I described a word's "fun, mischievous connotations." As I listened, I thought, "I think I have added a syllable to that word." Sure enough: While the spelling *mischievous* indicates just three syllables, my pronunciation had four, with the stress on the second syllable as opposed to the first ("mischievious"). I looked in dictionaries. *The American Heritage Dictionary of the English Language* online, as well as *Collins English Dictionary* online, have only one pronunciation of *mischievous* listed: mĭs'chə-vəs. *Merriam-Webster* online includes the pronunciation I used in the recording—and labels it nonstandard.

I started interviewing friends, and many of us had both pronunciations, with three and four syllables. And we had many theories. "Mischievous" (with three syllables) perhaps feels more playful, full of mischief, whereas "mischievious" (with four syllables) feels more devious—because of the shared ending *-ious*? We were speculating. But the point remained: Here were a whole lot of educated speakers who all had a "nonstandard" pronunciation. How many speakers does it take for a pronunciation to become standard? How educated do they have to be? As I said, there isn't a straightforward answer to this question, but it is just the question that wordies ask—or aks.

In this one chapter, I cannot go through all the stigmatized pronunciations out there. What I can do is give you a framework for thinking about what is happening, as a natural part of language variation and change. I've already shown you examples of metathesis, and there are many more, from historical changes (*bird* used to be *brid*, and *third* used to be *thrid*—which makes total sense: *three, thrid*) to current changes in progress ("perscription" for *prescription*).

Sounds and syllables sometimes get deleted: historically the initial /g/ in *gnat,* and currently for some speakers the medial /d/ in *sandwich* and /o/ in *police*. Sounds can also be inserted: a /p/ in *hamster* to create "hampster" (I absolutely do this!) or a /k/ in *espresso* to create "expresso" (which makes sense given how common the *ex-* prefix is). Do you see what I did there? I approached the pronunciation "expresso" with curiosity and openness, to understand what is happening, as opposed to going grammando on it—and this pronunciation of *espresso* is one of the peeves I hear about often. Why judge someone who wants an expresso to start their day? Be the wordie: the bird-watcher who does not try to kill the new bird.

Sometimes new pronunciations arise through analogy. There's a good chance that the pronunciation of *nuclear* as "nucular" (which President George W. Bush was chastised for—and see chapter 29 if you're concerned about my stranded preposition at the end of the clause) is modeled after words like *molecular, circular, popular, muscular*—you get the idea. It is conforming to a pattern. My mother said the word *height* "heighth." Yes, my very prescriptively correct mother had this "nonstandard" pronunciation, which is much more widely attested than just my mother. And it makes total sense: *breadth, width, length, depth, heighth.*

In retrospect, pronunciation changes seem interesting, rather than worrisome and/or worthy of scathing critique. In the mid-nineteenth century, poet Samuel Rogers described the pronunciation of *balcony* with the stress on the first syllable as enough to make him sick. Now we think his concern is odd and perhaps endearing. (The word was borrowed into English from Italian with the stress on the second syllable.) Some English spellings capture sounds that have since been lost, such as the initial /k/ in *knife* and the final /b/ in *lamb* (and the initial /g/ in *gnat,* as I mentioned above). How fun that we used to say those consonants! And did you know the *p* in *empty* was added to the spelling, because so many people had added the sound /p/ to the word *emti*? Say the word *emti* ten times fast and you'll see why! I'm just waiting for *hamster* to be respelled *hampster.*

the bottom line

If you can, let your inner wordie lead and approach variation in pronunciation with a willingness to embrace different ways of saying the same word. The good news: You actually do this much of the time. Your brain doesn't notice much of the pronunciation variation out there. So for the pronunciations that irk your inner grammando or someone else's, step back and consider whether there are good grounds to judge that pronunciation as wrong. Does it actually impede communication, or do you know exactly what the speaker means? Does someone's pronunciation reflect their dialect and community—an important part of them? Do not assume that new or unfamiliar pronunciations are lackadaisical (which many of us say "laxadaisical," as the brain creatively connects the two etymologically unrelated words *lax* and *lackadaisical*). Let your inner wordie be curious about how these pronunciations evolved, and know that some of them may already be or may become (because that is up to us) standardized. A key takeaway: The diversity of our pronunciations is part of the diversity of us.

12

....

counting less/fewer things

Blame the supermarket. No, actually, please don't blame the supermarket, even though the sign above the checkout lane may read "10 items or less." If that sign makes you want to go grammando—to pull out a red marker and change *less* to *fewer* even though you are not someone who would normally deface other people's property—pause for a moment and consider this glaring inconsistency. Many, many college admissions applications ask for "an essay of 500 words or less," yet irate parents aren't complaining about that. Technically, the same rule about *less* and *fewer* should apply. What's going on here?

The traditional rule about *less* and *fewer* is relatively straightforward and relies on a fundamental grammatical distinction for nouns: countability. When a noun is countable (e.g., *books*—we can count them as *one book, two books,* etc.), the rule tells us to use *fewer*: "I have read fewer books than my sister" (she tears through books—I don't know how she does it). When a noun is uncountable (e.g., *sleep, water, clothing*), the rule tells us to use *less*: "I got less sleep than I wanted to" (almost always true, isn't it?). We often find ways to count uncountable things by adding a countable noun to the mix. For example, we can count nights of sleep, drops or cups or glasses of water, and pieces of clothing.

Here's an important thing to know about the "less-fewer" rule, though: While it's often presented as straightforward and clear-cut, it doesn't always hold. While *fewer* minds its business and keeps company only with countable nouns, *less* is more promiscuous and shows up with both uncountable and countable nouns. We see it in common expressions like "500 words or less" or "less than two weeks." It also shows up in novel constructions, such as this headline from Reuters in July 2014: "Fist Bumps Relay 90 Percent Less Germs Than Handshakes." Some grammarians argue that this is a new "problem," but *less* has been behaving this way since Old English—that is, for over a thousand years.

The "rule" that aims to create a sharp distinction between *less* and *fewer* seems to have started out as a personal preference, committed to paper in 1770 by Robert Baker in *Reflections on the English Language*:

> This Word [*less*] is most commonly used in speaking of a Number; where I should think *Fewer* would do better. *No Fewer than a Hundred* appears to me not only more elegant than *No less than a Hundred*, but more strictly proper.

As you'll notice, Baker is openly expressing his opinion about what he thinks would be better and more elegant. But by the time William Strunk published the first edition of *The Elements of Style* in 1918, this opinion was no longer framed as a personal preference: It had become a hard-and-fast rule: "**Less.** Should not be misused for *fewer* . . . *Less* refers to quantity, *fewer* to number." Disregard this rule and you are "misusing" the language. Ouch.

Strunk did recognize one exception: When a noun like *one hundred* functions as a collective (i.e., we're thinking about one hundred as a nice round number as opposed to an actual count), it can take *less*. This exception accounts for common expressions like "500 words or less." Percentages can function similarly: We can say or write "less than 20 percent of people" because we're referring to a collective amount of people, not counting them out individually. The editors of the *American Heritage Dictionary of the English Language* point out a slew of other exceptions in a usage note for *less*:

Less than can be used before a plural noun that denotes a measure of time, amount, or distance: *less than three weeks; less than $400; less than 50 miles*. *Less* is sometimes used with plural nouns in the expressions *no less than* (as in *No less than 30 of his colleagues signed the letter*) and *or less* (as in *Give your reasons in 25 words or less*). And the approximator *more or less* is normally used after plural nouns as well as mass nouns: *I have two dozen apples, more or less.*

I would add the common expression *one less thing to worry about*. The alternate version *one fewer thing to worry about* sounds ridiculous! Or at least highly, highly unidiomatic. Things are clearly countable, but *fewer* doesn't like to appear right before a singular noun, which is why we say *one less thing to worry about*.

All that said, the *American Heritage Dictionary* Usage Panel vote from 2006 indicates that many highly educated readers remain conservative on this point of usage. For example, only 28 percent of the panel accepted the (at least to me) fairly idiomatic sentence "The region needs more jobs, not less jobs." Only 5 percent accepted "There are less crowds at the mall these days." That sentence doesn't strike my ear quite right either, but I am less bothered by "There are less than five cats in this room," which the editors answering questions for *The Chicago Manual of Style Online* say makes "our idiomatic ears say 'ouch.'" The point: What sounds idiomatic to us when it comes to *less* and *fewer* may not sound idiomatic to others.

the bottom line

Does it really matter whether we use *less* or *fewer*? No, not if we're concerned about confusion. No one in the checkout line at the grocery store is unsure about how many items they can have in their basket if they are in the "10 items or less" line; and we all know that if there are less than five cats in the room, there are, well, four or fewer cats in the room. It does potentially matter, however, in terms of how our audience may respond to our words.

As the Usage Panel votes reveal, sometimes using *less* with countable nouns will rub some linguistically conservative readers the wrong way, which can alienate them at least momentarily (and without good cause—and yes, I am speaking to you, linguistically conservative readers, on this point). At the same time, sometimes using *fewer* where our sense of idiom tells us to use *less* can sound pretentious—and alienate our audience yet again. The stiltedness of an email to a friend that says, "I look forward to seeing you in fewer than two weeks!" may undermine the expression of enthusiasm.

If your inner grammando is still trying to protect a clear-cut line between *less* and *fewer* and prop up the use of *fewer,* I hope you can help it let this one go.

13

·················

data and other disputed plurals

As an editor of my fellow linguists' writing, I am regularly confronted with the question of whether *data* should be treated as singular or plural. The linguists whose work I have edited do both, sometimes in the same article. I prefer *data* as a singular; to me, it functions as an uncountable mass noun, much like the nouns *information* and *research*. "The research suggests" and "the data suggests." But I know that many academics and academic readers have very strong feelings that *data* should be treated as a plural. "The data suggest," period. I got called in as a referee when a dispute about the singular/plural status of *data* got too heated in one of the social science departments at my university. What's a writer—or an editor, for that matter—to do?

The source of the "problem" with *data* is that the word is borrowed from Latin, which means that it does not follow the general pattern for creating plurals in English. Most countable nouns in English make the plural by adding *-s* (*book/books, raccoon/raccoons*). There are a few native English words that act differently for historical reasons. Some of them change the internal vowel to create the plural: *man* becomes *men, foot* becomes *feet,* and *mouse* becomes *mice* (don't let the different spellings of the final /s/ sound in *mouse* and *mice* fool you: All that happens in the plural is a vowel change). Three English nouns take plural *-en: children, brethren* (now highly specialized compared with *brothers*), and *oxen* (which odds are will give way to the more regular *oxes*). And a few nouns take the "zero plural"; in other words, they do not change form in the plural: *one deer/many deer, one fish/many fish.* An interesting historical side note: The plural of *fish* back a thousand years ago was *fishes,* which you will hear little kids say when they are learning the language; over time, *fish* took on a zero plural through analogy with other animal nouns like *deer* and *sheep.*

Now back to *data.* Technically, if we follow the Latin, *data* is plural; the singular is *datum.* But who says *datum*? Um, very few of us. So *data* exists in English largely without a singular counterpart. As a result, and given its meaning, many English speakers have reinterpreted *data* as a singular mass noun referring to the entire collection of data in question, not a lot of countable *datum*'s (so to speak). At this point, it is fair to describe both singular *data* and plural *data* as "common," with a preference for the singular in the spoken but plenty of examples of the singular in formal prose too, including academic prose.

Some of you may be thinking, "But this singular use is wrong. *Data* cannot just become singular." It can't? Don't be too sure. The history of another *-um* borrowing from Latin into English suggests that it can do exactly that. Technically, *agenda* is the plural form of the singular *agendum. Agendum* has become rare, and *agenda* has been reinterpreted as a singular, often to refer to a list of items to be covered at a meeting. Singular *agenda* is now completely standard, including in formal writing. This reinterpretation has given rise to the new plural form *agendas,* which has enjoyed a rapid increase in popularity over the past thirty years (check out the graph below from the Google Books Ngram Viewer). Notably, this new understanding of *agenda* as singular has met little to no resistance; in fact, it is rarely even mentioned in usage guides.

Media as a singular to refer to the press, in contrast, remains controversial, despite the fact that the use is widespread in spoken and written language. When the *American Heritage Dictionary* Usage Panel was polled in 2001, only 38 percent accepted this sentence: "The media has not shown much interest in covering the

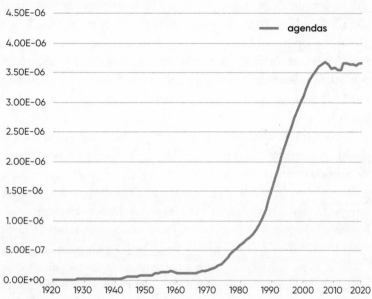

A Google Books Ngram Viewer search showing the relative frequency (with a smoothing of 3) of the word *agendas* from 1920 to 2019

trial." But a search of newspapers pulls up many similar sentences in edited articles, such as this one from the sports section of *USA Today* in 2004: "As the media has covered sports more closely and in more personal ways, fans have come to know details about players' lives that they didn't know years ago."

In the long run, odds are that *media* and *data* will come to be fully accepted in all usage guides and dictionaries as singular. At that point, the singular use will no longer be framed as "confusion" or "lack of agreement." It's not surprising that these words that end in *-a* not *-s* in the plural and that can refer to a collective singular entity have come to be understood as singular. And no one gets hurt—or even confused—in the process. The data (be that singular or plural) of actual usage show(s) us that many speakers and writers, even in formal settings, use these words as singular. It may not be etymologically accurate to the Latin, but it's actual English usage and far from unprecedented, as singular *agenda* demonstrates.

TRICKY LATIN -*US* WORDS

Most borrowings from Latin that end in -*us* take an -*i* plural in Latin: *fungus/fungi, focus/foci, stimulus/stimuli.* For all these words, the -*i* plural is still the most common in English, but some of them are starting to get Englishified. There is evidence of *focuses* not just in speech but also in edited prose; take, for instance, the opening of this sentence from a 2006 article in *The New York Times*: "Among their focuses will be helping the Iraqis process crime scenes." If you're feeling concerned about this new English plural *focuses,* it may help to remember it's joining good company, including *crocuses* (not *croci*), *abacuses* (not *abaci*), and *uteruses* (not *uteri*).

Syllabus is quirky because the Latin word itself is the result of a misreading of the Greek; but once that happened, the word *syllabus* started at least sometimes to take the plural *syllabi.* At this point, you can find both *syllabi* and *syllabuses* in English; and while statistically *syllabi* is more common in American English and *syllabuses* more common in British English, I regularly encounter both at my own university here in the United States—as well as questions from colleagues and students about which is correct!

At universities we also regularly talk about those who have graduated, which raises yet another plural formation conundrum: the *alumnus/a/i/ae* conundrum. The tricky part here is that the borrowed word *alumnus,* with its plural form *alumni,* has a feminine form, *alumna,* and its plural form is *alumnae.* If we're referring to a mixed group of people who have graduated, the Latin rule would tell us to default to the male *alumni.* The handy shortening *alum* helps us avoid this situation altogether, with its English plural *alums.* Right now *alum(s)* is considered colloquial, but its gender-neutral inclusiveness and usefulness may help it gain traction in more formal writing. And if you're concerned that the abbreviation is too informal, remember that informal abbreviations can sometimes lose that label. Consider the status of shortenings such as *lab* for *laboratory*, *limo* for *limousine*, or *flu* for *influenza*. Shortened forms don't have to remain strictly informal.

Okay, let's deal with the noun *status*, which I used in the previous paragraph. If we stayed true to the Latin, *status* should take a zero plural. It takes no ending to create the plural in Latin, so in theory the English plural of *status* would also be *status*. *Apparatus* falls into the same category: *one apparatus, many apparatus*—if we follow the Latin. But for the most part English speakers and writers have abandoned the Latin and use *apparatuses* and *statuses*, which standard dictionaries and the Microsoft Word spellchecker do not flag as having any problems at all, even though they do not adhere to the Latin.

It would seem irresponsible to end this section without talking about the wonderful non-Latin word *hippopotamus*. The word *hippopotamus* is Greek ('a water horse'), not Latin. Many dictionaries recommend *hippopotamuses* as the plural but also recognize *hippopotami*: Even though the latter is etymologically iffy, with its Latin plural, it has been used for centuries; many speakers and writers see it as the more correct, formal form. I myself am going with *hippos*! As I will continue to reiterate, correctness is not a stable notion, and we can usefully allow variation.

The Greek borrowing *octopus* is often treated in the same way, with both *octopuses* and *octopi* accepted as standard. The Greek plural would be *octopodes*, but that plural never seems to have gotten its eight legs under it in English. At the same time, the Greek borrowing *chorus* takes only *choruses*. For whatever reason, English speakers never tried to Latinize that plural.

the bottom line
....

For better or worse, we're living through a transitional moment with *data* and *media*, where not all language authorities have accepted the reinterpretation yet (as they have with, for example, *apparatuses* and *statuses*). By 2005, only 34 percent of the

American Heritage Dictionary Usage Panel still rejected *data* as singular in the sentence "Once the data is in, we can begin to analyze it." The editors conclude it is "safe to say that singular *data* has become standard usage." So not just common, but standard.

Be careful, though: Not all style guides are as liberal on this point of usage. For example, the *Publication Manual of the American Psychological Association* (colloquially known as "APA Style") deals with it as a straightforward issue of correctness and "proper use": *Data* is plural (no questions asked) and, therefore, is correctly followed by a plural verb. For any of us writing in the natural and social sciences, we do well to determine whether singular *data* is considered one possible standard usage or "incorrect" in the discipline.

As an editor in linguistics, I simply ask authors to remain consistent within the article as to whether the noun *data* is being treated as singular or plural. The widespread use of singular *data* in linguistics articles suggests to me that most readers won't find that in and of itself distracting. Flip-flopping between singular and plural agreement, though, seems potentially distracting. I recognize that my inner grammando may be getting the best of me here—I don't have evidence that the flip-flopping would be distracting to most readers. But I don't have evidence that it isn't either!

From questions and complaints that come in from radio listeners, I know that at least some readers have their antennae highly tuned in to this usage question about *data,* at least for now. And having your inner grammando tuned in to *data* isn't a bad idea; it allows you to make informed decisions based on context and audience, especially in more formal writing. In the end, we want readers to be able to focus more on the data and our arguments about the data than on our subject-verb agreement.

14

....

different from/than *between* and *among*

At a football tailgate a few years ago, I struck up a conversation with a genial-looking, white-haired alumna decked out in maize pants and a blue shirt, with a maize-and-blue University of Michigan scarf to boot.* She was a retired English teacher, and when she found out what I do for a living, she exclaimed, "Oh, you know what always gets to me: people who say 'different than' instead of 'different from.' It drives me crazy." I nodded sympathetically, even though in my head I was thinking, "Really? Huh. That's the one that gets your goat to the point that it distracts you from football?"

My goat notices *different than,* at least some of the time, and breezes right by. But one of my English department colleagues shares this pet peeve, fervently. She tells students not to use *different than* because it will make her grumpy, and grumpiness is not good for their grades. It's a reminder of what students are navigating as they move among (or between—we'll come back to this) classes where professors have different usage issues they notice—and sometimes "forbid." In this case, the choice rests between two

---

* The *boot* in "to boot" has nothing to do with footwear. It goes back to the Old English word *bōt,* which the *Oxford English Dictionary* defines as 'good, advantage, profit, use.' So the expression *to boot* originally referred to something that is added to one's advantage or into the bargain—or just added. Standard dictionaries now often define the phrase as 'in addition, besides.'

prepositions—*from* and *than*—and what makes the choice tricky is that we all have routinely heard both *different from* and *different than* in spoken American English.

You may be thinking, "Who cares?" Fair enough. That's the thing about language peeves: What riles up one person's inner grammando can slip right by someone else's.

So what could be seen as wrong with *different than*? The most common rationale for the peeve is that the adjective *different* does not live on a continuum: It does not set up a comparison on a scale the way that, say, *more than* or *less than* do. Something is either different from something else, or it's not. As a result, the preposition *than,* which suggests a scale or continuum, is inappropriate. With *different,* the argument goes, we are distinguishing one thing *from* another thing.

Adding fuel to the grammando fire, we say "X differs from Y," not "X differs than Y." So, the grammando position goes, we should say "X is different from Y."

Okay, okay, okay, let's pause and consider these arguments. First, it's not clear that *different* doesn't involve some kind of continuum. In my experience of the world, some things can be more different from, say, a squirrel, than other things. On the continuum of difference from squirrels, rats seem less different than kangaroos.

Second, prepositions don't hold across parts of speech—as in, just because we say *differs from* doesn't mean we have to say *different from*. For example, we *sympathize with* others, but we can express *sympathy for* them. And no one is going grammando on the *for* in *sympathy for*. Now. But they did! In the nineteenth century, essayist Thomas De Quincey called *sympathy for* a "monstrous barbarism." This now seems weirdly picky and even possibly irrational.

Third, prepositions in English are not a totally rational, logic-following bunch of words. Instead, they are highly idiomatic. Why is it *due to* instead of *due by*? Why is it *in addition* instead of *on addition* or *by addition* or *through addition*? We could come up with a rational argument for each of those (e.g., things are added *on* top of one another, or it is *through* addition that numbers get bigger), but idioms don't bow to logic (see chapter 8). And idioms can change over time. Right now, older speakers generally use the expression *by accident*, and many younger speakers use *on accident*. And guess what: The younger speakers will likely win this. You could try to turn the train around through resistance or put the train on a different track by popularizing *by purpose* to create grammatical symmetry with *by accident* (good luck!). Or you can jump on the train and embrace *on accident* alongside *on purpose*, even if you continue to be a *by accident* speaker (this is where I am).

Fourth, British English speakers often use *different to*, rather than *different from* or *different than*, and this is simply seen as a legitimate regional difference as opposed to an error.

In this list, I've now provided the three most common variants: *different from, than*, and *to*. The variant *different to* is the oldest (back to the 1500s), with *different than* and *different from* both appearing in the next century. All are arguably standard.

So when did *different than* start to get criticized? By 1770 for certain. Robert Baker, in *Reflections on the English Language* (which also contained his thoughts about *less* and *fewer*—see chapter 12), calls *different than* "not English." Whoa. Clearly hyperbole. What Baker meant was "I don't like it," and this opinion did not pick up a lot of steam until the late nineteenth century, at which point *different than* came to be widely critiqued. Note that by contrast, the critique of *sympathy for* as a "monstrous barbarism" did not turn out to have legs.

Different than remains a construction many American editors will correct, for the sake of tradition. But even the correcters have come to recognize that there are times when you really have to use *different than*. If *different* is followed by a noun or noun phrase, you can use either preposition, if you're willing to upset the grammandos out there. For example:

Millennials aren't all that different from Gen Xers.

Millennials aren't all that different than Gen Xers.

You may not agree with the statement, but for many of us, both prepositions sound idiomatically fine here.

Then consider *different* followed by a full clause. Here we really need *different than*. For example:

So much about college admissions for Gen Xers was different than it was for Millennials.

Different from doesn't work here. Just try it. It requires an awkward rewrite:

So much about college admissions for Gen Xers was different from how it was for Millennials.

In sum, *different from/than/to* can all be considered within the realm of standard, especially if we look at speech, and all have been used by well-known authors for several centuries. *Different from* is still often seen as the most formal and standard in written American English, but there is nothing wrong with *different than,* and it is the standard alternative when there is a clause following the adjective *different*.

There are three other preposition questions that merit attention because they have attracted the attention of grammandos, and so you need to be prepared to help your inner grammando and inner wordie sort it out.

BETWEEN AND AMONG

At some point in junior high school, I learned the rule (wait, let me rephrase that: *a* rule) about when to use *between* and when to use *among,* and it has been lodged in my head ever since, empowering my inner grammando in ways that, it turns out, are misguided. The rule I learned, which seems wonderfully straightforward: Use *between* for two things and *among* for three or more things. So when I get home from work and don't feel like cooking, I might be choosing between cereal and a sandwich, or I might be choosing among several takeout menus that have accumulated in a drawer in the kitchen.

But you know by now that when I say a rule seems straightforward, all odds are that then I'm going to say it isn't. And that's just what I'm going to do here.

Here's another, more accurate, descriptive way to phrase the rule, which captures how *between* and *among* behave out there in the world: We use *between* when talking about two things, and we can use *between* or *among* when talking about three or more things depending on whether we're talking about them individually or in individual relationships with each other (*between*) or whether we're talking about all the things collectively. In other words, I could say, "I am choosing between pizza, a burrito, and pad thai for dinner." I'm considering each one individually, against the others, among the many takeout options.

Your inner grammando may be up in arms right now: "But that is wrong!" It's important for your inner grammando to know that style guides won't consistently back you on this. I'm talking Strunk and White's *The Elements of Style* and *Garner's Modern English Usage*: They recognize that *among* can be used for more than two when we're describing the relationship of one thing to several others. And while it's true that, etymologically, *between* goes back to the meaning 'by two,' it has been used for more than two things since Old English.

Given this, you can judge whether sometimes there might be a difference in meaning when we're referring to three or more things. Take these two sentences:

Anne ran among the cars.

Anne ran between the cars.

The first may suggest I am weaving in and out among the cars stopped in a traffic jam or parked in a parking lot; the second may have rows of cars on both sides and, for whatever reason, I'm running between the rows. But could running between the cars involve weaving? You decide. There is some ambiguity here, so if it matters, you'll need to add enough context to clarify.

While we're here, let me say that I read *amongst* in a lot of student papers now. Bryan Garner says this is old-fashioned and even pretentious, but I would keep your eye on this resurrected word. It may have reenergized legs.

TOWARD AND TOWARDS

As I read across many kinds of writing, I also see a lot of *towards* in addition to *toward*. The bottom line here is that both are standard. *Towards* is more British and *toward* more American. Someone once said to me, just remember that Brits like to make the word longer—which, for the record, is not always true, but it works in this instance.

Interestingly, we're currently seeing an upswing in the use of *toward* in British English, and since 2000 an upswing in the use of *towards* in American English, so perhaps we'll meet somewhere in the middle of the Atlantic.

We similarly see variation between *backward* and *backwards, forward* and *forwards.* And yet some gatekeepers' inner grammandos are entirely inconsistent. This was captured in the 2012 *American Heritage Dictionary* usage survey about the adverbs *towards, backwards,* and *forwards.* As described in the usage note for *backward*: "*Backwards* and *towards* were deemed acceptable by 72 percent and 69 percent of Panelists, respectively, but only 38 percent found *forwards* to be acceptable." Good grief. We can rock backward and forward or backwards and forwards—and there are no good grounds for judging anyone any which way.*

---

* Then there is *anyway* and *anyways.* One of my colleagues used to make students chant, "Anyways is not a word." She was not pleased when I noted that it is,

Standard dictionaries and some usage guides note that when *backward* and *forward* are used as adjectives, they don't have the *-s*: It's a *backward* belief system, not a *backwards* belief system. But if we're going to be forward-looking, this is a usage to watch, at least with *backwards,* which is starting to show up as an adjective in edited prose.

BASED ON/OFF/OFF OF

About ten years ago, university colleagues started expressing concern to me about *based off (of),* rather than *based on.* One colleague in the humanities started her email this way: "I'm losing my mind reading papers with the expression *based off of,* which has become very widely used (rather than *based on*). What do you know about where it came from and how its meaning emerged?"

Its emergence is relatively recent. The graph below from the Google Books Ngram Viewer shows that the rise in use of *based off* and *based off of* starting in the 1980s has been dramatic. At the same time, don't let the scale here fool you: The variant *based on* is still thousands of times more common.

Is there a logical problem here? Not particularly. *Based on* makes sense because we physically build things *on* bases. But in the same way that we use ideas as jumping *off* points and we build *off* other people's ideas, we could base our arguments *off* things as well. If I were betting, I would put money on the young *based off* becoming more and more entrenched in writing and more standard.

What about *off of*? This compound preposition has been the focus of negative attention for over a century, with some complain-

---

of course, a word. It goes back several hundred years as an adverb meaning 'in any manner' (e.g., "He will do it anyways possible"). As a sentence adverb meaning 'in any case,' *anyways* has about two hundred years under its belt. This use of *anyways* has been relegated to the informal—and for many the "incorrect"—but there is no good reason to judge the final *-s* as inherently informal, and it is not incorrect.

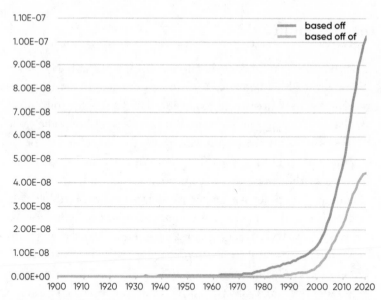

A Google Books Ngram Viewer search showing the relative frequency (with a smoothing of 3) of the phrases *based off* and *based off of* from 1900 to 2019

ing about the redundancy. Of course, some other compound prepositions such as *ahead of* and *because of* get to peacefully appear in their grammatical habitats with no judgment. Going grammando involves some cherry-picking.

It's hard for me to think about *off of* without a tune in my head: Frankie Valli's "Can't Take My Eyes Off You," which omits *of* from the song's title but absolutely has *of* in the lyrics: "can't take my eyes off of you." And notably, some of the artists who have covered this song, such as Lauryn Hill, have put the *of* into the title. We can find examples of *off of* (what a symmetrical phrasing that is!) back to the 1500s, with luminaries such as Shakespeare and Daniel Defoe writing it down. And the compound preposition is currently on the rise in American English. If we put on our wordie bird-watching hats, we can fairly say that *off of* usually occurs in more informal contexts (its most common habitat right now), but it is finding its way into more formal writing too.

the bottom line
· ·

Prepositions do fundamental grammatical work in the language and are highly idiomatic. Your inner grammando may want to fight the idiosyncrasies of prepositions and argue for some more "logical" use of a preposition. But prepositions are going to be prepositions. They aren't always going to "make sense," or we can make as much sense of the use of a new preposition as we could of the one it is replacing. As a reader and listener, I encourage you to let your inner wordie, the skilled bird-watcher, drown out the cries of your inner grammando. Observe the prepositional idiosyncrasies and be interested in the ways idiomatic preposition usage can defy logic and shift over time.

This is difficult territory for writers and speakers to navigate because we can't always know what prepositional peeve a reader or listener may be clinging to (or to which they may be clinging—see chapter 29). Given the low odds of confusion based on preposition variation in these idiomatic constructions, the gatekeepers could allow more variation through the gates. Remember that many of us play a role in deciding what is standard, in terms of both the language we use and the language we choose to "correct."

15

....

driving safe or safely

Advertisements succeed when they get our attention, and provoking our inner grammandos is one effective strategy. Any publicity is good publicity, right? Two well-known company slogans have raised some grammatical hackles—and propelled emails into my inbox over the years—based on their use, or nonuse, of adverbs. What are the slogans? Subway restaurant has long used the slogan "Eat Fresh," and in 1997 Apple rolled out "Think Different." Do we have a grammatical problem here? Let's puzzle it out as curious wordies do.

The slogan "Eat Fresh" sounds like "eat right" or "eat well," and there is nothing wrong with the latter two. But the words *right* and *well* can clearly be adverbs (e.g., "This fits right/well") as well as adjectives (e.g., "She is right/well"). This leaves us with the question of whether *fresh* can be an adverb. It is usually an adjective: "fresh flowers," "the fish is fresh today." But *fresh* can also be an adverb: "The bread is baked fresh every day." That said, in the expression *baked fresh*, *fresh* means something like 'newly' or 'recently'—which is not what Subway is going for in "Eat Fresh." Does Subway mean 'eat fresh food,' and this is a shortening of that phrase? Or are they drawing on a nonstandard meaning of the adverb along the lines of 'in non-stale, not preserved, and/or recently made ways'? The answer to both questions is probably yes. And the bigger point from the advertiser's perspective: We made you look!

In terms of "thinking different" in an Apple kind of way, standardized English grammar would be "think differently"—but this might mean differently too. Thinking differently involves thinking in different ways, but thinking different might also mean thinking different things or thinking about what it means to be different. Thinking big involves thinking in big ways about big things—because *big* can be both an adjective and an adverb. So is *different* in "Think Different" an adjective or adverb? I don't know, and that's the point. This ad didn't win an Emmy for nothing—the ambiguity is brilliant. And the ambiguity is possible because English has words that can be both adjectives and adverbs without changing form (e.g., *big, fast*)—what are often called "flat adverbs," and we'll come back to those because they are at the heart of some common peeves.

Let's quickly review the nature of adverbs. As I mentioned in chapter 7, adverbs may be "the trash can category" of English grammar, because the category contains so many kinds of words that can function in several different ways within a sentence. A definition from the editors at Merriam-Webster captures this heterogeneity: 'a word that describes a verb, an adjective, another adverb, or a sentence and that is often used to show time, manner, place, or degree.' Unlike adjectives, which modify only nouns, adverbs modify multiple parts of speech (but not nouns): verbs ("protest peacefully"), adjectives ("very peaceful"), adverbs ("ridiculously peacefully"), and full sentences or clauses ("Frankly, this whole situation is a mess").

Adverbs can also be hard to pin down in terms of where they appear in the clause/sentence. "Frankly, this situation is a mess." "This situation, frankly, is a mess." "This situation is, frankly, a mess." "This situation is a mess, frankly." In this sentence, *frankly* (which modifies the entire sentence) just can't appear in the middle of a noun phrase like "this situation" or "a mess." This flexibility also characterizes adverbs that modify verbs: "She wrote the email quickly"; "She quickly wrote the email"; "Quickly she wrote the email." The one version that would raise eyebrows for many: "She wrote quickly the email."

Most of the time this flexibility in adverb placement is not an issue, and if only that were always the case. But then there's *only* and guidance about where it should appear.

ONLY

Bryan Garner, in *Garner's Modern English Usage,* describes *only* as "perhaps the most frequently misplaced of all English words." When you hear a description like this, I encourage you to put on your wordie hat and ask: If this word is "misplaced" so frequently, is it really misplaced? Or are grammando-informed attitudes being overly inflexible about placement?

Concerns about the placement of *only* go back centuries, as early as Bishop Lowth (1763), who went after the phrasing "I only spake three words" instead of "I spake only three words." What was his objection? The sentence is ambiguous if we apply strict logic to the grammar. If the focus is that it was just three words, then *only* should come before "three words." If the focus is on what you spoke (versus wrote), then *only* should come before "spoke." If the focus is on *you* speaking (and not others), then *only* can also come before "spoke." In speech, intonation would typically indicate what is being emphasized; in writing, we sometimes need to use word order to minimize ambiguity. That said, some later grammarians called Lowth "hypercritical" on this—English grammar shows a general preference for *only* before the verb.

H. W. Fowler defends "misplaced" *only* in the sentence "[The man] only died a week ago." And we can find "misplaced" *only*'s in countless famous authors' works, not to mention almost all the rest of our prose. Here's just one example from the lexicographer Samuel Johnson: "Every other author may aspire to praise; the lexicographer can only hope to escape reproach." Is that sentence confusing, or are grammandos quibbling over too fine a point?

The *Merriam-Webster Concise Dictionary of English Usage* points out that in edited prose, *only* does tend to appear before the phrase it modifies. Here is an example from author James Thurber: "Indeed, we spent so little time in bed most of us had only one child."

So in formal writing, is it worth editing for the most accurate placement of *only*? I think the most judicious answer is yes, some of the time. If there is the possibility of genuine ambiguity, then it can be helpful to ensure your *only* is placed as unambiguously as possible. For example, consider this sentence:

The governor only says positive things about the new bill.

Right now this could mean that the governor only says positive things but doesn't believe them (*only* modifying *says*); the governor says only positive things and not negative ones (*only* modifying *positive things*); or the governor is not positive about anything other than the new bill (*only* modifying *the new bill*). In writing, if you mean one of the latter two, it is worth moving the *only* so that the reader is less likely to misinterpret the sentence. That said, context around the sentence will also often provide this clarity.

FLAT ADVERBS

Now let's circle back to those flat adverbs: adverbs that have the same form as their adjective counterparts (e.g., *fast, big, up, down*). If I am a fast eater, I eat fast. There is no *fastly*. So if I am a slow eater, can I eat slow? Or do I have to eat slowly?

One of the common markers of adverbs is the suffix *-ly*, which can be added to an adjective to make an adverb: *quick/quickly, beautiful/beautifully*. There are also a few adjectives that have that *-ly* ending (e.g., *homely, comely, manly, friendly*), and this is for historical reasons: The historical source of modern *-ly* had an adjective and adverb form (the latter distinguished by a final *-e*), and that distinction has been lost over time. The suffix *-ly* has come to be used to form adverbs, which leaves an adjective like *friendly* in an awkward position: What is the adverb form? *Friendlily?* In a friendly way? Yikes.

There are, though, many adverbs with no distinctive *-ly* marking, such as *soon, up, down, straight, hard, fast, slow.* Wait, wait, wait! (you say): *Slow* is an adverb? But there is the adverb *slowly,* so that must be the correct form.

While there is some controversy over the phrasing "drive slow," and you can find images of people going grammando on street signs to add an *-ly* to DRIVE SLOW, historically there is no problem here. Historically, *slow* was both an adjective and an adverb. Here's Shakespeare, from *Midsummer Night's Dream*: "But oh, methinks, how slow This old Moone wauns." At this point, *slow* as an adverb is often seen as nonstandard, but that is just a judgment that has been added over time. And for many of us, the warning "Go slow," when someone is, say, learning to drive, sounds better than "Go slowly."

What about "Drive safe"? Historically the adverb here has been *safely,* but why not let *safe* be a flat adverb? Dictionaries do not agree with each other: Merriam-Webster recognizes this adverbial use, but American Heritage and the *Oxford English Dictionary* do not (yet). I find both useful. For me, it's the difference between a public service announcement ("Drive safely!") and the words I say from my doorway when I am wishing friends safe travels home after a dinner party ("Drive safe!"). I don't want to sound like a PSA.

What about "play nice"? I was asked about this expression a few years ago when I was giving a talk at the Ann Arbor City Club, where there is a sign during the Bridge Club meetings that says PLAY NICE. *Nice* historically has been an adverb, although now it would be considered nonstandard in a sentence like "He sings really nice." Again, Merriam-Webster recognizes *nice* as an adverb and American Heritage does not. It's also worth noting that the verb *play* works in an idiosyncratic way here, when we think about potential parallels such as "play dirty" and "play clean."

Some flat adverbs mean something different from the *-ly* form. As the expression goes, working hard is very different from hardly working. And when we wish someone good night, we can say "sleep tight," which seems like a different message from "sleep tightly," the latter of which doesn't sound very comfortable at all.

It's also worth noting that the *-ly* form isn't always the preferred form because sometimes usage commentators are fickle. What am I talking about? Oh, *firstly*. The word has been around since the fourteenth century, and criticism of the word has been around since at least the nineteenth century. Samuel Johnson didn't put it in his dictionary in 1755. In 1847, Thomas De Quincey called *firstly* a pedantic neologism—and while it might be pedantic, it certainly wasn't a neologism (a new word) in 1847. The 1864 edition of Noah Webster's *American Dictionary of the English Language* called the word improper, an evaluation that was repeated over the decades. This objection lost momentum after H. W. Fowler dismissed it in his influential usage guide in the early twentieth century. He wrote, "The preference for *first* over *firstly* in formal enumerations is one of the harmless pedantries in which those who like oddities because they are odd are free to indulge, provided that they abstain from censuring those who do not share the liking." Both *first* and *firstly* are grammatical options; it is a question of style and perhaps of parallelism if the word is followed by a *second* or a *secondly*.

INTENSIFIERS

The intensifiers subset of adverbs can be helpful in some contexts and unnecessary in others. It's a fast-moving set of words, as we need to create new intensifiers as older ones lose some of their intensity. Two of the most common right now are *very* and *really*, with *so* moving up on *really* in terms of popularity. *Super* is also on the rise in informal contexts. And then there are the really informal intensifiers, such as *hella, uber, wicked, flipping, chuffing,* and the list goes on, including some taboo ones (I'll let you come up with those!).

In speech, intensifiers do a lot of emotive work for us, and they can be playful, slangy, and fun. In formal writing, it is worth looking at all intensifiers and seeing if you need them. I'm here to tell you that most of the time you don't. If you have written "This finding is quite remarkable," remember that it will be equally if not more dramatic to write "This finding is remarkable." The "very dramatic decrease" could be simply a "dramatic decrease." Removing some adverbs can tighten up your formal prose in effective ways. But this does not mean you should omit all adverbs!

Over the years, students have told me that past writing instructors have advised them to avoid all adverbs. This is not good advice. Some adverbs work to boost our claims: for example, *clearly, obviously.* Equally importantly,[*] adverbs can hedge our claims: for instance, *perhaps, possibly, potentially, arguably.* Part of academic writing is negotiating our commitments to our arguments and our assessment of others' claims. "Strong" arguments tend to be sophisticated in where they boost and hedge claims to make space for readers, for uncertainty, for additional evidence, and the like.

the bottom line
· ·

First, don't shun the adverb. And don't feel you have to shun the adverb *firstly* either, if you like its style. In general, remind your inner grammando that we're playing with style, rather than grappling with issues of grammaticality. Your inner grammando is right that a well-placed *only* can minimize ambiguity in writing in helpful ways—and that can be worth doing. Your inner wordie is also right that in some cases, a flat adverb will feel

* There has been debate since the 1960s about *more important* (or *equally important*) versus *more importantly* as sentence adverbs, even though they are both fine. The 1960s were a moment when *more importantly* was on the rise, and some usage commentators responded negatively—as opposed to being wordies and just watching and admiring the newly popular usage. Of course, without the *more* or *equally,* the sentence adverb would be *importantly.*

more informal or more playful, and that doesn't make it un-grammatical. Flat adverbs have been around for centuries. They can be a useful part of our repertoires—because they are the right choice for a given social context or perhaps because when they are used in creatively ambiguous ways, they can make us think different.

16

....

well, i'm good

A dear friend of mine is convinced that it is incorrect to say "I'm good" when someone asks her how she is. Her mother drilled into her from an early age that she is supposed to say "I am well"—assuming that she and things in her life really are, generally, fine. If and when she slipped up as a kid and blurted out an "I'm good," her mother would remind her: "No one asked you about your moral goodness, honey. It's not about whether you're a good person."

All these years later I still feel sorry for the younger version of my friend who was just trying to provide a positive and routine answer to a routine question—and was undoubtedly not trying to say anything about her moral stature. I hope this chapter might convince her, her mother, and anyone else still uncomfortable with saying "I'm good" that, well, it is all good.

The question "How are you?" (or its variants such as "How are ya?" or "How ya doin'?") typically helps open a conversation—or it can be just a part of a passing greeting on the street where you've already walked by before someone can respond. Given this, let's take a brief detour on greetings.

Greetings have a routine to them. In American English, we often start with "Hi" or "Hey" or "Yo" or "Hello"—and any one of these would be an appropriate response to any of the others. If the opening question is "What's up?" (or any of its variants such as "What up?" or "Wassup?"), some of the routine, generic responses are "Not much" or "Nothing." By "generic" I mean that the response generates no special notice, so that we as speakers can move right past the greeting to the rest of the conversation. Imagine how differently the conversation would go if someone asks you "What's up?" and you respond "So much you wouldn't believe it." It would be weird to just pass that response over without a follow-up question.

The question "How are you?" works much the same way, most of the time. Unless you are in a doctor's office or you have just been ill or through a hard time, the question isn't usually designed to elicit a genuine response in which you detail how you are. If and when "How are you?" is part of a greeting ritual, we can keep things simple and answer with one word: "Fine," "Okay," "Good," "Exhausted," "Fantastic," "Ducky." As long as we stay out of serious negative territory (e.g., "Terrible" or "Messed up"), these responses can pass without comment.

Now back to grammar. You'll see that the word *good* appeared in the list of one-word responses to "How are you?" And if we just say "Good," grammandos don't usually pounce on us. But if we say "I'm good," suddenly grammandos get grumpy. It's "I'm well," they say.

As a speaker, I can and do say both "I'm well" and "I'm good." It depends on the day! When I say "I am well," I am (at least it seems to me) referring to my health, my state of wellness. As a result, that response doesn't work if I want to answer the question more generally, about my general state of being in the world. If I want to say that I am in a good place, that my life is overall free of troubles, that I'm having a week of more good news than bad, I say, "I'm good." And you and I and anyone else who wants to has the right to ask why we can't say "I'm good" in the same way that I could say "I feel good" or "Life is good."

The answer is that we can. The prescription that "I'm good" is somehow grammatically wrong does not hold up under scrutiny, and let me explain why.

The verb *to be* is a linking verb: a verb that sets up an equivalence relationship between the subject (before the verb) and the predicate noun or adjective that comes after the verb. So in the clause "I am _____" in response to "How are you?" we should expect an adjective: "I am tired" or "I am happy." (The verb *feel* is also a linking verb, which is why we can say "I feel tired" or "I feel happy.") *Tired* and *happy* are adjectives, as is *fine*. As is *well*. As is *good*. Now you can start to see why things get confusing.

Most of the time, the word *well* functions as an adverb. For historical reasons we aren't going to get into here, *well* is the adverb form of *good* in standardized varieties of English. If I am a good poker player, I play poker well. If you are a good singer, you sing well. But *well* can also show up as an adjective in reference to health, meaning 'in good health.'

The word *good*, most of the time, functions as an adjective. *Good* is an adjective when we say, "These grits are good!" It is also an adjective when we reminisce later about those "really good grits." In some nonstandard varieties of English, though, *good* can also be an adverb, as in "He runs good." Now I realize that some of your inner grammandos just cringed: Adverbial *good* is stigmatized at this point, often seen as not only nonstandard but also uneducated and "wrong." I'm not about to suggest here that you pepper your formal writing with adverbial *good*, given current grammando grumpiness about it, but I do want to point out that there is nothing grammatically wrong with adverbial *good*.

As I talked about in chapter 15, English has "flat adverbs": adverbs that share the same form as their adjective counterpart. They are called "flat" because they do not add the adverbial suffix -*ly*. Flat adverbs accepted in standard varieties of English include words like *fast, hard,* and *wrong*. If, for example, we answered "wrong" (adverb), it means we provided the wrong answer (adjective). Why wouldn't *good* want to behave the same way? And why won't we let it? It is a collective decision—and has been for quite a while now—that adverbial *good* is nonstandard, but there is no grammatical obstacle to it becoming a more standard form.

Now how is this relevant to the belief that we can't say "I'm good"? My guess is that concerns about *good* as an adverb have bled over to this different construction, where *good* is actually an adjective. If you think about "I ran good" and "I am good," they look very similar: In both sentences, the word *good* occurs right after the main verb. It's a completely logical conclusion. But the verbs work very differently in these two sentences: *Run* is not a linking verb so it requires an adverb, whereas *be* is a linking verb and it takes an adjective. The similarity between the sentences, though, may have encouraged a sense that there is something wrong with "I am good," even though there is not.

So, in fact, we can say either "I am well" or "I am good," depending on what we mean. If we mean that we are in good health—perhaps we recently had the flu or a migraine or some such unpleasant thing—then "I am well" is an excellent choice. But if we're just having a good week, "I am good" sums that up well, and it will probably feel more colloquial to folks. If anyone challenges you that they didn't ask about your moral goodness, stand firm. After all, when we said the grits were good, did anyone think we were talking about the moral goodness of the grits? Good grief.

While we're talking about feeling things, let's talk about feeling bad. Yes, feeling bad. Does that sound wrong to you? Feeling bad? It makes my inner grammando wake up and wonder whether we have a problem here. I run into this question sometimes when I'm sending an apologetic email. For example, I want to say, "I feel bad that we didn't catch that error." Then I find myself staring at the sentence on the screen, thinking, "That sounds too informal. And it sounds kind of wrong. I feel badly? This other person is going to think I am wrong. Which is not going to help with this apology." I usually end up changing the sentence to something like "I feel real regret" or just "I am sorry." But did I need to change the sentence in terms of the grammar?

The answer is no. My angst over "I feel bad" and my sense that perhaps it should be "I feel badly" is an example of hypercorrection, when we overcorrect because we are so worried about getting it right. In "I feel _____," when we're talking about our emotional state, we want an adjective, and *bad* is an adjective. You can feel good for someone else, and you can feel bad for someone else. This is *feel* as a linking verb.

Badly would actually—or at least theoretically—change the meaning of the sentence into something a bit odd that means that you have a bad sense of feeling. This would be *feel* as a transitive or intransitive verb, where it refers to sensing things in the world (by touch, for example). Let's imagine that someone asks you to run your hand over something rough because, they promise, it will tickle, and you say, "Oh, it won't work for me. I feel badly with my hands." Okay, that example is fairly implausible. Here's a slightly better one. You had an unfortunate incident in which you burned the tip of your finger badly (no reason not to use the adverb here) and you lost feeling in it. Over time, you regain some ability to feel in that finger, but you remain discouraged: It still feels things pretty badly.

Now let's get real about acceptability. Is "I feel badly that I forgot your birthday" a grammatical fail, in addition to being a friendship fail? I don't think so. At this point, "I feel bad that I forgot your birthday" feels overly informal in many contexts, if not downright wrong. And "I feel badly" sounds more formal and more right. So with this one, I would say that you can go with either "I feel bad" or "I feel badly."

the bottom line
. . . .

As we try to talk about feeling good and feeling bad, all the historical grammando-going has muddied the waters. There is absolutely nothing wrong with "I'm good," and for many of us it usefully differentiates our general state of being from our state of health. Don't let anyone make you feel bad about this one.

And if you would rather feel badly than feel bad, I don't think you are going to run into a lot of grammandos on that path.

having proved or proven it

There's the variation in language that we notice: the colorful grammatical birds that catch our attention and make us pull out our binoculars. And there's the language variation that flies under the radar: the grammatical birds with varied plumage that manage to blend into the linguistic foliage. If you add an *-s* to *anyway*, you may get grammandoed, but does anyone care if you have proved or proven something? For many speakers and writers, both *proved* and *proven* are standard; they use both and don't judge others based on whether they are a *proved* or *proven* user. Yet, as we will see, *proven* has been the target of grammandos in the past.

Before we dive into the history of *proved/proven* so you can know if grammandos still lie in wait here, let's talk about past participles more generally. At the beginning of my grammar courses, I sometimes ask students which terms stump them, and *participle* (along with *gerund* and *subjunctive*) usually sits near the top of the list. "What in the world is a participle?" students ask. Luckily for all of us, the answer is relatively straightforward.

There are two types of participles: present and past. Present participles are one of the most regular forms in the language: Take the infinitive form of the verb (e.g., *juggle*) and add the suffix *-ing* (*juggling*), and now you have the present participle. We use the present participle to create the progressive, which describes actions in progress. For example:

I was juggling multiple jobs at the time.

The past participle, which is formed by adding a final *-ed* or *-en* to the infinitive form of the verb or with an internal vowel change (I'll come back to this), shows up in two different grammatical constructions. It occurs after a form of *have* in the perfect:[*]

I have _____ for three years. (juggled, eaten avocados, shrunk)

And it shows up in the passive after a form of *be*:

The bananas were _____. (juggled, eaten, shrunk)

It quickly becomes apparent that the past participle is not as regular as the present participle; after all, you have a final *-ed* on *juggled* and a final *-en* on *eaten*—and then *shrunk* has no ending at all: It has just changed the vowel (*shrink/shrunk*).

Rather than dismiss this as a hopeless mess, it's more fun to see it as a grammatical puzzle, and the key to the puzzle lies in the history of English verbs. So let's take a brief detour for the benefit of our inner wordies. I promise it is worth the trip: You'll learn when

[*] The perfect aspect seems worth explaining—and I recognize this is the densest footnote in the book. Hang on! Let's start with "the perfect," which is not a tense but an aspect in English grammar. The perfect describes an action in the past and its relation to another moment in time. The present perfect is used for an action that began in the past and is still happening or remains relevant now: for example, "I have read half the book." If you imagine a timeline, this sentence places the action of reading the book as starting in the past and continuing up to this moment—and at this moment I have finished half the book. The past perfect describes an action that began in the past and ended at another moment in the past: for example, "I had read half the book when I decided it wasn't worth finishing." So in this case, the starting and ending of the reading both happened in the past, in the left-hand part of the timeline if time is moving from left to right, with the present in the middle and the future to the right. (I don't know about you, but I almost always feel bad about not finishing a book I start. And see the previous chapter if you have concerns about *feel bad*.)

Americans introduced *snuck* and why people go grammando on *have went*, and you'll get to hear about one of my goofier teaching moments.

The story starts with how we make the past tense of English verbs. It seems like a question with a straightforward answer: Just add *-ed*. Sure, except for all the verbs where you don't do that, such as *eat/ate, drink/drank, ring/rang, bring/brang* (oh wait, no, that's not it: *bring/brought*—I got distracted by the pattern!), *come/came, go/went*, and on and on. Now, it is true that the vast majority of verbs make the past tense by adding a final *-ed*: *talked, walked, played, dined, stayed out late*. This is why we call *-ed* verbs "regular" verbs. And usually, when we make a new verb, it follows this pattern. So, for example, when the noun *wine* became the verb *wine* (as in *wine and dine*), the past tense was *wined*, not, say, *wone* (like *shine/shone*).

Then there is a not small set of verbs (it just isn't big enough to justify a description beyond "not small") that create the past through an internal vowel change. If English is your first language and you have never studied linguistics, you may not have noticed the pattern in these "irregular" verbs. First, they all change nothing other than a vowel within the verb to make the past tense. Second, you can see some similarities in how the vowel changes. For example, the vowel change in *sing/sang* looks the same as *ring/rang, drink/drank, spring/sprang, swim/swam*. Huh, go figure. *Bear/bore* has the same changes in the vowel as *wear/wore*. *Speak/spoke* has a vowel change like *weave/wove*. *Drive/drove* parallels *write/wrote*. It's pretty cool. And the takeaway: There is a method to the madness among these seemingly irregular verbs. Here's why.

Over a thousand years ago, back in Old English, English had two kinds of regular verbs: those that took the equivalent of a final *-ed* (our modern "regular" verbs) and those that underwent an internal vowel change (what we now think of as "irregular" verbs). The vowel-change verbs never outnumbered their peers, but there were many more of them back in the days of *Beowulf*. Over time, some of them just died and another good number became regular—

that is, they stopped taking a vowel change and created the past tense with *-ed* instead. The verb *help* is a good example. The past tense used to be *halp* or *holp,* but now, in standardized English, it is *helped.* The past tense of *swell* used to be *swoll,* and now it is *swelled* (although we have the newly derived *swole/swoll* to describe those who are super muscular). We can still see the change in progress with the verb *shine,* which has two past tenses: *shone* and *shined. Shined* is the newer past tense, and some style guides say that you should use *shone* when there is no object (e.g., "The sun shone brightly") and shined when there is an object (e.g., "We shined the light into the corner")—but when you look at edited prose, it doesn't consistently follow this "rule." We do, though, generally use only *shined* when talking about shoes, at least right now.*

Are you now thinking about the verb *sneak?* I wouldn't blame you if you were. I mean, I did mention it a few paragraphs ago, and it is another verb with two past tenses: *sneaked* and *snuck.* The regular past tense *sneaked* must be newer, right? It would fit the pattern of vowel-change verbs becoming regular verbs over time. But no. Not this time. In this case, Americans are creating an irregular verb. Historically, the past tense of *sneak* has been *sneaked,* but starting in the twentieth century, Americans started to use *snuck.* And it took off! Check out the graph below from the Google Books Ngram Viewer, where you can see *snuck* now competing almost neck and neck with *sneaked* in American English. (I'm not sure why, in general, we're doing more sneaking these days!)

Garner's Modern English Usage described *snuck* as nonstandard until the most recent edition, which recognizes the dramatic increase in this form. In 2008, 75 percent of the *American Heritage*

---

* This historical detour helps disentangle the mess of *lie* and *lay. Lie* ('to be in a horizontal position') historically is a vowel-change verb: *lie/lay/have lain.* Its transitive counterpart *lay* ('to put into a horizontal position') is a regular *-ed* verb: *lay/laid/ have laid.* The forms of these verbs are frequently mixed up, and one confusing part is that the past tense of *lie* is the infinitive/present tense of *lay* (which is because the two verbs are historically related). I have my eye on the expression *lie low,* as I think *lay low* is becoming more standard.

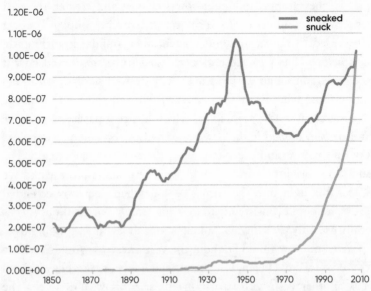

A Google Books Ngram Viewer search showing the relative frequency (with a smoothing of 3) of the words *sneaked* and *snuck* from 1850 to 2010

Dictionary Usage Panel accepted *snuck* (and, as you know, the panel is not known for its liberalness on these issues), which showed a significant increase from the 33 percent who accepted it in 1988. *Snuck* has quickly snuck its way into standard usage, so to speak.

Sneak isn't alone in jumping off the regular verb ship either. The past tense of *dig* used to be *digged,* before it became *dug.* And the past tense of *dive* was *dived*—which you can still see and hear, although it is becoming overwhelmed by the newer past tense *dove.* With *dive,* we can quickly see the analogy that may have caused the change: *drive/drove,* so why not *dive/dove?* With *sneak,* it is much harder to find the analogy. *Peek/puck?* No. *Seek/suck?* No. There is the past tense *stuck,* but it's not a perfect analogy because it would need to be *steek/stuck.* (If you figure out the analogy, please do write me!)

This history also gives context to understand nonstandard past tenses like *drug* for *drag.* Which leads me to the memorable teaching story. A few years ago, on the first day of my undergraduate introductory linguistics course, I was talking with students about *sneaked* and *snuck,* and the graduate teaching assistant for the course said, "You know, the other day I heard someone say that they had drug someone along with them." What a great example of another regular verb becoming irregular, I responded, and then I turned to the class. "How many of you are *drug* users?" I asked innocently. And as soon as the question left my mouth, I realized that wasn't the question I meant to ask at all! "Never mind! Never mind!" I exclaimed. "I don't want to know." The students thought linguistics might not be boring after all.

It's also worth noting that there are some super irregular verbs, such as *go*. Why does the *g-* in *go* become a *w-* in the past tense *went*? Because the verb *go* stole the past tense *went* from the verb *wend*. Seriously. We then created a new past tense for *wend*: *wended,* as in "We wended our way through the neighborhood."

Okay, now back to *proved* and *proven*. Here we're talking about variation in the past participle, but you'll see the detour about the past tense was not for naught. The two are related. Regular verbs that make the past tense with *-ed* also typically have an *-ed* past participle. We saw that with "I juggled" and "I have juggled." Verbs that change a vowel in the past tense also usually change the vowel in the past participle, and some of them also add *-en*. Consider:

I *write*. I *wrote*. I have *written*.

We *eat* avocados. We *ate* avocados. We have *eaten* avocados.

It seems logical, then, that *proven* must be the older form, given that it is irregular, and then *prove* developed a regular past participle, *proved*. But *prove* is another idiosyncratic verb, swimming upstream against regularization. The verb *prove* was borrowed into English from French, and early on it had a regular past tense and past participle, *proved*. But then *proven* appeared, originating in the past participle of Scottish English *preve*, through analogy probably with *cleave/cloven, weave/woven*. When *proven* was newer, it met with resistance, to say the least. Here is Richard Grant White in *Words and Their Uses, Past and Present* (1870):

> PROVEN, which is frequently used now by lawyers and journalists, should, perhaps, be ranked among words that are not words. . . . *Proved* is the past participle of the verb *to prove*, and should be used by all who wish to speak English.

Proven isn't even English? That seems harsh. And while criticism is now more tempered, there remain concerns about *proven*—which I will admit that I didn't know until a few years ago. *The Associated Press Stylebook* states: "Use *proven* only as an adjective: *a proven remedy*." Bryan Garner has only recently removed the description "ill-advised" from *proven*, acknowledging its frequent use in nonlegal contexts as well as in legal ones (e.g., *innocent until proven guilty, not proven*).

But, of course, many of us use *proven* as a past participle, and editors regularly let it pass. Consider this sentence from an academic publication, the *Journal of International Affairs*: "The above mentioned measures have been implemented half-heartedly and for the most part have proven to be ineffective." Many dictionaries include both past participles as standard. *Proved/proven* is a useful reminder that views on what is good and bad usage change over time, and *proven* is now unremarkable for many if not most of us.

Interestingly, the verb *shaved* does something similar: *Shaved* is now the past participle in a construction such as "He has shaved," but we often use *shaven* as the adjective (e.g., *clean-shaven*). But the history of *shave* is different: It was an irregular verb that became regular over time—but clung to the old *-n* form with *shaven*. The verb *mow* has done the same thing, gradually shifting its past participle from *mown* to the regular *mowed*—although undergraduate students tell me it is an open question whether the old form *mown* remains a recognizable word! They laugh at me when I talk about a freshly mown lawn.

It's tempting, then, to think that the verb *sew* must follow the same pattern of becoming more regular over time, which is how we have the past participles *sewed* and *sewn*—but no, we must resist temptation here. We as English speakers (well, actually, English speakers of several centuries ago) went rogue with *sew. Sew* started its life in English as a regular verb, with the past tense and past participle *sewed*, but over five hundred years ago the irregular form *sewn* showed up, probably through analogy with *sow/sown*. And right now, *have sewn* is more common than *have sewed*.

While we're talking about past participles and speakers trying to make things more regular (at least some of the time), let's address the much-criticized construction *have went* (or *have ran* or *have drank*—you get the idea). With regular and irregular verbs under our belts, it's easier to explain what is happening here. With regular verbs like *juggle*, the past tense and the past participle are identical (*juggled*). Hold on to that idea because it is key to the explanation. With irregular verbs, the past tense and past participle are typically different (*we went/we have gone; we drank/we have drunk*). As speakers, we can seek out regularity and even change things to make them behave more regularly. So sometimes, with irregular verbs, speakers will try to make them a little more regular, not by adding *-ed* to make the past tense and past participle (people aren't saying *goed* and *drinked*), but instead by making the past tense and past participle the same. As a result, we see *have drank* (rather than *have drunk*) and *have went* (rather than *have gone*). These constructions remain nonstandard, but they are far from illogical in their formation.

the bottom line

It is very hard to argue that *proven* poses a usage problem at this point (to create a highly alliterative sentence). You are well within standard usage to use both *proved* and *proven* as the past participle of *prove*, with *proven* being the preferred form when it is functioning adjectivally (e.g., *a proven remedy*). With *proved* and *proven,* I have even managed to quiet my inner grammando such that when I'm copyediting, I don't require authors to be consistent in using one or the other as the past participle. This variation is flying largely below the radar at this point, causing no confusion and requiring no editorial attention.

As a bigger takeaway, remember that sometimes we as speakers seek to create more regularity, such as when we say "They have went," and then sometimes we introduce brand-new irregularities, such as the new past tense *snuck*. Audience members at public talks sometimes ask me if English is getting more streamlined and regular over time. My response: English is getting more regular except for the places where it is not.

part 4

which pronoun to pick?

18

....

the singularity of *they*

The phrase "singular *they*" seems to be a siren song for inner grammandos, even with some of the most socially liberal people I know.

"*They* can't be singular!"

"*He or she* is awkward!"

"This is all a lot of PC nonsense!"

Just how big a problem do we have on our hands here? The answer: not as big as many people think we do. And it's getting smaller every day.

Let's start with the widely held belief that English has no singular generic or gender-neutral pronoun. If this were true, then it would pose a real grammatical conundrum. As the website Grammar Girl (by Mignon Fogarty) has described the problem: "English has a big, gaping pronoun hole—we have no word to describe a single person if we don't know whether he or she is male or female." We have *he* for people who identify as male and *she* for people who identify as female. We have *it* for inanimate things—and, if we're honest about it, occasionally for babies if they are dressed in yellow and we're just not sure which pronoun to use. But *it* doesn't work in reference to adults of unknown, irrelevant, undisclosed, or nonbinary gender.

So is it true that English has no gender-neutral singular pronoun? No, not if you look at what real speakers say in real time.

English speakers have solved the generic pronoun problem—and in fact, they solved it hundreds of years ago. When presented with a person whose gender is unknown or irrelevant or not to be disclosed, the majority of speakers know just what to do:

> "Someone who knows where they're going should give you directions."
>
> "A teacher should learn their students' names as quickly as possible."
>
> "I was just talking to a friend who sold their house in two days for more than the asking price."

If you're thinking, "I would never say that," I would urge you to suspend your certainty and listen closely to your own usage. Studies show that *they* is the most common singular generic pronoun in spoken American English, and the same pattern holds in British English and other varieties. Even the folks who think they would never use singular *they* sometimes use singular *they*. It is just that natural to our spoken grammar.

Singular *they* now regularly appears in edited prose too. A search of newspapers in the Corpus of Contemporary American English turns up hundreds of examples. For instance, a 2001 article in the *Chicago Sun-Times* about what *hooking up* means (a good question—students tell me they don't all agree on what this means) includes this sentence, with both a singular *their* and a singular *they* referring back to *someone*:

> Ask someone in their late 20s or early 30s and they might tell you that it simply means to meet someone.

It made headlines in 2015 when *The Washington Post* announced the change in their style guidelines that permits singular *they* when making the sentence plural would be "impossible or hopelessly awkward." More and more newspapers are sure to follow.

Given the evidence of widespread use of singular *they*, I am struck by the wording of critics who ponder whether the pronoun *they* "can be" singular. When you step back to think about it, the question makes no sense. Clearly speakers can and do use the pronoun *they* as a singular (e.g., "Someone who knows where they're going should drive," or "My neighbor washes their car every day"). It is not a debatable question. And *they* is not the only plural pronoun to simultaneously take on a singular function: The second-person pronoun *you* used to be only plural, complemented by the singular pronoun *thou*. As *thou* died in most varieties of English, *you* took on the singular function too, so that now the pronoun *you* can refer to one person or many people—and in standardized varieties of English it takes the plural verb *are* in both cases.

So, if we're going to debate the use of singular *they*, let's focus on debatable questions. For example, is it too ambiguous? Or is it too informal?

In terms of ambiguity, let's consider three points. First, in many instances, we employ singular *they* exactly because the gender of the antecedent noun (the person we are referring to) is unknown or irrelevant; the ambiguity about gender, therefore, is intentional. And there is usually no ambiguity about number: In a sentence like "My neighbor washes their car every day," it is unambiguous that I am talking about one person, and that person is my neighbor.

Second, in the cases where there genuinely is ambiguity about the referent of singular *they* (e.g., "I was talking to my mother and her friend, and they said . . ."), we can rewrite the sentence. That is simply solid writing advice about any potentially confusing sentence. And it is important to note that this kind of ambiguity can arise with any pronoun (e.g., "I was talking to my mother and her friend, and she said . . .").

Third, when *they* is the pronoun of a person who identifies outside the male-female binary, the meaning of the pronoun is not ambiguous: It means that the person does not identify as *he* or *she*. Perhaps you are someone who prefers the nonbinary pronoun *ze* to *they*, but that does not make *they* ambiguous. In 2017, *The Associated Press Stylebook* accepted this nonbinary singular use of *they*, and odds are that soon editors will accept all other uses of singular *they* too.

The question of informality is intriguing and potentially circular. Singular *they* often does feel more informal because it is characteristic of spoken language (including in more formal settings) and informal written language, not formal written language. It is not in formal written language because many style guides tell us we shouldn't use it—for many reasons, one of which is that the pronoun is too informal. One of the only ways for singular *they* to become recognized as both formal and informal is to allow its use in formal edited prose (as some editors are starting to do). The circularity becomes apparent.

Calling singular *they* "bad grammar," as *The Princeton Review* did in 2015, unproductively dismisses the grammar of many, many English speakers. It's not a question of whether this pronoun *can* be singular; it's instead a question of whether we should and will let *they* be used in its singular form in formal, edited prose without comment. That decision is within our control.

So when did singular *they* start and when did it get relegated to the category of "bad grammar"? If you search the internet for Jane Austen and singular *they*, you will find a website with dozens of examples of the construction in Austen's novels. For example, here is Jane Bennet in *Pride and Prejudice*: "But to expose the former faults of any person, without knowing what their present feelings were, seemed unjustifiable." The nineteenth century, however, does not take us back nearly far enough. What about Shakespeare? Examples of singular *they* pop up there too, such as these two lines from *The Comedy of Errors*:

> There's not a man I meet but doth salute me
> As if I were their well-acquainted friend

And recent historical research has traced examples back at least three centuries earlier, into the Middle English period. In other words, English speakers solved the "generic pronoun problem" centuries ago. Singular *they* has over eight hundred years of history in the English language; interestingly, so do generic *he* and generic *he or she.*

It was an eighteenth-century female grammarian, Ann Fisher, who was one of the first to propose the idea that the masculine pronoun not only could function as a generic but should. In *A New Grammar* (1750), the first published book on contemporary grammar by a woman, Fisher wrote: "The *Masculine Person* answers to the *general Name,* which comprehends both *Male* and *Female; as, Any person who knows what he says.*" In other words, the pronoun *he* can be understood to mean 'he or she' and function as a generic.

This statement about singular generic pronouns was picked up as a rule by subsequent grammarians and made prominent once it was included in Lindley Murray's widely popular *English Grammar* (1795). The book went through sixty-five official editions in less than eighty years, and Murray even had a board game named after him ("The Journey to Lindley Murray's"—a game that looks not even as exciting as the grammar book, which might explain why almost no copies have survived). In the grammar, Murray presents a sentence with singular generic *they* and corrects it to include generic *he* instead. The original sentence is "Can any one, on their entrance into the world, be fully secure that they shall not be deceived?" Murray then provides the prescribed alternatives "on *his* entrance" and "that *he* shall." Almost two hundred years later, the belief about the pronoun *he*'s ability to "embrace both genders" had become such common sense that William Strunk and E. B. White could write in the third edition of *The Elements of Style* (1979) that generic *he* "has become seemingly indispensable. It has no pejorative connotation; it is never incorrect." Wait, what? Never incorrect?

Second-wave feminists, beginning in the 1970s, begged to differ. Generic *he,* they argued, was sexist and unacceptable because its meaning was clearly male, not gender-neutral. By the 1990s, most standard usage guides had changed their tune on generic *he* and were recommending against it. For example, Andrea Lunsford and Robert Connors write in their widely used book *The Everyday Writer* (1997):

> Indefinite pronouns often refer to antecedents that may be either male or female. Writers used to use a masculine pronoun, known as the generic *he*, to refer to such indefinite pronouns. In recent decades, however, many people have pointed out that such wording ignores or even excludes females—and thus should not be used.

While there have been many new generic pronouns suggested over the past two hundred years or so, including *e, thon, heshe, huh, hu, co,* and *ze,* none of them has caught on as a viable generic pronoun. It's hard to introduce a brand-new pronoun into a language. The pronoun *ze* (with *zir* for the object and possessive form) has gained some momentum as a useful pronoun, in addition to *they,* for transgender individuals and those who do not identify within the male-female binary. Efforts to promote a specific transgender or nonbinary pronoun are often conflated with efforts to promote a "gender-neutral pronoun," but it is useful to distinguish the two.

In terms of the singular generic pronoun, style guides today regularly provide a few alternatives: (a) Use *he or she* as a singular generic pronoun; (b) Alternate between *he* and *she* by sentence or paragraph; (c) Make the antecedent plural and use *they;* or (d) Rewrite the sentence to omit the need for a pronoun. None of these solutions completely works.

The conjoined phrase *he or she* is not fully inclusive, and it can get cumbersome if it appears multiple times within a sentence or two—for example, "A teacher should learn his or her students' names as soon as he or she receives the class roster, even if he or she claims to be bad at learning names." Alternating pronouns by paragraph can be jarring for a reader: Given that neither *he* nor *she* functions well as a generic, readers may be distracted by the shifts in gender reference. Making the sentence plural can work in many instances, but sometimes we really do need to refer to individual people of unknown or irrelevant gender, in which case we need a singular generic pronoun. And some of the grammatical gymnastics involved in omitting the pronoun can contort a sentence's meaning as well as its syntax.

A few more progressive style guides now recognize the ubiquity of singular gender-neutral *they* in speech, even as they adhere to more conservative guidelines for writing. And this recommendation for formal prose is not without cause. The *American Heritage Dictionary* usage survey has been tracking attitudes about singular generic *they* for decades. In 1996, 80 percent of the panel rejected a sentence like "Each student must have their pencil sharpened." In the 2011 survey, only 55 percent of the Usage Panel disapproved of the sentence. In other words, resistance to singular *they* with an antecedent like *student* or *person* dropped 25 percent in just fifteen years. Perhaps even more striking is that now more than half the panel accepts singular *they* with antecedents such as *everyone* and *anyone*. The editors of the dictionary conclude: "Writers who choose to use *they* with a singular antecedent should rest assured that they are in good company—even if a fair number of traditionalists still wince at the usage."

Here's a problem, though: Many of these wincing traditionalists are in positions of power and can reject your job application because it contains a singular *they*, seeing it as evidence that you don't control "good grammar." It may not be fair or accurate, but as the Usage Panel reveals, this kind of judgment remains a real possibility. It is much less of a problem at this point in journalistic writing, but it remains a conundrum in some of the most formal genres.

the bottom line

I have been employing singular gender-neutral *they* in my formal writing for years, and I used to footnote it the first time the pronoun appeared, using the footnote to briefly explain my ra-

tionale.* I have told students they can do this too and encourage
them to direct questions to me if they want to (which they do—
and I have received some wonderful emails from across campus
with queries about these footnotes). All of you are welcome to
cite me too! This footnote accomplishes at least three things: It
shows readers that the author is consciously making a choice to
use singular *they;* it informs readers about legitimate reasons for
using singular *they,* even if they disagree with its use in this context; and as importantly, it asks us to be careful, self-conscious
writers, reflecting on and explaining our choices in our writing.

As more and more newspaper style guides accept singular
they, I think my footnote is becoming less and less necessary. In
fact, as dean of the liberal arts college at the University of Michigan, I have changed our style guide to use singular *they* as an
inclusive singular third-person pronoun.

With job letters and the like, where footnotes are not really
an option, you may want to make the sentence plural. Honestly,
even though I am probably the most fervent advocate of singular *they* that you will ever meet, I will sometimes reword the
sentence because I suspect the audience of the text may have
conservative views on the construction, and I don't have time to
get into it. But I no longer use *he or she* because it isn't inclusive.

If we're speaking or writing about individuals whose pronoun is *they,* it is an important signal of respect to use their
pronoun. Good writing is cognizant and respectful of potential
readers, and pronoun choices matter. It's as disrespectful to dismiss someone's pronoun as it is to dismiss their name: "You go
by Andy? Well, that isn't convenient for me: I'm going to call
you Al." That would be weird and rude.

---

* Here's what my footnote looks like: "I am choosing to use singular gender-
neutral *they* in this text. It is the most widely used singular generic pronoun in the
spoken language and provides a useful, inclusive, concise solution to the issue in the
written language as well."

In general, keep an eye on how quickly prescriptions are changing on this front. I'm predicting it won't be long before it will be unremarkable to use singular generic *they* in all written registers, just as it is unremarkable to say it in all spoken contexts. And as writers and editors, we can help make that happen if we choose to. Which I honestly hope we will.

for who(m) the bell tolls

How can something that is technically "right" sound sometimes so very, very wrong? That is the situation we're now in with the pronoun *whom*.

Let me show you what I mean. Given my professional title (English professor) and the fact that I study grammar (and do things like write usage guides), some folks like to read my emails very carefully looking for, from their perspective, grammatical slip-ups. And then email me about them, with messages like "I can't believe that you of all people would write . . ." It makes me a very self-conscious email writer! So I find myself in something of a conundrum when I need to open an email with something like "I wasn't sure who to send this message to, so please forward it as needed."

Technically I should use *whom,* not *who*: "I wasn't sure whom to send this message to." But, wow, that sounds hopelessly stuffy if not pretentious or downright wrong. If I take the *to* and move it forward, it sounds less wrong ("I wasn't sure to whom to send this message") but perhaps even more stuffy. I find myself, then, between a grammatical rock and a hard place: keep *who* and risk people going grammando on me for not knowing my *who*'s from my *whom*'s, or use *whom* and risk damage to my social life for being the grammatically fussy English professor who is going to be judgy about other people's emails. Hmmm.

Because it is email, which is a less formal kind of writing, I stick with *who*. I also know that we're living through an extended change in progress in the language and that in the long run, *whom* is likely not going to survive. Some of you are probably cheering and others are gritting your teeth. For the latter group, let me flip the tables: Rather than lamenting that *whom* may finally disappear, we could look in awe at how long it has managed to survive.

Let's start with the rule about how to use *who* and *whom,* and then I'll explain why things get so confusing. *Who* is an interrogative pronoun (a pronoun used to ask questions) and a relative pronoun (a pronoun used to introduce relative clauses, which modify nouns—we'll come back to that). For the moment, let's focus on interrogative *who,* as the issues with the interrogative and relative are similar. *Who,* which is used in subject position, has two derivative forms: *whom* when the pronoun is in object position, and *whose* when it is possessive. That is the traditional rule. So we would ask:

Who invited you to the *Star Trek* party?

Here, *who* is the subject—the person who invited you to the party. Let's imagine you borrow a fantastic *Star Trek* costume for this party, and I am oohing and aahing over the costume. I ask:

Whose costume is that? I love it!

The question is focused on who possesses the costume, hence the use of *whose.* Then off you go to the party, and the next day, you reveal that you may have had too much to drink and spilled a secret. I ask:

Whom did you tell?!

Or at least, that is what I ask if I am following the rule about using *whom* in object position. If we turn the question around and use the declarative form with question intonation, it is easier to see that *whom* is in object position, after the verb:

You told whom?!

In my own education, I had teachers suggest substituting in a personal pronoun (e.g., *she/her, I/me*) to see if you need the subject or object form. For example, you would ask "You told her?" not "You told she?"—which helps you know that you need the object form. Now if I am trying to express my shock that you spilled the secret, "Whom did you tell?!" may not seem colloquial enough. Even on the page, the juxtaposition of *whom* and the punctuation ?! looks odd. "Who did you tell?!" may sound better in terms of what we would actually say, but "Whom did you tell?!" follows the technical rule.

What is happening when what sounds right isn't technically right and we find ourselves unsure of which form to use? There are two parts to the answer: (a) the nature of how we make *wh-* questions in English, and (b) the history of subject and object forms in English. We'll start with how we make questions. You'll notice that we needed to "undo the question" to see that *whom* was the object in "Whom did you tell?!" When we make questions with *who, what, where, when,* and *why,* we typically start the question with that *wh*-word:

Where was the *Star Trek* party?
When did you get invited?
Why in the world did you spill that secret?!

With *who* and *whom,* then, the *who* or the *whom* is always going to appear at the beginning of the question, whether it is the subject or the object. We get:

Who saw you there?
Whom did you see there?

That's where things get confusing for us. English speakers typically tell their subjects from their objects by whether they come before or after the verb. At this point in its history, English is a language that depends highly on word order. As a clichéd quip about word order goes: "The dog bit the man" is not news, but "The man bit the dog" is news. We know who did the biting by which noun appears before the verb and which noun appears after the verb. *Wh*-questions, though, behave differently and can throw us off the subject-object scent. Because the *wh*-word always appears at the beginning of the question, it always appears where we expect a subject. Sure, we can undo the question "Whom did you see there?" to get "You saw whom there?" and see that the *wh*- word is in object position. But when we ask the question with the *wh*-word in the beginning, it looks like a subject. And that is a big part of why we want to use *who*: "Who did you see there?" or "Who did you tell?!"

Now for the second part of the story. You may have noticed that I said "at this point in its history," English depends highly on word order to tell what is the subject and what is the object in a sentence. That hasn't always been the case. And how clever of me to use the word *case*, because it's exactly what I'm talking about: English used to have grammatical case, just like German, Russian, Latin, and many other languages. What this means is that all nouns and pronouns used to take different inflectional endings to indicate their grammatical role in a sentence. For example, the Old English word for 'name' was *nama* when it was in subject position and *naman* when it was a direct object. So, in Old English, if you said the equivalent of "My name is Ishmael," where *name* is in subject position, you would use *nama,* and if you said, "She called my name," you would use *naman* because it is the direct object of the verb *called.* In Old English the word for 'boat' was *bāt* when it was in subject position (e.g., "The boat sank"), *bāte* when it was an indirect object (e.g., "We gave the boat a name"), and *bātes* when it was in the possessive (e.g., "the boat's name"). This whole case system for nouns disintegrated over time so that now a name is a name is a name—and a boat is a boat—whether it is a subject, a direct object, or an indirect object. The only endings we kept are the -s for possessive (e.g., *name's, boat's*) and plural (*names, boats*).

But (and this is a big but) pronouns in English have retained case much longer. They are tenacious, those pronouns. In the personal pronouns, we still distinguish subject and object for most of them (e.g., *I/me, she/her, he/him, we/us*), as well as the possessive (e.g., *mine, hers, his, ours*). And the interrogative pronoun *who* does the same thing: *who* for subject, *whom* for object, and *whose* for possessive. But because *who* and *whom* both tend to show up in what looks like subject position, we're losing the distinction here earlier than we're losing it with other pronouns. It is a harbinger of things to come. (For more on that, turn to the next chapter, where we'll talk about "between you and I.")

What's amazing to me, in all honesty, is that *whom* remains alive at all. We have evidence of *who/whom* confusion as early as the fifteenth century—so over five hundred years ago! In his 1768 edition of the book *The Rudiments of English Grammar,* Joseph Priestley explains that we often tend to use subject forms of pronouns when they appear before the verb, no matter what grammatical function they play, and notes how common it is to hear phrasing such as: "Who is this for?" and "Who should I meet the other day than my old friend." He concludes, "This form of speaking is so familiar, that I question whether grammarians should not admit it as an exception to the general rule." Yet, through education and correction, *whom* is still around. It is healthiest when it occurs right after a preposition because it is clearer that it is in object position (e.g., *to whom*). But you can find examples of *by who* and *to who,* without working all that hard. In sum, much of the time, we see *who* used for *whom,* as in the example above: "Who did you tell?!" But sometimes we get hypercorrection, where speakers and writers overuse *whom* in subject position because they are worried that they have it wrong and don't use *whom* enough.

And sometimes it's downright confusing, especially with relative clauses. As we close this chapter, let's look at an email I received with a *who/whom* question. The writer wanted to know what was correct in this sentence:

> We have chosen the candidate [who or whom] we believe can meet our needs.

What does your gut tell you? It can be tempting to use *whom*, because it looks like it might be the object of "we believe." But it's not. It helps if we remove "we believe," because it is functioning almost parenthetically; then we get:

> We have chosen the candidate [who or whom] can meet our needs.

Once we do that, it becomes more obvious that the pronoun is in subject position and we need *who*. So when might we need a relative *whom*? Here's an example:

> I voted for the candidate whom the president endorsed.

Okay, does that sound awkward to you? It gets us back to where we started: *Whom* sometimes just sounds too formal. The good news here is that you can just omit it. With interrogative *whom*, we don't have this option, but with relative *whom*, it is optional (it is a quirk of English syntax). So if you don't want someone to go grammando on a *who* and you don't want to use *whom*, you can say or write:

> I voted for the candidate the president endorsed.

Or, gasp, you could use *that*.

We'll end with that peeve, which I used to have. I long felt strongly that people should get *who/whom*, and inanimate things could get *that*. In students' papers, I used to underline constructions like "the student that wrote the essay," and write *who* over *that* as a preferred alternative. Then about twenty years ago, a graduate student brought his essay to me and asked, "Why do you keep underlining this? I checked usage guides and they say there is nothing wrong with it." He was completely right about usage guides, and as a historian of the language, I should have known better. English speakers have used the equivalent of *that* with people for centuries, including in the Lord's Prayer ("Our Father that art in heaven . . ." in early versions). So now I just notice it, and I keep my pen quiet.

the bottom line

. . . .

While I continue to let my inner grammando have some say with *who/whom* and adhere to the prescriptive notion of when to use *whom* in my most formal writing, I find that at this point, *whom* can sound fussy in many contexts. I tend to avoid it in email or text, either by reworking the sentence or just by using *who*: for example, "Who did you call about getting the washing machine fixed?" We're all navigating grammandos here as well as, for many of us, a desire to sound unpretentious. It is impossible to say that *whom,* at this point, is unequivocally the right choice for a grammatical object in many, many contexts.

20
....

between you and me/i/myself

n the Q&A after my public talks and in listeners' questions to the radio show, I hear regularly about constructions such as "between you and I" and "me and my team went." A lot of people are concerned that our personal pronouns are a hot mess.

The good news: The concern is more circumscribed than all personal pronouns. The concern focuses on conjoined constructions (*X and Y*), in which we're collectively struggling to keep case straight. (Please turn back to the previous chapter on *who/whom* for a quick summary of case systems.) The bad news for your inner grammando: Our personal pronouns, in conjoined constructions, *are* a bit of a hot mess. The news you likely won't be surprised to hear at this point in the book: This hot mess is not new in the history of English.

We could go earlier than Shakespeare, but it's always fun to quote Shakespeare. Here is a line from *The Merchant of Venice*: "All debts are clear'd between you and I." My mother's inner grammando wants to leap up and shout "between you and me" from the audience! And here is Othello: "Yes, you haue seene *Cassio,* and she together." We could say that Shakespeare wasn't masterful with his language, which would run counter to all arguments about Shakespeare, or that this was a "slip of the quill," as one commentator has argued. Or we could acknowledge that Shakespeare was masterful at capturing the language around him; this is what was happening with pronouns in conjoined constructions at the time; and Shakespeare did not judge these constructions as unworthy of the page or the stage.

Because they are not unworthy. And it's not clear they're ungrammatical. Or a hot mess for that matter. Let me explain.

SUBJECTS, OBJECTS, AND CASE

The most robust remnants of the case system in English are in the personal pronoun system, and "robust" might be generous at this point. For the majority of personal pronouns, we still distinguish between the subject form and the object form: *I/me, he/him, she/her, we/us, they/them*. The pronoun *it* has always been identical in the subject and object form, all the way back to Old English. The pronoun *you* lost the distinction a few hundred years ago. Yes, you heard me right: The case distinction has already collapsed for the pronoun *you*. In Old and Middle English, *ye* was the subject form and *you* was the object form, before *you* took over all grammatical functions.

Shakespeare lived through the late stages of this particular language change, and he struggled to keep his *ye*'s and *you*'s straight—or he was masterfully capturing that everyone around him was having trouble keeping their *ye*'s and *you*'s straight. He could use *ye* in subject position, as Banquo does in *Macbeth*: "Are ye fantasticall, or that indeed / Which outwardly ye shew?" He could also use *you* in subject position and *ye* in object position, as captured in this line from Antony in *Julius Caesar*: "I do beseech yee, if you beare me hard." To use modern parlance, his *ye*'s and *you*'s are a hot mess. To put it the way a linguist would, his pronoun variation (or some might say "confusion") reflects a language change in progress.[*]

---

[*] Shakespeare was living through another change with *ye* and *you*. Historically *ye/you* was the second-person plural pronoun and *thou/thee* was the second-person singular pronoun. By the Renaissance, *ye/you* had taken over both the singular and plural functions, but *thou/thee* wasn't completely obsolete (and even to this day it is

Over time, *you* replaced *ye* and can now be used as both the subject and object pronoun—and nothing catastrophic happened to English grammar. Keep that in mind as we return to "between you and I/me."

BETWEEN YOU AND I/ME

In American and British English, and most standardized varieties of English around the world, the subject/object distinction generally remains intact for *I/me, he/him, she/her, we/us, they/them* when these pronouns appear alone. "She geeks out on grammar" (subject), and "Language delights her" (object). As kids learn English, they will sometimes produce sentences like "Him wants the cookie," rather than "He wants the cookie," as they master the fact that unlike nouns, most personal pronouns (other than *it* and *you*) are not identical in subject and object position. In the English-based creole language Jamaican Creole, the subject/object distinction has collapsed for all personal pronouns—so, for example, it's *mi* in the first-person singular in both subject and object position.

Where we see personal pronoun variation in American and British English (and many other varieties) is in conjoined pronoun constructions—when *I* or *she* or the like do not appear alone. It can be a subject form in object position ("for you and I" or "my mother called my sister and I") or an object form in subject position ("me and the team reviewed the document"). These constructions have been labeled "wrong" or "ungrammatical" based on the assumption that conjoined constructions function the same way as pronouns on their own. When I was growing up, I was told, "Substitute in the pronoun by itself and see what form you need, and then use

---

not fully obsolete given its use in the Quaker community). In the singular, *thou/thee* could be used as an informal pronoun of address, with *ye/you* as the formal pronoun of address. And if you read Shakespeare carefully, you'll find him playing with *thou* as a subtle put-down. He even uses the verb *to thou* to refer to the use of the pronoun as an informal dig.

that in the conjoined construction." So because it would be "for me," then it should be "for you and me." Because it would be "my mother called me," it would be "my mother called my sister and me." In the same way, in subject position, because it would be "I reviewed the document," it would be "my team and I reviewed the document."

But . . . does it really work that way? Some eighteenth- and nineteenth-century grammarians took it upon themselves to tell us that the English language works that way, but when you listen to us talk, it doesn't always align. And even some of the nineteenth-century grammarians knew that! Here is Joseph Priestley, who in addition to making many scientific discoveries as a chemist took a notably descriptive approach in *The Rudiments of English Grammar* (first published in 1761, and republished with "improvements" in 1768, which is how he can quote a work, *The Fair American,* from 1767 here):

> The nominative case is sometimes found after verbs and preposi-
> tions. It has even crept into writing. *The chaplain intreated my*
> *comrade and* I *to dress as well as possible.* . . . *He told my Lord*
> *and* I. Fair American, vol. I p. 141. This aukward construction is
> constantly observed by the author of this romance. On the other
> hand, he sometimes uses the oblique case instead of the nomina-
> tive. *My father and* him *have been very intimate since.* Ib. vol. 2
> p. 53. This last is a French construction.

The variation in these conjoined constructions is not new, nor is the commentary on them.

So what's going on here? Many linguists have spilled ink on this question, and I'm going to give you a few theories, without one definitive answer. Sorry: I recognize that may be frustrating, but I don't want to simplify what is a fascinating linguistic question.

Let's start with what we know, and here I'm going to be adapting some material from a 2003 study by Philipp S. Angermeyer and John V. Singler, linguists at New York University. We have three basic grammatical patterns (yes, I did say *grammatical*— *grammatical* in the sense that these are constructions English speakers use regularly, recognize as patterned language use, and interpret without difficulty):

- *me and X* in both subject and object position (vernacular or informal usage)
- *X and I* in subject position and *X and me* in object position (standardized usage)
- *X and I* in both subject and object position (polite usage)*

I know: It's a very non-judgy way to think about it. Stick with me. You will notice one pattern that is not there: *I and X.* For most speakers, this construction is not grammatical, in the sense that we don't use it, and it can strike us as awkward when we see or hear it. It's not that *I and X* isn't linguistically possible; we just don't seem to use *I* first in these conjoined constructions.

Angermeyer and Singler propose a couple of principles at work in the variation in conjoined constructions. In terms of order, we as speakers prefer the first-person pronoun first in the informal construction (*me and X*) and the first-person last in polite constructions (which include standardized and polite usage): *X and I.* In terms of case, we prefer the object case in the informal (*me*); we prefer the subject case in the polite (*I*); and we follow the case of a single, stand-alone pronoun in standardized usage (*me* in object position, *I* in subject position).

The informal construction (*me and X*) is where young children start when they are learning the language. And one explanation of polite usage (*X and I,* everywhere) is hypercorrection: Kids spend part of their childhood being corrected from saying "me and X" in subject position to "X and I" ("Honey, not 'me and my friend went,' but 'my friend and I went'"), and then they start overapply-

---

* You'll sometimes see the reflexive pronoun *myself* get substituted for *me* and *I,* perhaps as a way to skirt the decision about which pronoun is "correct."

ing the correction and using *X and I* not only in subject position but also in object position. It's an attractive theory. The problem is that the evidence of polite usage (*X and I*) predates prescriptive attention to this construction in usage guides.

Another theory is that these conjoined constructions are acting as one unit. In other words, we have routinized "chunks" of language in the form *X and I* and *me and X,* whether they appear in subject position or object position. So we find "You and I are best friends," and "This trip is designed for you and I." If you're a mathy person, it's the difference between the preposition *for* distributing across both pronouns ("for you" and "for me"—which is how I learned it when I was told to see what happened if I put just one pronoun after the preposition) and "for [you and I]" where *you and I* is an independent, invariant unit, unaffected by the preposition. *

Other factors can also affect order. For example, while standardized usage prefers that the first-person pronoun comes last, it will often come first if the other part of the conjoined construction is long. What do I mean? Let's imagine you are talking about the person who used to live next door. You could say: "The package came to the person who used to live next door and me." Totally possible, but it is equally or more likely that you will put the heavy noun phrase last and say: "The package came to me and the person who used to live next door."

If you're looking for me to tell you which one of those is right, I can't. They are both grammatical, and it can be helpful to have the flexibility to change the order if one sounds better to you as a speaker and writer. And I hope that the framework for thinking about this as informal, standardized, and polite usage will be liberating. It's not that one of these constructions has to be grammati-

---

* An interesting construction that shows some speakers are treating *X and I* as a chunk occurs in the possessive. For example: "I hope you'll listen to my friend and I's idea." The possessive *-'s* is getting attached to the conjoined chunk *my friend and I.* If you're thinking, "No one says that," I hope your inner wordie will start listening for it. It's out there!

cally "wrong." Our grammar can allow variation, and none of this variation is confusing in terms of what a speaker is trying to convey about who did what. And our own sense of correctness may shift over time. I'll be honest that while standardized usage would dictate that I write "Please send the memo to Jay and me," this now feels a little off to me. Not off enough to change it to *Jay and I* yet, but off nonetheless.

IT IS I

As I mentioned in the introduction, I was taught it was proper grammar to respond, "This is she speaking" if someone called and asked, "Is Anne there?" Never mind that this felt over-the-top formal to me and my sisters.

But is it proper grammar? The basis for the prescription goes as follows. *To be* is a linking verb. Linking verbs roughly equate, semantically, the subject with the predicate noun phrase or adjective phrase that follows it. (If Anne is a wordie: Anne = wordie.) Linking verbs must also, then, equate the subject and the predicate noun phrase grammatically. So, given that the subject is in the nominative case (e.g., *I, she, we*), then the predicate noun must also be in the nominative case (e.g., "It is I," "This is she speaking").

Why does it sound so odd, then, to say, "It is we," rather than "It is us"? And while we're at it, here's another awkward sentence: "I asked who called yesterday, and it was he." My gut wants to say "It was him," just like I want to say "It's me" when someone asks for me on the phone. At the same time, my inner grammando channels my mother and winces.

If you have a similar battle going on in your head, here's the good news: Many usage guides now say that both "It is me" and "It is I" are acceptable. It is, rather than an issue of grammaticality, an issue of formality. If your inner grammando is not convinced that "It's me" could possibly be grammatical, remind it that other languages show the predicate noun doesn't need to be nominative. In

French, for example, it is only grammatical to say "C'est moi" ('It is me'), not "C'est je" ('It is I'). Joseph Priestley, the descriptively inclined grammarian I mentioned earlier in this chapter, brought up exactly this example from French in the 1700s to defend "It's me" in English.

Did you, like me, learn that you should say "She's taller than I" rather than "She's taller than me"? Either is fine. The question is whether we interpret *than* as a subordinating conjunction or a preposition. If it's a subordinating conjunction, the argument is that the full sentence is "She's taller than I am," so when it is shortened, it becomes "She's taller than I." But *than* can also function as a preposition (in which case it takes the object case), and there isn't an especially compelling reason not to let it be a preposition here, so "She's taller than me." There are occasionally sentences where there will be ambiguity—for example, "My father called my sister after me." *After* can also be a subordinating conjunction or a preposition. So the question is: Did your father call your sister after you called your sister or after he called you? My best advice here: Rather than trying to legislate that everyone, all the time, use *than* and *after* and the like as subordinating conjunctions in these constructions, reword the sentence if it might be ambiguous.

the bottom line

If your inner grammando is still struggling to accept all this variation in the pronouns, here's a useful question to ponder. I first heard this question posed by my linguist colleague Geoff Pullum: How many educated speakers have to use constructions like "between you and I" in their speech (and email!) before we call it educated usage? Or, put another way, how often do we need to hear "between you and I" in both informal and formal contexts before we recognize it as formal usage rather than a mistake?

We have two options: We can continue to tell all these speakers that they have it all wrong in their speech and writing, and they've had it all wrong for centuries. Or we could accept that in these conjoined constructions with personal pronouns, we have variation that signals levels of formality. The standardized constructions can float across the continuum, from less to more formal situations. And then we have informal and formal constructions available. These kinds of stylistic choices can be a helpful part of grammar.

21

none is/are confusing

I t seems like it should be straightforward to determine whether the subject of a sentence is singular or plural. One octopus is, and many octopodes are. Done! But sometimes it isn't that easy. Consider these two examples:

None of my friends is/are coming until after eight P.M.

For dessert, either cake or cookies is/are fine.

Do you have a clear sense of which verb is "right" in each sentence?

I grew up being told that the word *none* is singular. If we accept this premise, the first sentence technically should be "None of my friends is coming until after eight P.M." But the sentence feels plural to me, because it implies that not just one but more than one friend—it could be three or thirteen or thirty—are not coming until after eight P.M. "Feels plural, Anne?" my inner grammando smirks. "Feelings shmeelings." Because my inner grammando and I thought I knew what was right, I corrected my own writing to the singular and suggested the change to students for years. Then I looked into the history of the *none* rule and discovered that my inner grammando needed some reeducating, and I didn't have to ignore my feelings about these sentences.

With the second sentence, it matters for the grammar whether we mention the cake or the cookies first. Here's the teaser: It's called "the proximity rule." We'll come back to that and dive into the complexities of *either*. We'll also look at agreement issues with *there is/are*. Is it ever okay to say or write: "There's lots of reasons grammatical agreement can be confusing"? If you're a fan of both/and approaches, as opposed to either/or approaches, you will like this chapter.

NONE

Questions about how the word *none* works grammatically take us into the land of indefinite pronouns. Indefinite pronouns do not refer to a specific person or thing—they stand in for a vague or undetermined person (*anyone/anybody, everyone/everybody, someone/somebody, no one/nobody*) or thing (*something, anything, everything*) or both (*either, neither*), or an amount of people or things (*few, many, some, none, each, every*). Most indefinite pronouns are straightforward in terms of agreement with verbs: For example, *anyone* is singular ("anyone is") and *few* is plural ("few are").

None is trickier, perhaps especially in a phrase where it is referring to none of a plural group of things or people, such as "none of my friends is/are." So, can *none* be both singular and plural? To ruin the punch line, here's the answer: Yes. I told you: This is the both/and approach!

While many of us have been taught at some point in our schooling that *none* must be singular, the "rule" here seems to be bogus. The etymology of *none* is 'not one,' but that doesn't mean that *none* must behave exactly like *one* now. As far back as 1795, in Lindley Murray's highly prescriptive, best-selling grammar book (which, as chapter 18 describes, was key to the promotion of singular generic *he*), even Murray said: "*None* is used in both numbers." He knew and noted *none*'s etymology, and then he added there was "good authority" for using it in the plural, as well as the singular.

Somewhere along the way this balanced approach got lost. By the late nineteenth century, some guides had started advancing a strict rule about *none* as singular. Luckily others were pushing back. J. Lesslie Hall was a literary scholar at the College of William and Mary and translator of *Beowulf;* he knew the history of the language. In his 1917 book, *English Usage,* he describes *none is* as "rather puristic" and predicted that the plural will "eventually be almost universal in spoken English and increase its ratio in literature." Thomas Lounsbury, a fellow literary scholar at Yale University from 1871 to 1906, was even less forgiving of those clinging to notions of singular agreement. In *The Standard of English Usage* (1908), he wrote:

> There is no harm in a man's limiting his employment of *none* to the singular in his own individual usage, if he derives any pleasure from this particular form of linguistic martyrdom. But why should he go about seeking to inflict upon others the misery which owes its origin to his own ignorance?

What is especially wonderful about this quote is that "linguistic martyrdom" is limiting ourselves to just one option. It's not that using singular agreement with *none* is wrong either. There is just no good reason not to have both singular and plural agreement at our disposal, especially because *none* can mean different things in different contexts.

Bryan Garner, in his authoritative guide, *Garner's Modern English Usage,* distinguishes between *none* meaning 'not one' (singular) versus 'not any' (plural). So, for example, let's imagine a context in which I am sure that *plog* is a word (because I grew up with it), and you challenge me that it is not. I check the online versions of the American Heritage and Merriam-Webster dictionaries, and I can't find an entry for *plog.* Determined that some dictionary is going to contain this word, I go through the dozens on my shelves, and finally I admit, "None of the dictionaries has *plog*."* Not one. So singular verb agreement. But with the sentence that started this chapter, the implication is plural, so it's fine to say (or write), "None of my friends are coming until after eight P.M."

EITHER

The indefinite pronoun *either* is straightforward if both nouns are singular ("either my sister or my brother is") or both plural ("either my sisters or my brothers are"). But sometimes we want to talk about a choice between a singular entity and a plural entity. For example:

Either the players or the owner is/are going to have to cave for the strike to end.

Which do you prefer: *is* or *are*? And does it matter if we switch the order of the subjects?

Either the owner or the players is/are going to have to cave for the strike to end.

With the second, I think many of us prefer *are*, so that we don't have the sequence "the players is." With the first, we may have a more split opinion. So what's the answer?

There isn't one right answer here. The widespread convention is "the principle of proximity": Whichever noun is closer to the verb governs agreement. This principle holds for straight up *or* construc-

---

* I grew up in a home where both noses and toilets could be plogged. A blend of *plug* and *clog*, *plog* has a playful emphatic element to it, and I had no idea this wasn't a shared term until students called me on it, claiming it wasn't "a real word" (see chapter 2). With the help of editors at the *Dictionary of American Regional English* and word sleuths around the globe, we have located one dictionary entry: In James Halliwell-Phillipps's *Dictionary of Archaic and Provincial Words* (1846), there is an entry for *plog* with the definition 'to clog, or hinder. Sussex.'

tions too: "The cake or the cookies need to be gluten-free"; but "The cookies or the cake needs to be gluten-free." That said, if you prefer a plural verb in the latter sentence because the semantics feel plural, you're not wrong. There simply isn't consensus here. In 2009, only 64 percent of the *American Heritage Dictionary* Usage Panel accepted proximity as the way to resolve agreement in these situations. And it gets even trickier when *either* pairs with two pronouns: "either you or I am/are"? Common usage suggests *are,* and usage guides tend to punt!

THERE IS/ARE

High on the list of peeves I hear about regularly is "incorrect" agreement with "existential *there*": *there is* + a plural noun. Here's an email I received a couple of years ago from a public radio listener with a strong grammando streak (I serve as the linguistic expert on a Sunday morning show on words):

> Nobody—not the evening newscasters or pundits, not NPR, not even The NY Times—says "there are" anymore. Everyone says "There's so many" no matter how many there is (see what I did there? :-)). "There's a bunch of them"—OK. "There's three of them"—not so OK. "There's more than ten . . ." "There's lots of reasons . . ."—I could go on.

No need to go on! I would guess some of you share this peeve about *there's.*

We call the grammatical subject of these sentences existential *there* because it is functioning as a grammatical placeholder, filling up the subject position of the sentence and allowing the notional subject to come after the verb. Why is that helpful? Because often we as speakers and writers want to put something grammatically heavy (i.e., relatively long) or semantically heavy (i.e., full of important information) into the predicate. (See chapter 33 for further discussion.)

Here's the prescriptive rule with existential *there*: The notional subject governs agreement. So it's no problem if there is only one spider on your head: "There's a spider on your head." Now let's imagine the unfortunate situation (or fortunate if you are a spider aficionado) in which three spiders are sitting on your head: "There are three spiders on your head." But could you say or write: "There's three spiders on your head"?

Many of us would say it. We often contract *there is* to *there's*, and this has become formulaic enough (some would say "grammaticalized") that the number of the following noun doesn't matter: "There's a reason for that" and "There's three reasons for that."* The role of *there's* is simply to introduce the highlighted information to come, whether that information is grammatically singular or plural. In a 2005 study, the linguist Bill Crawford, who works at Northern Arizona University, showed that existential *there* constructions with plural nouns appear with the singular *there's* 50 percent of the time in speech. Half the time! This is what the radio listener was hearing on NPR and elsewhere. This use of *there's* mirrors other colloquial expressions such as "Here's your shoes" and, for some of us, "How's things?" In formal writing, we're less likely to contract *there is* to *there's*, given long-standing conventions that discourage contraction; and without the contracted form, it's more likely that the following noun will govern the agreement (some of which is also due to strict editing).

---

* What about contracting *there are* to *there're*? Most standard dictionaries include independent entries for contractions such as *won't, haven't, shouldn't, can't,* and *ain't*. Merriam-Webster includes *there've,* and Collins and American Heritage do not. All three include *it'll,* but American Heritage omits *there'll,* while Merriam-Webster and Collins have an entry for it. Yet for all this variation, all three dictionaries agree on this: They don't include *there're*. There's nothing inherently wrong with the double *-re,* and it's hard to argue *there're* is more difficult to say than *there'll* (and, of course, we say both in informal speech). My inner grammando is coming to terms with *there're*.

Some of my fellow linguists have pointed out that the proximity principle can come into play with *there is/are* as well, if the existential *there* construction is followed by a list. Imagine a (delicious) sentence such as:

> There are cookies, a chocolate cake, and an apple tart on the dessert tray.

All fine. But what if we change up the order of the list?

> There are a chocolate cake, cookies, and an apple tart on the dessert tray.

For some of us, the grammar here feels off because of the sequence "are a chocolate cake": a plural verb (*are*) next to a singular noun (*cake*) that could be seen as governing agreement—except that it's part of a list. Oy! What are we to do? Well, first I would say that we shouldn't lose a lot of sleep over these constructions in speech. There is no compelling reason not to allow *there's* to function as a static, formulaic placeholder in subject position, with either singular or plural nouns or a variety of lists after it. In theory, there's no compelling reason not to allow this in formal writing too, but right now editors will still likely edit it out. So if we're writing and avoiding the efficient contraction *there's,* and then we run into this list conundrum, we can revise and reorder the list to put a plural noun first, if possible.

THE JURY SAYS . . . (OR DO THEY SAY?)

We're not finished with agreement conundrums yet. Collective nouns (i.e., singular nouns that describe a group of people) such as *jury, group, family,* and *couple* present their own set of agreement challenges. There are (see what I did there?) two ways to think about agreement with these nouns: meaning and geography.

In terms of meaning, agreement can depend on whether we're talking about the collective as a single unit or as separate individuals. It's the difference between "Her family is highly educated" and "Her family are all doctors." Perhaps you're thinking, "Wait, does that really mean I can't get this wrong?" Yes, and I hope that feels like a relief. In terms of geography, if you're from the United States, you're likely to use singular agreement (e.g., "the jury is"); if you're from the United Kingdom, you're likely to use plural agreement (e.g., "the jury are").

Agreement can get muddy when the collective is followed by a prepositional phrase with a plural noun such as "a jury of my peers is/are." American grammar guides often allow some variation here based on meaning, depending once again on whether a noun phrase like "a group" refers more to the individuals than to a unit (e.g., "My group of friends are going different ways after college").

the bottom line
....

There's an important lesson about what counts as standard usage in all these examples if we're prepared and willing to listen: Variation is okay.

Inner grammando, are you listening?

With some of these tricky constructions in which grammatical number and word meaning conflict or when different elements of the subject noun phrase have different grammatical number, even prescriptively minded usage guides often acquiesce to the variation we find in common usage. First, verb agreement often reflects what we mean in a given sentence—whether, for example, we're talking about a group as a unit or as a set of individuals. In that way, verb agreement provides the audience with useful information about what we as writers or speakers mean. Second, the language sometimes relies on fixed expressions that do grammatical work, and it's efficient to let them be fixed, in the way that *there's* is working for many speakers. If we can say "It's three more miles to get there," why not "There's three reasons"? When we ask, "Says who?" in response to the idea that there must be only one right way with these agreement questions, we don't get a very convincing answer.

22

....

which-hunting

The Microsoft Word grammar checker has strong feelings about the difference between *that* and *which* as relative pronouns—and it expresses those feelings in the green squiggly lines under our *which*'s and *that*'s. It is no wonder that a good number of writers, many of them unsure exactly what the "rule" is here, change *that* into *which* or *which* into *that* until the grammar checker has been appeased and the green squiggly line disappears. Why are so many of us getting these pronouns "wrong"? And could that many of us really be wrong, or is there something not quite right about this rule?

Here's an example of a sentence that gets flagged as a "problem" by many versions of the grammar checker in Microsoft Word:

Anne wants to meet a duck-billed platypus which can talk.

The grammar checker wants to change *which* to *that,* to give us "that can talk," because it is a restrictive relative clause. The grammar checker would allow *which* in a sentence with a nonrestrictive relative clause, such as "Anne wants to meet a talking duck-billed platypus, which is not a thing."

Clearly the difference between restrictive and nonrestrictive relative clauses lies at the crux of this usage issue, so let's back up and define a relative clause, and then distinguish restrictive from non-restrictive members of that relative clause club.

A relative clause is a clause (that is, it has a subject and a predicate) that modifies a noun or noun phrase.* In English it always comes after the noun or noun phrase, so we say "a duck-billed platypus that can talk" as opposed to "a that can talk duck-billed platypus."† Relative clauses are often introduced by a relative pronoun that stands in for the noun being modified; relative pronouns include *that, which, who, whom, whoever, whomever,* and *whose.* We'll come back to when we can omit that relative pronoun, which can get you out of at least some of the *that/which* conundrums you might face.

Now let's think about duck-billed platypuses (or *platypodes,* if we want to go back to the Greek; *platypi* is a faux Latin plural). Imagine a world in which there are platypuses that can talk and platypuses that can't talk. I have just used two *that* relative clauses to distinguish two different groups of platypuses: those *that can talk* and those *that can't talk.* In other words, those two restrictive relative clauses have, in each case, restricted the set of platypuses, allowing us to compare the two sets. In writing, restrictive clauses occur without a comma before them, and in speech they typically happen without a pause to introduce them.

Now it's time to burst the bubble of the imaginary world in which some platypuses can talk. A duck-billed platypus expert, who has been studying the creatures for twenty-seven years, states definitively that platypuses have never been seen or heard using lan-

---

* This is a slightly simplified definition, but I didn't want to slow us down. Relative clauses can refer back to any grammatical construction that acts like a noun as well as a full clause (e.g., "It is snowing, which means school might be canceled tomorrow").

† Perhaps you're someone who believes that a platypus should be referred to with *who* rather than *that* or *which.* There isn't a clear usage rule—it's more about how you feel about the animal in question. With dogs, cats, elephants, turtles, platypuses, and the like, it is much more common to use *that* or *which,* but you can find *who,* especially if the reference is to, say, a pet.

guage. As you may have noticed, I just used a nonrestrictive relative clause ("who has been studying the creatures for twenty-seven years") in order to enhance the expertise of the platypus expert: The length of the expert's career is additional, optional information; in this context it is not being used to distinguish this platypus expert from another platypus expert. Nonrestrictive relative clauses are typically preceded by a comma in writing and by a pause in speech.

I could easily talk about the platypus expert with a restrictive relative clause:

> The platypus expert who agreed to be interviewed states definitively that platypuses have never been seen or heard using language.

In this sentence I seem to be setting up a contrast between the expert who agreed to be interviewed, and perhaps some other platypus expert who did not pick up the phone or refused my request.

To summarize the difference between restrictive and nonrestrictive relative clauses, let's imagine two scenarios, one with multiple cars and one with only one car. You and I are trying to leave a party and sort out the key situation. In scenario one, you and I came to the party in different cars, and I want to let you know that I have keys for the car I drove and put in the garage, but not keys for the other. I use a restrictive clause to let you know that I am not taking responsibility for the location of the keys for the car that you parked on the street:

> I have the keys to the car that is in the garage.

In scenario two, I drove to the party and parked the car in the garage; you got a ride to the party with a friend. We're ready to go and I want to make sure you know where the car is, given that you didn't drive with me. I use a nonrestrictive clause to kindly share this information:

I have the keys to the car, which is in the garage.

Many of you undoubtedly noticed what I did with *that* and *which* there, in addition to adding a comma: I used *that* for the restrictive relative clause and *which* for the nonrestrictive clause, following the rule that the grammar checker is trying so hard to make us all follow.

The *that/which* rule appears to have been an attempt by grammarians to create complementary distribution for *that* and *which* with relative clauses. A key point here: Such a tidy distribution of *that* and *which* has probably never existed in English. It is not that this rule preserves some tidier system from a past moment; it tries to create tidiness in an area where it's not clear speakers or writers require it. Here's where the "rule" generally lines up with usage: Most speakers typically use *that* only in restrictive clauses. That is, we tend not to use *that* after a comma (or a pause) for nonrestrictive relative clauses—although you will certainly see it sometimes. But here's where the "rule" breaks down: A whole lot of us can use *which* for both nonrestrictive clauses and restrictive clauses. Remember the opening sentence: "Anne wants to meet a duck-billed platypus which can talk."

So, stepping back, why not let *which* do double duty? *Who* and *whom* already can introduce both a restrictive and nonrestrictive relative clause. And *which* has been able to double up for hundreds of years. There is no good reason other than tidiness: If grammarians (and the grammar checker) can get us as speakers and writers to use *which* only for nonrestrictives, then there would be no overlap with *that*.

The roots of this imposition of *which/that* tidiness is relatively new in the history of English. We can trace the prescription back to 1908 and the Fowler brothers' usage guide *The King's English*. Here is what the Fowlers wrote:

This confusion [between *that* and *which*] is to be regretted; for although no distinction can be authoritatively drawn between the two relatives, an obvious one presents itself. The few limitations on 'that' and 'who' about which every one is agreed all point to 'that' as the defining relative, 'who' or 'which' as the non-defining. . . . 'Who' or 'which' should not be used in defining clauses except when custom, euphony, or convenience is decidedly against the use of 'that.'

Did you catch what else is happening in this quote, beyond distinguishing *that* and *which*? The Fowlers are recommending *that* as the restrictive relative pronoun with animate and inanimate nouns, with *who* and *which* for nonrestrictive relative clauses. *That* for animate nouns? Circle back to chapter 19 to read about me getting over that peeve. The Fowlers never got traction on limiting *who* to nonrestrictive clauses; we all use *who* for restrictive and nonrestrictive clauses, and no one gets hurt—and I'll come back to that.

In his subsequent and highly influential *A Dictionary of Modern English Usage* (1926), H. W. Fowler clarifies his preference for complementary distribution of *that* and *which* and yet shows his awareness that actual usage and his preferred order for things do not necessarily align. He starts by acknowledging that grammarians have less influence on usage than they may realize, but that it's hard to resist having preferences about what would be best usage. He then notes:

The relations between *that, who,* & *which* have come to us from our forefathers as an odd jumble, & plainly show that the language has not been neatly constructed by a master builder who could create each part to do the exact work required of it, neither overlapped nor overlapping.

So he accepts the jumble, but he says it doesn't mean we couldn't, at least theoretically, do better. He explains:

If writers would agree to regard *that* as the defining relative pronoun, & *which* as the non-defining, there would be much gain both in lucidity & in ease. Some there are who follow this principle now; but it would be idle to pretend that it is the practice either of most or of the best writers.

Even as he claims that writers would gain lucidity and ease, Fowler recognizes that "good usage" as practiced by "the best writers"—and even most of the best writers—does not always follow this. It raises the question of whether it is, in fact, easier to let it be more of a jumble.

The jumble that Fowler describes, however, gets lost in Strunk and White's version of the "rule" in *The Elements of Style.* They make a clear distinction: *That* is restrictive; *which* is nonrestrictive. They then note there are exceptions, such as this sentence from the Bible: "Let us now go even unto Bethlehem, and see this thing which is come to pass." But in the end, we as writers are not allowed to do as our predecessors have done for "euphony or convenience": Strunk and White tell us to go *which*-hunting to improve our work.

This definitive advice about *that* and *which* now appears in lots of places. *The Associated Press Stylebook,* for example, makes no exceptions to the restrictive/nonrestrictive rule for *that* and *which*:

> Use *that* for essential clauses, important to the meaning of a sentence, and without commas: *I remember the day that we met.* Use *which* for nonessential clauses, where the pronoun is less necessary, and use commas: *The team, which finished last a year ago, is in first place.*

Garner's Modern English Usage (fifth edition, 2022) is worth quoting in full on this, given its strong stance on this historical jumble:

> You'll encounter two schools of thought on this point. First are those who don't care about any distinction between these words,

who think that *which* is more formal than *that,* and who point to many historical examples of copious *whiches.* They say that modern usage is a muddle. Second are those who insist that both words have useful functions that ought to be separated, and who observe the distinction rigorously in their own writing. They view departures from this distinction as "mistakes." Before reading any further, you ought to know something more about these two groups: those in the first probably don't write very well; those in the second just might.

This kind of prescriptive language can encourage language gatekeeping—and make a whole lot of educated people feel like they don't know what they're doing as writers. The idea seems to be that if you follow this rule, you are detail-oriented as a writer and care about niceties. I beg to differ. To be detail-oriented with *that* and *which* is to know the history of the rule and make informed decisions about what sounds best in a given sentence. Sometimes, as in legal writing, we need to be very careful to distinguish our restrictive relative clauses from our nonrestrictive ones. Sometimes, in other genres, a restrictive *which* sounds better. For example, as the usage note in the *American Heritage Dictionary* points out, writers and editors may prefer a restrictive *which* to avoid two instances of *that* appearing too close together. Consider the sentence: "We want to assign only that material *which/that* will be most helpful."

If you're thinking, "Can I just avoid this whole situation?" the answer is sometimes. English grammar provides one escape hatch where we as speakers and writers can just omit the relative pronoun. It's called the "zero relative" and it's a lovely way to get out of the *that/which* conundrum. It can only happen when the relative pronoun functions as the object in the relative clause and when it is restrictive. So you can omit the pronoun here:

I loved the platypus that/which I had as a child.

I loved the platypus [Ø] I had as a child.

And look how this helps with the *who/whom* conundrum too:

I can't remember the name of the person who/whom I met last night.

I can't remember the name of the person [Ø] I met last night.

But because we can omit the relative pronoun only when it functions as an object, we can't use this strategy all the time when faced with a green squiggly line under a *which*.

the bottom line

In writing, it can be useful and sometimes very important (e.g., in legal documents) to distinguish nonrestrictive from restrictive relative clauses. This is when your inner grammando's sense of alertness in the realm of relative clauses is helpful. In writing, the most consistent tool for doing so is the comma. Yes, the comma. The pivotal role of the comma often gets lost in the kerfuffle about *that* versus *which*. The comma separates the nonrestrictive relative clause from its antecedent. We could think about a clear-cut distinction between *that* and *which* as a backup system to the comma, providing some redundancy to indicate this clause really is restrictive or nonrestrictive. If you're writing a legal contract, you have good reason to minimize ambiguity, and this is one tool for doing so. For most of us, in most writing situations, this is unnecessary given how we use the comma, and we could save ourselves the time of replacing restrictive *which*'s. After all, we make do with just the comma when the relative pronoun is *who*, which covers both restrictive and nonrestrictive relative clauses with no grumbling from grammandos.

part 5

where does that
punctuation go?

commas, commas, and commas

The website FiveThirtyEight conducted a poll of Americans in 2014 about, of all things, the Oxford comma. That's the comma after the penultimate item in a list. It's the comma I used in the chapter title ("Commas, Commas, and Commas") when I could also have omitted it ("Commas, Commas and Commas"). Does putting those two versions of the title next to each other already make you want to vote about which one is better? People have strong enough feelings about this comma that it is not absurd to poll them. And vote they did. Of 1,129 Americans who voted, 57 percent preferred the Oxford comma and 43 percent preferred to omit the Oxford comma. But what if you are on the fence about the Oxford comma—or don't have strong feelings about commas at all? We'll come back to that.

Commas deserve their own chapter because they are, to be hyperbolic, everywhere, and the rules about how to use them, at this point, have become intricate. (I managed to get five commas into that sentence alone!) In both American and British English, according to a study in 1987 by linguist Charles Meyer at the University of Massachusetts–Boston, the comma and the period are neck and neck for most common punctuation mark (40 to 45 percent each), with the comma winning by a nose (or the width of an exclamation point?). The period, though, is relatively straightforward: It marks abbreviations (e.g., *etc., Dr.*) and the end of sentences. The comma: not so much.

If you're wondering what comes after the comma and the period in terms of frequency, it is the dash, coming in at 2–3 percent; the semicolon, at 1.5–2 percent (after all, it gets to appear in lists like this one); and then the question mark, colon, and exclamation point. In terms of which punctuation marks people are most confused about, I think the comma, the semicolon, and the apostrophe are at the top of the list—perhaps also the dash, which can feel like a free-for-all. This cluster of chapters will cover all these squiggles on the page. And before we do that, let's talk a bit about the history of punctuation.

PUNCTUATION: THE BRIEFEST OF HISTORIES

Punctuation is a key part of how we organize language on the page. Of course, we manage just fine in spoken language without punctuation. We use intonation (e.g., rising or falling pitch) and pauses to help our listeners understand how to chunk the information and when, for example, we're asking a question rather than making a statement. It's not always clear in spoken discourse when a sentence ends. On the page, though, sentences end with periods, question marks, or exclamation points; they do not end with commas, colons, semicolons, or dashes. Commas, colons, semicolons, and dashes help to show how information clusters into phrases and clauses within a sentence, and how a set of words is related to the words before and/or after it. (Slashes now have very little role to play other than in phrases like *and/or,* but that has not always been the case, as we'll return to.) All these punctuation marks play a major role in disambiguating meaning on the page—and that is an important point to keep in mind.

As context for English punctuation, let's turn to early Roman antiquity, when manuscripts typically did not have punctuation. There weren't that many readers (literacy was a precious and hard-earned commodity), and readers often were already familiar with the texts, which makes it easier to read without punctuation. And without punctuation, the scribes who were copying down the manuscripts could rest easy that they were not prejudicing the reading by adding in punctuation where they thought it should be. When punctuation marks were added, they were guides to phrasing, aimed to help read texts out loud. They were designed to help readers know when to pause and how long as well as whether the intonation should be rising or falling. This is largely how punctuation works in medieval English texts. It is a modern notion that punctuation should align with grammatical structure as opposed to spoken phrasing—and, as we'll come back to, not everyone agrees on this.

For English, the arrival of the printing press, which was brought to England in 1476, was a watershed moment for punctuation. Not that anything dramatic happened in 1476, but the ability of the printing press to churn out identical copies of a manuscript, with no worries about a scribe getting sloppy or sleepy as he (yes, he) copied a text, encouraged more and more standardization of written English, including both spelling and punctuation. It took centuries and, as I'll cover in chapter 26, there is some punctuation that never fully settled down (I'm talking about you, apostrophe). In Shakespeare's day, there remained lots of variation in punctuation, with the comma alternating with the virgule (that's this symbol: /), although by the sixteenth century the comma was starting to win the popularity contest among writers.

To give you a small taste of the similarities and differences in punctuation some four hundred years ago, let me share a couple of lines from a story titled "How the Witch Served a Fellow in an Alehouse," which was published in 1606 in a pamphlet called *The Most Cruell and Bloody Murder*. These popular pamphlets in the Renaissance catered to the same human interests that sell tabloid magazines today—and I have often incorporated this pamphlet into my History of English course to show what non-Shakespearean language looked like. The witch (who was undoubtedly not a witch but rather a woman being unfairly called a witch—and by the end of the story hanged for it) has come into the tavern and confronts the drunkard. Here is the passage:

> At last the witch got so much time to cal to him, Doest thou heare good friend (quoth she?) What sayst thou ill face (quoth he?)

It can be easy to get distracted by the nonstandard spelling (*cal* for 'call' and *heare* for 'hear') and the now-archaic-looking inflectional endings on the verbs (*doest* and *quoth*), but let's focus instead on the punctuation. The dialogue is framed by "quoth she/he" in parentheses, and you'll notice there are no quotation marks; the question mark is also in the "wrong place": It is in the parenthetical as opposed to at the end of the question. There is no comma to set off the vocative each character uses to address the other: "good friend" and "ill face." There is also no period after "(quoth she?)" or "(quoth he?)" to end the sentence. In current edited prose it would look like:

> At last the witch got so much time to call to him. "Do you hear, good friend?" she said. "What do you say, ill face?" he said.

It was the rise of prescriptive grammars in the eighteenth century that started to set down stricter standards for how punctuation should and shouldn't be used—but if you read eighteenth- and nineteenth-century texts, you'll still see punctuation used in ways we wouldn't see as standard now. And often that is because there is more punctuation than we're now accustomed to. Yet no one talked about this when I read Jane Austen in high school! Let's consider the first sentence of Jane Austen's *Pride and Prejudice*:

> It is a truth universally acknowledged, that a single man in possession of a good fortune, must be in want of a wife.

Today's copy editors would likely strike both of those commas, with a laser focus especially on the second one: "that a single man in possession of a good fortune must be in want of a wife."

The twentieth century witnessed some reining in of punctuation, and we'll focus on the modern rules about commas in this chapter. In general, commas are designed to mark or set off phrases or groups of words that are shorter than a sentence (and this is the etymology of *comma* in ancient Greek rhetoric). It helps to know a bit about the history of punctuation because the modern rules about commas reflect a hodgepodge of historical rules based on signaling pauses for those reading aloud and rules based on grammatical structure, which sometimes have no correlation with pauses. And I promise to explain the "comma splice."

The comma is asked to do a lot. And yet we now curtail some of its versatility and power. It's a bit like putting curfews on a rebellious teenager, and you'll see that even in edited prose, the teenager sometimes breaks curfew. And some of the rules of the curfew are more recommendations than rules, which makes the whole thing a bit of a muddle. Let's actually start with the dreaded comma splice, which usefully captures the current limits on the comma's power.

COMMA SPLICE

A modern-day comma is not allowed to connect two full clauses all by itself. So, a comma is not allowed to do this:

> Boston got twenty inches of snow in two days, they called it Snowmageddon.

Why not? Why can't we just connect those two clauses with a comma? Because we have decided the comma is not allowed to do that. If you're thinking there must be a more elaborate answer than that, I'm sorry to disappoint. Commas work by convention. They are just a specific kind of squiggle on a page, and a community of writers—especially editors, educators, and authors of usage guides—decide over time which squiggles can do what work. And while the comma is allowed to do a lot, it hits its limit when it comes to connecting two independent clauses. It's called a "comma splice" because the comma is trying to connect—or splice—those two clauses together all by itself. The comma was given more freedom to splice together two clauses into a sentence until the twentieth century, but no longer—unless you are licensed due to your stature as a writer (because we assume the writer knows the rule and had good reason not to follow it—and there is no way to know when you have reached this stature as a writer!).

Just to make sure, at this moment, that we're all on the same page with the more technical grammatical language here: Remember, an independent clause is a unit that can function as a freestanding sentence (if asked to do so) because it has both a subject noun phrase and a verb phrase (e.g., "Boston got twenty inches of snow in two days," where the subject is *Boston* and the verb phrase is *got twenty inches of snow in two days*). Now, obviously, it's not that in English we can't connect independent clauses on the page. If we want to put them next to each other in one sentence, as I did in the example above about Snowmageddon, we just need to use a semicolon rather than a comma:

> Boston got twenty inches of snow in two days; they called it Snowmageddon.

Why the semicolon? Because that is what we have decided the stacked squiggle and dot of the semicolon can do (see chapter 24).

There's another way to avoid a comma splice in this Snowmageddon situation, and that's a coordinating conjunction (sometimes called a coordinator):

Boston got twenty inches of snow in two days, and they called it Snowmageddon.

Coordinators are those little words that connect equal units. If you remember "Conjunction Junction" from the *Schoolhouse Rock!* television shorts, this is what we're talking about. *And, or,* and *but* are the most famous of the lot, but the list also includes (at least for some grammarians—this is contested territory) *for, nor, yet,* and *so.* Coordinators can connect nouns (e.g., "snow and sleet") or verbs (e.g., "slip and fall") or adjectives (e.g., "cold but beautiful")—you get the idea.

They can also connect full clauses.

When two full clauses are connected by a coordinator like *and, or,* or *but* (I am feeling very self-conscious about the use of a coordinator in a list of coordinators!), we're told to put a comma after the first clause, before the coordinator and the second clause. For example:

He played tennis for four hours yesterday, and his back and arm muscles are letting him know about that today.

But . . . you wouldn't use a comma if the second clause is not a full clause but just a second verb phrase referring back to the same subject. Here's what I mean:

He played tennis for four hours yesterday and won two of three matches.

Here's the way to think about the rationale for this rule: A comma should not separate the subject of a sentence from the predicate. That is why modern editors would remove the comma after *fortune* from Jane Austen's clause so that it reads: "a single man in possession of a good fortune must be in want of a wife." And it holds even when there is a compound or coordinated predicate: "A single man in possession of a good fortune might be in want of a wife or might be looking for a life partner who is not a wife." Even if we might pause before the coordinator *or* when saying this sentence, we're told to skip the comma when we write it down. As I told you, we're working with a hodgepodge of rules here.

MORE COMMA RULES

The no-commas-between-the-subject-and-predicate rule is good as far as it gets us, but there are kinds of intervening material that will justify commas. Here are two:

- Commas around a nonrestrictive clause: As we covered in chapter 22, commas are the primary way we indicate that a relative clause is nonrestrictive. In this case, the comma corresponds with a pause in speech. It's the difference between Paul having one sister, and I've decided to tell you a bit more about her ("Paul's sister, who is an attorney in Atlanta, paid him a surprise visit") and Paul having more than one sister and I want to make sure you know which one I'm referring to ("Paul's sister who is an attorney in Atlanta paid him a surprise visit").

- Commas around any kind of parenthetical phrase: Whenever we're adding some optional information, commas can function like parentheses (e.g., "Snowmageddon, as mentioned earlier, arrived in Boston . . ."). Here again the comma reflects a pause in speech.

Another spot where the comma usually corresponds to a pause in spoken language is the comma after an introductory subordinate clause. A subordinate clause begins with a subordinating conjunction or subordinator, such as *because, while, if, when, before, after, although*. These clauses are called subordinate because they cannot stand alone as sentences. If you try to use a subordinate clause this way, you'll be leaving your reader or listener hanging: "While I was flying to San Francisco." While you were flying to San Francisco, what? Not fair. The initial *while* indicates that more is to follow to complete the sentence. Okay, fine, here's the whole story: "While I was flying to San Francisco, the dog in the seat next to me (yes, the dog had its own seat) decided to climb into my lap."

Don't worry: I haven't forgotten that we're talking about commas, not dogs. The point is that after that initial subordinate clause ("While I was flying to San Francisco"), we use a comma. So there would also be a comma here:

> After the mayor met with citizens from the neighborhood, she approved a zoning change that would allow a high-rise hotel.

What if the subordinate clause comes after the main clause? You're on your own there! There is not agreement in style books about whether a comma should separate a subordinate clause at the end of a sentence. My own preference is usually not to put in a comma, but I allow myself some stylistic discretion:

> The mayor approved a zoning change that would allow a high-rise hotel (,) after she met with citizens from the neighborhood.

Stylistic discretion? What about consistency? That is my transition to the infamous Oxford comma.

THE OXFORD COMMA

People sometimes ask me how I feel about the Oxford comma. And here's the thing: I do have feelings about the Oxford comma! I like it. I am not an advocate of comma proliferation—I'm on the more minimalist end of the comma spectrum. But the Oxford comma can support clarity and even usefully disambiguate some lists. For example, if I'm writing about "my brothers, the doctor, and the nurse," it's clear there are at least four people (two or more brothers, a doctor, and a nurse). If I had written "my brothers, the doctor and the nurse," there could be four or more people, or there could be only two: my brother the doctor and my brother the nurse.

Now, of course, it can take some effort to create a list that has that kind of ambiguity built into it, where the Oxford comma does essential work in disambiguating the list. Here's one of the famous examples that floats around the internet: "This book is dedicated to my parents, Ayn Rand and God." As far as I know, no one has ever seen the actual book that contained this dedication, but real or not, it still illustrates the pitfalls that can come, every once in a while, with comma parsimony. At the same time, we can create an equally ambiguous list with an Oxford comma: "my brother, the doctor, and the nurse." Are there two people (your brother is the doctor) or three? I rarely see this potential ambiguity discussed when people are defending the Oxford comma.

The Oxford comma is called the Oxford comma because Oxford University Press has been following this stylistic convention since 1893—a holdover from the heavier punctuation of the eighteenth and nineteenth centuries. With attempts to streamline or minimize punctuation in the twentieth century, the Oxford comma was taken out in some style guides, especially newspaper style guides. Journalistic writing tends to minimize punctuation, as part of concision more generally. So at this point, the Oxford comma is typically a question of "house style" or personal style.

I tend to use the Oxford comma in my own prose, and I tend to notice when others don't. Note the verb there: I *notice*. I don't judge those who do not use the Oxford comma. I do not hold out that using the Oxford comma is inherently better than not using the Oxford comma. In the end, it's just a comma.

But here's a question: Should one be consistent about the Oxford comma? In other words, if you start your text not using the Oxford comma, should you stick with that style all the way through the text? Or if I'm copyediting a magazine or an edited volume of academic articles, should I make sure that all articles consistently use or don't use the Oxford comma? The answer from copy editors right now is a resounding yes. In fact, it might be seen as heresy that I'm even asking the question.

Okay, I'm going to make an argument here that even I can't yet wrap my head around, but I think it's an important one for us all to consider. What if we don't privilege consistency in the use of commas at all costs? Why couldn't I or anyone else opt to use the Oxford comma when it seems useful and not use it when it seems unnecessary? Couldn't we respond to the aesthetics or the logical requirements of each list on a more local basis instead of requiring a global stylistic rule about comma use? We could. Our brains could totally handle it. The question is whether editors and English professors and the like, given our training, can loosen up to let it happen.

Linguist Deborah Cameron, at Oxford University, has provocatively—and usefully, I think—pointed out that the emphasis on complete consistency in punctuation conventions, as well as other formatting guidelines, leads to the expenditure of many, many hours of academics' and editors' time, which could productively be spent in other ways. House style guides lay out rule after rule about when to use commas (and other punctuation marks) in published text and its citations, and we spend hours trying to adhere to the rules precisely. This laser-like focus on the consistency of each comma is relatively new to English. And in some places we just let the comma be variable.

VARIABLE COMMAS

For all the rules about commas, introductory adverbials are a bit of a free-for-all. The introductory adverbial phrase *In addition* often gets a comma after it, but not always. The introductory phrase *By contrast* is also a mixed comma bag. If something happens suddenly, does it get a comma?

> Suddenly the parties came to the table for peace negotiations.
> Suddenly, the parties came to the table for peace negotiations.

It feels like an aesthetic question, and there's no reason it shouldn't be. If the adverbial phrase gets longer than a couple of words, a comma often feels helpful:

> In addition to higher pay for all employees, the new contract provides dental insurance.

Part of each of our decisions about commas is going to depend on whether we prefer lightly or more heavily punctuated text. I'm in an ongoing discussion with a colleague about whether the email greeting should read "Hi Eileen" or "Hi, Eileen." There is no right answer here. It's about aesthetics, not correctness.

the bottom line

As we think about punctuation in formal writing, I find it helpful to remember Bishop Lowth's wise words from the mid-eighteenth century: "The doctrine of punctuation must needs be very imperfect: few precise rules can be given, which will hold without exception in all cases; but much must be left to the judgement and taste of the writer." There are guidelines, but the very creativity of human language and of effective prose requires some flexibility and some application of good sense to punctuation.

I'm not arguing for comma anarchy by any stretch. And I still allow my inner grammando to romp around in the comma space, copyediting my own work to ensure consistency of comma use throughout. But I think it is worth asking whether these feelings we harbor about the importance of getting our commas "right" and of getting them "right" in the same way each time are the best use of our time and energies. The effectiveness of the comma might even benefit from a bit more flexibility, allowing it to respond to the rhythm, logic, and punctuation needs of any given sentence.

24

. . . .

rolling stops with semicolons

The semicolon may have the power to connect two independent clauses all by itself, but it has a problem: an image problem. Some people really don't like it.

We're talking aesthetics here, and the semicolon has regularly
been relegated to the displeasing and the ugly. Kurt Vonnegut, author of *Slaughterhouse-Five*, had strong feelings about this punctuation mark; in *A Man Without a Country*, he advises against
using semicolons at all, insults them by going after their sexuality in
offensive ways, and concludes: "All they do is show you've been to
college." (I couldn't resist putting a semicolon in that sentence.)
George Orwell decided to test his own sense that semicolons are
unnecessary and write his novel *Coming Up for Air* without any
semicolons.

But the semicolon also has its staunch defenders. The American
physician Lewis Thomas, who was also an accomplished essayist
and poet, writes evocatively about the semicolon in "Notes on
Punctuation":

> It is almost always a greater pleasure to come across a semicolon
> than a period. The period tells you that that is that; if you didn't get
> all the meaning you wanted or expected, anyway you got all the
> writer intended to parcel out and now you have to move along. But

with a semicolon there you get a pleasant little feeling of expectancy; there is more to come; to read on; it will get clearer.

Look at all those semicolons in the last sentence! Well played, Mr. Thomas.

The eighteenth century witnessed the explosion of the semicolon. American grammarian Lindley Murray, writing near the end of that century, described the semicolon as the punctuation mark that divided a compound sentence into two or more parts, "not so closely connected as those which are separated by a comma, nor yet so little depend on each other, as those which are distinguished by a colon." The semicolon has lost popularity since then, but we can find some heavy use of semicolons certainly into the first half of the twentieth century. An oft-cited example comes from Evelyn Waugh's 1945 novel *Brideshead Revisited,* including these lines:

> "I have been here before," I said; I had been there before; first with Sebastian more than twenty years ago on a cloudless day in June, when the ditches were white with fool's parsley and meadowsweet and the air heavy with all the scents of summer; it was a day of peculiar splendour such as our climate affords once or twice a year, when leaf and flower and bird and sun-lit stone and shadow seem all to proclaim the glory of God; and though I had been there so often, in so many moods, it was to that first visit that my heart returned on this, my latest.

A sentence of 108 words, with four semicolons, six commas, and finally one period. Most contemporary editors would break this into multiple sentences, to avoid that many clauses strung together with semicolons. And Waugh's use of semicolons also creates one "clause fragment" ("first with Sebastian . . ." is a long prepositional phrase, not a full clause), which you get to do if you're Evelyn Waugh in 1945, but contemporary editors would likely challenge most of us on it.

At this point in their history, semicolons have two main uses:

- Semicolons can join two independent clauses that have a close semantic relationship. As one of my students put it years ago, the semicolon is like a "California stop" at a stop sign: Unlike the period, which would represent a full stop at a stop sign, the semicolon involves putting on the brakes to slow down but still rolling through the stop sign. The semicolon can be followed by a conjunctive adverb such as *nevertheless, thus,* or *however* (see more below), but it doesn't have to be. The semicolon can show readers that you, as a writer, see the ideas in two clauses as tightly linked.

- Semicolons can usefully separate items in a long list, especially when some of the items in the list have punctuation within them (e.g., "I went to Vegas with my friend Auden, who had never been to Vegas; my sister, who loves Vegas in a way I don't understand; and my mom, who just wanted to spend time with us").

That's the semicolon, whether you're a fan or not. With those long lists, it can be helpful, so I wouldn't recommend swearing off its use even if you're not a semicolon enthusiast. But if you prefer to show tight connections between clauses through other means, and you feel like it's important to slim down your punctuation toolbox, there are plenty of other options.

The colon, when introduced at the end of the sixteenth century, was used to mark a pause longer than a comma or semicolon but shorter than a period. It is now used to introduce explanatory material: a list (like this one!), an example, a definition, or other material that helps explain the assertion in the introductory clause. If the semicolon, as Lewis Thomas describes, creates a feeling of expectancy that more related material is to come, the colon could be seen as urging the reader forward, foreshadowing that what is to come is going to explain or exemplify what we have just read.

The colon and semicolon barely figure in the written English of texting: Their formality makes them a bad choice rhetorically and aesthetically. But they do serve an important role in the smiley and winky face (pre-emoji).

HOWEVER TO PUNCTUATE *HOWEVER*

The conjunctive adverb *however* is one of those words that we write much more often than we say—along with its conjunctive adverb friends *therefore, thus, consequently, moreover,* and the like. What do I mean? In the Corpus of Contemporary American English, which allows us to compare speech from recorded television and radio programs with writing in newspapers, magazines, fiction, and academic prose, the word *therefore* appears five times more often in academic writing than in magazines or in spoken language. *However* shows up almost ten times more frequently in academic writing than in speech. *Thus* is more than thirty times more common in academic writing than in speech. In speech, we're more likely to say *so* or just *and* to show that consequential relationship. And speaking of consequences, *consequently* is twenty-five times more common in academic writing than in speech.

This is one of several reasons why we should be wary of the advice often given to writers who are struggling to get an idea onto the page: "Just say it out loud and write that down" or "Just write it like you would say it." That advice is fine as far as it gets us—it might help us get an idea out of our head initially, combatting writer's block or a fear that we aren't sure how to get the wording right yet. But in any formal register of writing, we are expected to use different vocabulary and different syntactic structures (e.g., more subordination), as I'll talk about more in chapter 30. Part of that different vocabulary encompasses some of these more hifalutin conjunctive adverbs. Our inner grammandos can sometimes forget to differentiate between speaking and writing, and between more and less formal and informal registers of both.

Conjunctive adverbs conjoin two clauses semantically—that is, they show their relationship to each other. The clauses can remain independent, with a period in between them; however, they can also be conjoined by both a semicolon and a conjunctive adverb. As I did right there (did you notice?) with the semicolon and *however*.

So why does this section focus specifically on *however*? Because this conjunctive adverb in particular is creating punctuation headaches for editors. Many writers, including many students I have taught over the years, want to make *however* behave like *but* in between clauses, which means that we can put a comma before it, not a semicolon, like this:

> The comma is powerful, however it cannot connect two
> independent clauses by itself.

That sentence will get caught by most editors and changed to:

> The comma is powerful; however, it cannot connect two
> independent clauses by itself.

What is going on here? I got very interested in this question a few years ago and wrote an article about it with Lizzie Hutton, now a professor at Miami University. Why is *however* so confusing? To begin, *however* is a very common conjunctive adverb in academic writing (e.g., four times more common than *therefore*). *However*, like other conjunctive adverbs, can move around in a clause. Take a look:

> However, the marriage is not working.
>
> The marriage, however, is not working.
>
> The marriage is, however, not working.
>
> The marriage is not working, however.

But, looking at the past few decades, *however* has become more and more common at the beginning of the clause. Why does that matter? Because when *however* comes at the beginning of the clause, it looks a lot like a coordinator such as *but*. So when *however* appears first, some writers are treating it like a coordinator, which means it gets a comma before it, not a semicolon.

Maybe I have touched a nerve here for your inner grammando if you've been aggravated about "mis-punctuated" *however*'s. But did you realize there is a history of prescription about not using *however* at the beginning of a sentence? Here are William Strunk and E. B. White in the now-classic 1959 first edition of the co-authored *The Elements of Style*: "Avoid starting a sentence with *however* when the meaning is 'nevertheless.' The word usually serves better when not in first position." Bryan Garner more recently has called it a "stylistic lapse." These criticisms seem odd given how common sentence-initial *however* is now, even in formal writing.

What does the *American Heritage Dictionary* Usage Panel say? The question first appeared on the 2015 ballot (and it was not coincidental that Lizzie and I were investigating the question at the time—I asked the editors to put the question on the ballot!). Only 10 percent of the Usage Panel reported that they always follow the rule prohibiting sentence-initial *however*, and another 30 percent said that they usually or sometimes follow it. Sixty percent said that they rarely or never do so. (I was part of that 60 percent.)

As the restriction on sentence- or clause-initial *however* fades, now usage guides must police the use of the semicolon before *however* when we use it to connect two clauses within one sentence. And police it they do! *However* gets special attention in usage books and online grammar guides. What does the Usage Panel have to say? The 2015 survey asked whether it is ever acceptable to have a comma before *however*. Here is the sentence:

> Main Street will be closed to traffic for the parade, however, the stores along it will remain open.

Eighty-six percent of the panel called this unacceptable. I'm struck that 14 percent didn't! This clause-initial *however* is worth watching, as punctuation requirements may shift over time. Language changes and peeves fade.

the bottom line
. . . .

It's worth knowing current conventions about the semicolon, and then you can decide whether it matches your style in different kinds of writing. It will bring with it a certain formality, so don't let your inner grammando persuasively argue the semicolon is always the right choice. Sometimes a dash may be what you want (see chapter 25).

With *however,* for right now I recommend treating it like its conjunctive adverb peers, such as *nevertheless* and *therefore*—which means it needs a semicolon to connect two clauses into one sentence. But your inner wordie has good reason to be paying close attention to when this advice may become stodgy. I've been seeing more and more uses of *however* with a comma in edited writing online, and I predict that at some point in the foreseeable future, *however* will be allowed to work like *but* between clauses. You heard it here first!

25

·················

the wild west of dashes and hyphens

f I had to pick a favorite punctuation mark (and how is one to pick among so many good ones?), it would be the dash, or more specifically, the em dash. It is one of the most versatile punctuation marks we have: It can function like a comma, a semicolon, a colon, or parentheses, but with a different, less formal, sometimes more dramatic connotation. It has a bit of flair, a dashing style, so to speak. It's hard to get wrong. What's not to like? I have at least one answer to that question—but it's easily managed.

First, a little terminology. The em dash—so called because it is the width of a typed *M*—is the punctuation mark that serves to separate phrases and clauses within a sentence. The en dash (yes, you guessed it: which is the width of a typed *N*) is the shorter mark that, among other roles, separates dates (e.g., 2023–2024) or other inclusive numbers (e.g., pages 34–39) and connects entities in a directional relationship (e.g., the New York–Boston train). The hyphen is the shortest of the three and is used in compound words or a compound modifier (although some style guides prefer the en dash here)—or (just to throw in an em dash) when a word breaks at the edge of a printed page. There isn't much more to say about the en dash, but the em dash and the hyphen sometimes invite grammatical stickling.

EM DASH

Once you embrace the em dash as a useful punctuation mark, it's hard to go back. It's the utility player of punctuation baseball. Adding a new but related thought, with some emphasis? Put in an em dash. Interrupting the sentence to add an explanation? Put in two em dashes. Adding nonessential information about something, but it feels more important than parentheses? Put in two em dashes. Connecting two clauses but the semicolon feels too formal? Put in an em dash.

You may now be thinking, "Okay, that's a lot of dashes." That *is* a lot of dashes, and the extreme utility of the em dash ("Put me in, coach!") is perhaps the biggest potential pitfall of the dash: overuse.

Most style guides provide a good amount of leeway in terms of how the em dash can function—it can function like a colon (as it did right there), parentheses (such as when adding an explanation about why the em dash is called an em dash in this chapter's second paragraph), or a comma (as when I added a note about hyphens being used for word breaks at the edge of the page in that same paragraph). I sometimes see the em dash used in place of a semicolon—while that use strikes me as a bit less ideal, I am reluctant to call it wrong. And, obviously, I did it right there.

There are a couple of grammatical spots where an em dash can appear and no other punctuation mark will quite do the trick. For example, how should we handle an introductory list, followed by a full clause to explain something about all the items in that list? Here's an example:

> Drinking hot chocolate with whipped cream, reading a good novel in front of the fireplace, enjoying the quiet that comes with a snowfall—these are a few of my favorite winter things.

We could rewrite the sentence as a more straightforward list: Here are a few of my favorite winter things, colon. But rhetorically there can be good reason to put the list first, and then the em dash is there to help us pull it off.

Sometimes we also want to add a phrase that just wouldn't do as well with a comma. Here's a wonderful example from George Eliot's *Middlemarch*:

> He had done nothing exceptional in marrying—nothing but what society sanctions, and considers an occasion for wreaths and bouquets.

So what does it look like to overuse the em dash? First, it can be too many dashes in one sentence. It's one thing to set off additional explanatory material or a parenthetical note between two dashes. It's another to link clause after clause with dashes. Here's a sentence that I came across in my university life (I have changed some of the details to mask the identity of the sender!):

> The retreat will fall on the last Friday in June, which may not work for all faculty—but this will not be the only opportunity for faculty to discuss the curricular reforms—we'll hold another full faculty meeting to discuss the curriculum early in September.

Are you feeling an urge to replace that second em dash? A period could be a good option here. A sentence can also be overly dashed and confusing if we embed a parenthetical element surrounded by dashes within another parenthetical element surrounded by dashes: "The group of students—which included both graduate and undergraduate students—some of whom had traveled to Italy and some of whom lived there—couldn't leave their rooms during the pandemic."

Second, we as writers can start to make the em dash less effective—by overusing it. As an editor I have started to create informal rules about the em dash, such as no more than two sentences per paragraph with dashes—and certainly some paragraphs should have only one or—gasp!—none. And certainly avoid using the em dash in every sentence in a paragraph—even if arguably every sentence legitimately could take a dash—because otherwise you end up with a paragraph like this one, where the dashes have overrun the prose.

It's not that any one of those dashes is incorrect. The issue is distraction. Punctuation is designed to help readers navigate written material, subtly organizing phrases, clauses, and sentences on the page, minimizing ambiguity where it can. Ideally, it should be a supporting character in the prose, not a star. Is overuse misuse? I recommend being careful about equating the two. But overuse can deprive the em dash of its punctuational punch.

HYPHENS

In my head, the word *semicolon* has a hyphen in it: *semi-colon*. In this book it does not have a hyphen because *Merriam-Webster's Collegiate Dictionary* (tenth edition), spells *semicolon* without a hyphen, as does the fifth edition of the *American Heritage Dictionary of the English Language* and the *Oxford English Dictionary*. This word's spelling has been hyphen-variable since the beginning. The first example of the word in the *Oxford English Dictionary* is from Ben Jonson's *English Grammar,* published around 1640, and there is no hyphen. The next quotation is from Richard Hodges's *English Primrose* (1644), and there is both a hyphen and a delightful description of a semicolon: "At a comma, stop a little. . . . At a semi-colon, somewhat more."

Hyphens live with em dashes in the Wild West of punctuation. The use of hyphens is to some extent idiosyncratic—or downright "chaos," to quote H. W. Fowler in *A Dictionary of Modern English Usage*. David Crystal, in his book *Making a Point: The Persnickety Story of English Punctuation,* calls the hyphen "the most unpredictable of marks."

Hyphenation of specific compounds varies from dictionary to dictionary, style guide to style guide, and decade to decade. Sometimes changes in hyphen fashion make newspaper headlines—for example, when the *Shorter Oxford English Dictionary* removed hyphens from about sixteen thousand words in 2007. Not everyone would think this is breaking news, but all of us wordies were paying attention. So what happened when all those hyphens disappeared? If you're thinking all the compounds became one word, think again. Some compounds became two words (*ice cream*) and some became one (*pigeonhole*). Why? Because. Many standard dictionaries spell *storyboard* and *timescale* as one word, but *story line* and *time frame* as two words—and it's hard to find a rhyme or reason here.

Sometimes the hyphen is a way station as a compound becomes fully accepted as a lexical item (e.g., *start-up* is now often *startup*) or a combining form becomes assimilated (e.g., *e-mail* over time became *email*). It made headlines in 2013 when *The New York Times* changed *e-mail* to *email* in its style guide. Sometimes you need a compound not to have a word break so that, for example, a *bluebird* is distinguished from a bird that happens to be blue, a *shortfall* from a fall that isn't far or doesn't take long.

Sometimes hyphens can distinguish an established *re-* prefixed word from a newly created one in English in which *re-* means 'again.' For example, it's the difference between resigning from your job (i.e., you're not coming back) and re-signing to come back for another stint. Did you resent the memo you needed to send your colleague overseas, or was it that you re-sent it? You get the idea.

Sometimes, hyphens are about aesthetics. Does *glowworm* look weird to you? A hyphen can avoid that double *w*. Both British and American style guides generally prefer hyphens between two of the same vowel (*aa, ii, oo, uu*), so *anti-intellectual* and *pro-organic*. Wait, what about *ee*? Here we may have a trans-Atlantic distinction (and I used a hyphen in *trans-Atlantic* because the second part of the word is a proper name). Or it may be more in flux: a British resource like the *OED* uses a hyphen (*re-elect*), many American dictionaries have no hyphen (*reelect*), and AP style used to recommend a hyphen but then lost the hyphen in 2019. And *The New*

Yorker magazine has struck out on its own with diaereses in all these double-vowel sequences (*reëlect*).*

Okay, now let's talk about compound modifiers and why there is a hyphen in *double-vowel* when I wrote "double-vowel sequences." In this case, the noun *sequences* is modified by the two-word combination *double-vowel*. To indicate that *double-vowel* is working together to modify *sequences,* we insert the hyphen. This is why I wrote "two-word combination" in the previous sentence as well. In most cases, hyphens with compound modifiers are designed to disambiguate. Common three-word compounds like *chocolate chip cookie* exist without a hyphen because they are (arguably) widely recognizable, with little ambiguity about what is modifying what. Compare that with *a small business owner,* where *a small-business owner* is about the size of the business and *a small business owner* might (arguably) be about the size of the owner.

When the compound modifier starts with an *-ly* adverb (or with *very*), most style guides recommend no hyphen: *excessively expensive coffee* or *critically important question.* With other adverbs, go ahead and use a hyphen, many of these guides advise: *much-needed improvement* or *less-desired outcomes.* For this reason, I don't think any of us should be surprised to see hyphens now appearing with *-ly* adverbs too (e.g., *densely-populated area*). After all, it provides *often-sought-after* consistency. That said, some style guides are more minimalist when it comes to hyphens; others opt for the hyphen to avoid even a whiff of ambiguity.

the bottom line

First, try and help your inner grammando accept the relative Wild Westness of the dash/hyphen region of punctuation land.†

---

* If you wanted to call those two dots an umlaut rather than a diaeresis, you're in good company! Umlauts are about pronunciation; diaereses indicate that the second vowel in a sequence begins a new syllable.

† Did your inner grammando just balk at *try and*? I hear about this peeve a lot, from those who believe it should be *try to,* not *try and.* The construction *try and*

Em dashes provide helpful flexibility when the comma, semi-colon, colon, and parentheses don't seem quite right or when you're trying to add emphasis or flair beyond one of these more traditional punctuation marks. The only caution here is over-use, within a sentence, a paragraph, or a text. Your inner gram-mando has a point about the downsides of overuse. Experiment to see if the em dash works well for you, and allow others to do the same.

With the hyphen, I recommend focusing primarily on mini-mizing ambiguity on the page. You can tie yourself to a particu-lar dictionary and follow the editors' decisions on hyphens. Be aware, though, that those conventions will change over time, will not agree with all other dictionary editors' decisions, and may even allow variation within that dictionary (i.e., the editors provide a hyphenated and a nonhyphenated version, or a one word and a two-word version). It's also okay to follow your aesthetic preferences if/when a word looks odd to you on the page and a hyphen will help. After all, punctuation is about helping readers not get distracted from the content of the text.

---

goes back to at least the 1600s and may even be older than *try to*. *Try and* is also in good company with other "verb-and-verb" (look at all those hyphens!) idiomatic phrasing such as *go and see* or *come and visit*. And for *try and* to work, it has to be in that base form, with no inflectional endings on the verb; we can't be "trying and helping," and "we tried to do that," not "we tried and did that." This is the fascinat-ing descriptive grammatical knowledge that fluent speakers carry in their heads.

26

········

when it's *its* and other apostrophe conundrums

f we're honest about it (and this is a no-judgment zone!), pretty much all of us have mixed up our *it's* and *its*. Right? You were proofing a work memo or an email, and there it was: *it's* for possessive. That possessive *it's* just popped out as your fingers flew over the keyboard because, well, it makes sense. We know that to make the possessive, we take a singular noun and put *-'s* at the end: *Isaac* becomes *Isaac's, my mother* becomes *my mother's,* and *an elephant* becomes *an elephant's.* So why shouldn't *it* become *it's*? Because pronouns.

As we talk about apostrophes, let's just remember that we all mess them up sometimes and not get too high up on our apostrophe high horse. It makes the fall more painful.

Before we get into why the possessive is now *its* rather than *it's,* let's step back to get some context. In the conversations I have about punctuation (and I have many), there seems to be an underlying assumption that there was a moment in the history of the English language, say the mid-nineteenth century or so (different folks have different ideas about when this magic moment was), when English speakers and writers all agreed on how to use the apostrophe. *It's* then slid downhill from there. I hope it will be more reassuring than disappointing when I tell you that there has never been such a moment. The apostrophe is perhaps the most unstable punctuation mark in English, and it has long been unstable.

Yet we sometimes judge others severely based on how they use the apostrophe: poking fun at the so-called grocer's apostrophe in the plural *apple's* or deciding not to go on a date with someone because their online profile has a *their's*. Sure, I notice apostrophes that are missing or have gone astray from standard conventions, but I work hard to keep any conclusions I draw in check. Poor proofreading? Possibly. More important things on the writer's mind? Possibly. Sloppy? Possibly. Uneducated? Be careful. I spend my life contemplating these details of language, and I'm a very experienced copy editor. I also know I've sent an errant *it's*. I have to think about whether it is *masters degree* or *master's degree*. One of my closest and most brilliant colleagues just doesn't notice apostrophes when she proofreads, no matter how slowly she works through the sentences. And the rules for apostrophes are idiosyncratic, to put it kindly. For example, the Moses/Jesus exception? I'm being serious—stay tuned. . . .

The word *apostrophe* is a French borrowing, coming into English in the sixteenth century (etymologically from the Greek for 'turning away, elision'). The apostrophe has historically been used for contractions, which are relatively straightforward: When two words get smashed into one, letters and/or sounds can get left out, and when they do, we put in an apostrophe to mark their absence. *Cannot* becomes *can't, do not* becomes *don't, we have* becomes *we've, you are* becomes *you're,* and *it is* becomes *it's*. Some of the historical contractions that took the apostrophe feel very Shakespearean because, oh, they were: contractions such as *on't, refus'd,* and *i'faith*! We can also use the apostrophe to show that we have elided a letter or sound at the beginning or end of words, such as: *'tis, runnin'*.*

---

* What sound has been dropped from *-ing* words like *runnin'* is more complicated than you might think. We talk informally about "dropping our g's," but the fact is that most of us have dropped our g's in words like *running*. If you say the word and draw out the last sound, you won't hear a /g/ sound in the way that you hear at the end of *dog*. What you hear is a different kind of nasal sound, which is produced with your tongue fairly far back in your mouth—the same sound that you

From contractions, the apostrophe expanded its territory by the end of the sixteenth century to encompass possessives—both nouns and pronouns. Yes, pronouns. So historically you will find *your's* as well as *yours*, *our's* as well as *ours*. With standardization over the past two hundred years or so, the apostrophe has been kept for the possessive of nouns (e.g., *the cat's meow*) and removed from the possessive of pronouns (e.g., *yours*). Why isn't that inconsistency confusing most of the time? Because most of the personal pronouns change form when they become possessive, as well as adding a final *-s*. For example, *we* becomes *ours* (not *wes* or *we's*), *he* becomes *his*, *they* becomes *theirs*, *she* becomes *hers*, and *you* becomes *yours*. We're not just adding possessive *-s* to the subject pronoun (*theys*, *shes*, or *yous*). Unless it's *its*. In that case, we are just adding possessive *-s* to the subject form: *It* becomes *its*. In other words, the pronoun *it* acts like a noun such as *aardvark* or *grammando* in terms of not changing its form to make the possessive. No wonder we get confused!

The apostrophe's territory is said not to include marking plurals—except for the few cases where it does! And I'm not talking about the grocer's apostrophe here. Warn your inner grammando to be careful about enforcing apostrophe rules as if there are no exceptions. The apostrophe pops up in plurals with numbers and letters. For example, you can write *1960s* or *1960's*. The apostrophe-less *1960s* is gaining ground, but *The New York Times,* for example, still uses *1960's*. You'll also sometimes see the apostrophe in a phrase like "straight A's." Here it's optional, as "straight As" would not be especially ambiguous (although it looks a little odd). But imagine I am describing how to spell the word *aardvark*, which has three *a*'s; if I don't use the apostrophe there, it becomes "three *as*", which is potentially confusing. As a linguist, I also sometimes need to use the plural apostrophe when I am referring to multiple instances of

---

hear at the end of *king* or *song*. If you don't believe me, try saying the word with an actual /g/ at the end. So when we talk about "dropping our g's," we're actually talking about saying /n/ in *runnin'* rather than the backer nasal sound in *running*—and we drop the *g* in the spelling to reflect that.

a word—for example, there are eleven *the*'s in this paragraph (and two *this*'s, which is telling of, well, not much at all). The copy editors of this book valiantly attempted to dissuade me from this plural apostrophe (style guides do not all agree on this point), and I take full responsibility for its use and any aggravation it has caused your inner grammando.

So now the apostrophe is used for a handful of plurals, contractions, and the possessives of nouns. When you step back and think about it, it is not especially convenient that English now marks the possessive of both singular and plural nouns with a final *-s*. In speech, you cannot hear the difference, and in writing we mark the difference by moving the apostrophe: *one grammando's peeve, many grammandos' peeve*. The apostrophe in singular *-'s* represents the omission of *e* in the historical suffix *-es* (the earlier form of *god's*, for example, was *godes*). The plural possessive *-s'* didn't settle down until the nineteenth century, and it still causes fits with irregular nouns. Yale University, for example, had to correct Maya Lin's remarkable marble statue honoring women at the university from *Womens' Table* to *Women's Table*.

Those fits, however, are nothing compared with the conniptions caused by nouns that end in *-s*. Do we add another *-s* with an apostrophe (*Chris's aardvark?*) or just an apostrophe (*Chris' aardvark?*)—or try to avoid the whole thing by writing *the aardvark that Chris owns?* These final *-s* nouns get me every time, and my aesthetic preferences seem to change by the week.

In my book *Fixing English,* which was published in 2014, I wrote about Lynne Truss's book *Eats, Shoots & Leaves*. When I got the page proofs, I decided I didn't like how the possessive form *Truss's* looked (too many *s*'s in a row, I thought—too busy), and I changed every *Truss's* to *Truss'*. I sent off the page proofs and panicked. It should be *Truss's*! I emailed the editor and asked him to change it back.

There isn't one "right" answer here (sorry to disappoint!). There are at least three factors in play: aesthetics (do you like how the word looks on the page?); pronunciation (are you trying to capture whether the possessive -s is pronounced as an extra syllable?); and consistency (do you just want to do the same thing with all nouns?). There are some writers who don't like the look of -s's (which is understandable) and so they want to use just a final apostrophe (e.g., *Burns' poem, Chris' friend*). These folks run smack into the folks who want to make a distinction based on pronunciation. The pronunciation people want to make a distinction between possessives where the possessive is not pronounced (e.g., *Burns' poem*, assuming that *Burns'* remains one syllable) and possessives where the possessive ending adds a syllable (e.g., *Chris's friend*, assuming that *Chris's* is two syllables). As you can imagine, the pronunciation people run smack into the consistency folks, who want the same rule to be applied to all nouns. Given that nouns that don't end in -s take -'s, then let's just do that for all nouns (*Burns's poem, Chris's friend*).

Style guides run the gamut, from pronunciation to consistency. Some of the most influential ones, though, introduce an exception to the consistency principle. Strunk and White's *The Elements of Style*, for example, advises that we should always make the possessive of singular nouns by adding -'s, except for a selection of ancient proper names ending in -*us*, -*es*, or -*is*. They cite *Jesus, Moses,* and *Isis* (the goddess). So it is always *Moses'* and *Jesus'*—or you can take the escape hatch and go with something like *the laws of Moses*. I call this "the Moses/Jesus exception," and it may have been influenced by the King James Bible, which uses *Jesus'*. Other guides mention only Moses and Jesus, but not other ancient figures. I can't help but wonder how this rule applies to Socrates (is he ancient and famous enough?), a cat named Moses, or the twenty-first-century child named Jesús.

Bryan Garner, in *Garner's Modern English Usage,* defers to this tradition of always using -'s except for classical names like *Jesus* and *Aristophanes,* and names of companies and countries like *General Motors* and the *United States.* I would guess many of you prefer the look of company names and the U.S. this way: *General Motors' reputation,* not *General Motors's reputation; the United*

States' next president, not *the United States's next president.* We often slip out of this apostrophe issue with the United States because we use it as a noun modifier: *the U.S. economy, the U.S. military.* In other words, the construction no longer requires that the U.S. be in the possessive; if it comes before another noun, we assume it acts as a descriptive modifier. We can also rephrase with an *of* construction to avoid the apostrophe issue entirely: *the reputation of General Motors, the next president of the United States.*

Then these funny cases pop up where a word ends with the sound /s/ but the spelling doesn't end in -s. The rule about always adding -'s to a singular noun unless, maybe, it ends in -s means that nouns ending in -x and pronounced with /s/ get -'s: *Marx's ideas.* And French nouns where the final -s is not pronounced also get the -'s: *Descartes's philosophy, Illinois's governor.* I will admit that I think this is the way to go. Fewer decisions to make.

Finally, the icing on the possessive apostrophe cake: plural nouns that end in -s. What a nightmare. Let's imagine that there is a family with the last name Jones. This family has one car, and we want to refer to that car. Is it *the Jones' car* or *Joneses' car?* Many guides, believe it or not, say it should be *the Joneses' car.* Which means that the house owned by the Hastings family really is this unwieldy: *the Hastingses' house.* My advice when things get this aesthetically displeasing is take the escape hatch: *the Jones family's car, the Hastings family's house.*

THE FUTURE OF THE APOSTROPHE

Given that the story of the apostrophe is the story of instability and change, what does the future hold? Let me be honest: I have no idea, and I know better than to predict the future. But let me speculate a little.

John Richards, a retired copy editor and journalist in Boston, England, founded the Apostrophe Protection Society in 2001. In 2019, he announced that the society was being disbanded due to lack of caring about "correct" use of apostrophes—but it was revived in 2021 by a new chair.

At the other end of the continuum is the Kill the Apostrophe website, which calls apostrophes redundant, wasteful, and snobbish.

Some people thought texting would kill the apostrophe, but autocorrect has made that worry seem obsolete. In counterpoint, the U.S. Board on Geographic Names typically removes apostrophes from place names. Did you know that there are only a handful of place names in the United States that are allowed, as exceptions, to have an apostrophe? They include Martha's Vineyard (which got the apostrophe back in 1933), Clark's Mountain (2002), and Ike's Point (1944). Pikes Peak lost its apostrophe in 1891, and Harpers Ferry didn't get to keep its apostrophe either. The Birmingham City Council in the United Kingdom banned apostrophes from street signs in 2009. Its fellow British city Cambridge tried to do the same in 2014 but had to reverse the decision after a public uproar.

George Bernard Shaw famously and eloquently disliked the apostrophe. He wrote: "There is not the faintest reason for persisting in the ugly and silly trick of peppering pages with these uncouth bacilli." He believed in using the apostrophe in contractions only when there would be ambiguity without it (e.g., *I'll* versus *Ill*). Odds are that we overestimate the ambiguity that would happen without apostrophes. Sure, *she'll* and *shell* would become homographs (words written the same way), as would *he'll* and *hell*. In context, though, how ambiguous would it be? "Shell be here at nine." If we were used to seeing *shell* this way, it would not be very ambiguous.

I'm playing mind games here, stretching us to contemplate what we need in the written language versus what we're used to. I don't actually think the apostrophe will die entirely in contractions or the possessive (although a couple of linguists have suggested this). I do think its use will diminish. One factor is the increasing use of noun modifiers in English such that nouns appearing before other nouns are assumed to modify the noun afterward, often through possession but not always (e.g., *farmers market*): *book's cover* versus *book cover, the building's steps* versus *the building steps, the students' experience* versus *the student experience.* If the possessor noun always comes before the noun being possessed, do we need the possessive ending? I know this is radical, but this is what happens when you study the history of the language.

Some voice the concern that if we aren't careful, chaos will reign in the written language. John Richards posed the sentence: "Residents' refuse to be placed in bins." If you remove the apostrophe: "Residents refuse to be placed in bins." Ha! What excellent, witty ambiguity. And probably worth avoiding, especially without any context. That said, these ambiguous sentences are fairly hard to find/construct. And it is rare that we would get this sentence without any context to know if we were talking about the residents' garbage or stubborn residents. I'm not saying we should get rid of apostrophes; I am simply keeping our concern about impending chaos in check.

the bottom line
· ·

It's useful to know these standardized conventions about when and where to use apostrophes because judgment is rampant. That judgment is not especially well-founded, as I've described, and we're undoubtedly living through ongoing change in apostrophe conventions. So when your inner grammando is tempted to judge others' apostrophes, I would recommend exercising caution. There's good reason to be less judgy. Many brilliant writers are not great proofreaders, not everyone prioritizes proofing text messages, and almost all of us get mixed up at least sometimes on *it's/its*. Do you really want to write someone off over an apostrophe? I have one friend who said an emphatic "yes" to that, and I thought about the talented people she would never meet over an errant squiggle. We still read and celebrate historical texts that employ the apostrophe differently, with less

consistency than we insist on today. And even in that consistency, there are lots of exceptions and idiosyncrasies to the
"standard" use of the apostrophe.

With the apostrophe, I recommend listening intently to your
inner wordie and allowing yourself to be fascinated, rather than
frightened, by the evolution of this punctuation mark.

27

....

bequeathing capital letters

I will be the first to admit that the current conventions for capitalization of words like *president* or *dean* do not make sense to me. I can explain the rules, and I can follow the rules in my formal writing, but I don't like them. If I could wave my magic capitalization wand (where did I leave that again?) and change how we capitalize these words, we would do things differently. In this chapter, we'll look at the current state of capitalization within historical context, and you'll see why Benjamin Franklin also wouldn't be happy about the current state of things.

Here's where we are right now with a noun like *president* (or *dean* or *prime minister* or the like). If we're talking about a president in general, the noun is clearly not capitalized, as in "In the United States we elect a president every four years." When we refer to a president by name, where the noun is part of the person's title, it is clearly capitalized, as in "Yes, President Obama was in office for eight years." All straightforward so far. Things get less intuitive (at least for me) when we refer, for example, to the specific person who was in the White House, but we don't name them (e.g., President Lincoln). Instead, we write "The president/President issued an executive order." Which one is it?

Before I answer that (yes, I am using a capitalization teaser), I think it is helpful to get some historical perspective on capitalization. Otherwise, I fear I might be suggesting a stability and logic to the answer that would be wholly inappropriate.

Capitalization has been a moving target in the history of English. Our current rules emerged relatively recently and are still to some extent in flux—and not just because of texting and other electronic technologies! We won't go all the way back to Old English because capitalization was sparse and highly variable. It makes more sense to jump to the Renaissance. By the seventeenth century, some capitalization conventions were settling down in familiar ways: A word would be capitalized at the beginning of a sentence (which helps distinguish sentences on a page), in proper names (out of respect), for the word *I* (which is weird—we'll come back to that), and in important nouns like titles and personified nouns (e.g., *Virtue*). It also remained possible to capitalize a noun in the middle of a sentence because it was important—and that is a practice that increased in the eighteenth century. Ben Franklin was fond of this practice of capitalizing important nouns (much like German capitalizes nouns). We saw this in chapter 6 in the letter I quoted, which Franklin wrote to Noah Webster; it opens: "I cannot but applaud your Zeal for preserving the Purity of our Language, both in its Expressions and Pronunciation." An English teacher today would not let this stand uncorrected, and certainly would not see it as appropriate for someone who wanted to preserve the purity (no caps) of the language (no caps).

This fact about eighteenth-century capitalization provides a new perspective on the language of the Constitution and Declaration of Independence. Have you noticed how many nouns are capitalized in these important historical documents? The Declaration of Independence starts with this line: "When in the Course of human events it becomes necessary for one people to dissolve the political bands . . ." Perhaps you assumed that the capitalization of the word *Course* was the equivalent of a typo, or perhaps you just allow older documents to be idiosyncratic in their capitalization practices and look the other way. But it isn't completely idiosyncratic: It's about important nouns. One of the most quoted lines from the Declaration of Independence looks like this on the page: "We hold these truths to be self-evident, that all men are created equal, that they are endowed by their Creator with certain unalienable Rights, that among these are Life, Liberty and the pursuit of Happiness." At this point, I hope you're asking not why *Creator, Rights, Life, Liberty,* and *Happiness* are capitalized but instead why *truths* and *pursuit* are not! Part of the answer is that written language was not as hyperstandardized as it is now, and practices like capitalization of nouns were not entirely consistent. Take, for example, the fact that the noun *men* is not capitalized in the line I just quoted. The very next sentence in the document starts: "That to secure these rights, Governments are instituted among Men . . ." It's not that the men in the second sentence are more important than the men in the first sentence; it's about inconsistency in capitalization.

The preamble of the United States Constitution looks strikingly similar in terms of how it deploys capitalization:

> **We the People** of the United States, in Order to form a more perfect Union, establish Justice, insure domestic Tranquility, provide for the common defence, promote the general Welfare, and secure the Blessings of Liberty to ourselves and our Posterity, do ordain and establish this Constitution for the United States of America.

Almost all the nouns in this passage are capitalized, with the striking exception of *defence* (for which I have no explanation other than editors weren't as nitpicky about these things in 1787). And the spelling of *defence* with a *c* rather than an *s* occurs because Noah Webster hadn't yet reformed American spelling to differentiate it from British English spelling. Yes, we really can thank Noah Webster for many of our distinctive American spellings, which were from the very beginning designed to assert the independence of American English, a few decades after the country had declared independence: *realize* rather than *realise, theater* for *theatre, color* for *colour, traveled* instead of *travelled,* and *offense* for *offence.* And while we're talking about this passage, I want to note that I don't hear too many people complain about *more perfect union*, whereas they chide those who say or write *more unique* (see chapter 5).

In any case, back to capitalization. By the end of the eighteenth century, grammarians started to clamp down on this use of capital letters for nouns of "special note." Grammarians claimed that it "disfigures" one's writing to use capitals for all nouns. And capitalizing for emphasis came to be out-and-out proscribed in the nineteenth century.

So now capitalization is generally restricted to the start of a sentence, proper names, and titles when they occur with the person's name (e.g., *President Roosevelt*). And that description returns us to my teaser question about when we capitalize *president*. According to *The Chicago Manual of Style,* we are not to capitalize titles like president or dean even when the referent is specific, so long as it is not direct address (e.g., "Thank you, Senator"). Let me show what this looks like:

> President Rodriguez easily won re-election. Her supporters and opponents alike praised the president for her adept handling of the economic crisis.

Yes, seriously. Even if you are referring back to a specific president, in this case President Rodriguez, you would not capitalize *president* unless you write *President Rodriguez.* So in these two sentences, which are about the same person, in one sentence *president* is capitalized and in the other it is not. If this makes no sense to you, you're in good company—at least if you consider my company good company! And actually, as I was writing this chapter, I had lunch with two colleagues at the university (lowercase, not uppercase), and I was describing this rule to them. One exclaimed, "But I thought you *would* capitalize president in a sentence like that. It is referring to a specific president. That makes no sense!" And because the inconsistency is hard to make sense of, you will regularly see capitalization of *the Dean, the Senator,* or *the President* when it is used to refer to a specific person. I read this capitalization as an attempt to be formal and polite, in recognition of the position. Capitalization is one of the ways we show respect on the page.

Titles are also not the only place in the language where we see inconsistency in capitalization. Bryan Garner, in his usage guide, points out the contradiction of capitalizing *Stone Age* and not *space age.* He advocates minimal capitalization in general, although he does provide the leeway for capitalizing for "some rhetorical purpose." Many of us lowercased the word *Internet* years before usage guides decided it was okay to spell it *internet* (*The Associated Press Stylebook* and *The New York Times* didn't authorize *internet* until 2016). And are you now wondering whether I should have capitalized *The* in *The New York Times*? Believe me, in a chapter on capitalization, I checked to make sure I had that right. We are asked to remember that *The* is part of the title of *The New York Times* and *The Washington Post* but not of the *Los Angeles Times.*

Perhaps the most remarkable inconsistency in capitalization in English is the first-person pronoun, capital *I.* In Old English, the first-person pronoun was *ic* (pronounced "each"), and it was spelled like that, with no capital letter. The pronoun lost the *c* by the twelfth century (that final *c* was lost on lots of words, including the suffix *-lic,* which became modern *-ly*). By the late 1300s, the one-letter pronoun started to become taller. Historians of the language aren't sure why: Perhaps it didn't look good on the page as a lowercase *i,* or perhaps it helped distinguish the pronoun *i* from the shorthand *i,* which could be an abbreviation for *if* or *in.* It eventually got tall enough to be consistently written as a capital *I.*

The mysterious capitalization of *I* can strike non-English speakers as odd. In French, the singular first-person pronoun *je* appears just like that, with no capital unless it is at the beginning of a sentence. And given politeness conventions, which dictate that we are supposed to be humble about our own position, it is odd that the only pronoun that is capitalized in English is *I*. Remember, capitalization in English can be a way to signal respect. In German the formal 'you' pronoun, *Sie,* is capitalized, but *ich* for 'I' is not.

Speakers of French may also find it odd that *English* is capitalized in the English language; not all languages consider the names of languages to be proper nouns. In French, languages like *anglais* (English) and *français* (French) are not capitalized. In German, nationalities are not capitalized when they are adjectives, like *amerikanisch* (American) or *deutsch* (German). We wouldn't want to assume that in all languages capitalization works the same way.

the bottom line

In the end, for formal writing, choosing a style manual you like—or that is prescribed by the powers that be in your setting—will be helpful. The American Psychological Association still capitalizes *Internet,* but as of 2017, *The Chicago Manual of Style* switched to *internet. The New York Times Manual of Style and Usage* requires capitalization of a full clause after a colon; many other guides do not. As I hope is now clear, it is not that one of these styles is right and others are wrong. You may be more accustomed to one style and/or you may aesthetically prefer a specific style. In some situations we're required to follow one specific style book consistently (e.g., newspapers have their own style guides, as do academic journals). When left to your own rules in formal writing, I would recommend consistency in your practice.*

---

* The language historian in me needs to point out that the modern vigilance focused on persnickety capitalization and punctuation rules is a bit over the top. Hard-and-fast copyediting rules about absolute consistency seem to suggest that the human brain cannot process some inconsistency from page to page or even within the same page. But, of course, it can. I often use the example of my own handwriting, which is a mishmash of print and script letters at this point. This means that I have two different *f*'s and *r*'s, among other letters, and they appear to be in free variation across words and even within the same word. When I point this out to students midway through the semester, asking them to consider an example of my

Capitalization is undoubtedly not finished shifting, and we should be comfortable with that. It is, after all, a question more of aesthetics than anything else. Informal writing in texting and elsewhere is often playful with capital letters, sometimes using the lowercase *i* for the pronoun and capitalizing words for emphasis much like we did in the eighteenth century (although you'll see it applied to parts of speech beyond nouns). And as you know, if I had my way, we would capitalize titles like *dean, senator,* and *president* if we are referring to a specific person. If we all work together, perhaps we can make it happen.

---

writing on the board, it is regularly the first time they notice that their brains have processed my two *f*'s as the same thing, without missing a beat. Some usage experts and teachers and editors argue it's sloppy not to be entirely consistent. I contemplate how many editor hours are devoted to catching every capitalization inconsistency in the twenty-first century, while we frame the Constitution with its far-from-consistent capitalization.

part 6

how stylish is that
sentence?

28

....

to boldly split infinitives

When I teach writing courses, I ask students on the first day to share with me the usage rules they have learned from past English teachers and others. Most semesters, a student will chime in with "Don't split an infinitive" (along with "Don't use the pronoun *I* in formal writing," a rule I clearly violated in the first sentences of this chapter). One semester I asked the student who volunteered the rule, "What's an infinitive?" She paused and then said, "I'm not sure, but I know you can't split it."

So let's start by clarifying the basics of the rule that has been handed down from generations of English teachers to generations of students for almost two hundred years. In Modern English, the infinitive form of the verb is made up of the particle *to* and the base form of the verb (which is also called the infinitive form and has no additional endings on it): *to serve, to understand, to be, to go.*

The rule not to split an infinitive works from the idea that although the infinitive is two words, it is fundamentally one unit and should be treated as a unified whole; therefore, the rule prohibits our putting an adverb or an adverbial phrase between *to* and the base form of the verb, as in *to better serve* or *to more fully understand* or *to really be.* This rule suggests, then, that the original catchphrase of the television show *Star Trek* has a grammatical problem given that the adverb *boldly* is splitting the infinitive *to go* in "To boldly go where no man has gone before."

Hmmm. We should already be asking questions because "to boldly go" doesn't sound like a problem. In fact, it sounds so colloquial as to be unremarkable. In 1998, Oxford publishers lifted the ban on split infinitives with the *New Oxford English Dictionary,* and many style guides have relaxed their guidelines on this point of usage. And yet many editors and English teachers have not. The rule about not splitting infinitives remains one of the best known, strongest prescriptive rules in the popular understanding of grammar. It generates both interest and anxiety, as witnessed on the over one hundred thousand websites dedicated to split infinitives (seriously).

To figure out whether there is any reason to follow this rule anymore, it helps to know where it comes from. (If you want that sentence not to end in a preposition, be sure to read the next chapter. For perhaps obvious stylistic reasons, I decided against the alternative: "It helps to know whence it comes.") There's a widespread rumor among linguists that the rule about split infinitives comes from Latin grammar getting imposed on English. It is true that in Latin, infinitives are one word and, therefore, cannot be split; and it is true that a good number of Latin grammatical categories and rules got imposed onto English. However, the split infinitive rule doesn't appear to have started there.

Split infinitives were irrelevant in the time of the *Beowulf* poet because in Old English, infinitives were one word. A verb typically took the ending *-an* to mark the infinitive form, such as *swimman* for 'to swim' and *luvian* for 'to love.' When the infinitive is one word, it is downright impossible in English to split it. But by the thirteenth century or so, it had become more common to put *to* in front of the verb to create the infinitive, at which point it became possible to put an adverb in between the *to* and the verb. And we have evidence from as early as the fourteenth century of English writers doing exactly that; for example, the Wycliffe translation of the Bible includes this line: "It is good to not eat flesh and to not drink wine."

By the seventeenth century, some writers were trying to avoid split infinitives, but there was no explicit rule. Because people like to blame Bishop Lowth's grammar for all kinds of things, sometimes people have claimed that he banned split infinitives, but in fact the construction is not mentioned in his 1762 grammar. Or in Lindley Murray's best-selling grammar at the end of the eighteenth century. The editors at Merriam-Webster have located what may be the first published criticism of the split infinitive: It's in John Comly's *English Grammar, Made Easy to the Teacher and Pupil,* published in 1803. He writes simply: "An adverb should not be placed between a verb of the infinitive mood and the preposition *to* which governs it."

Richard W. Bailey (who, full disclosure, was my advisor in graduate school) found an anonymous letter to the editor printed in the *New-England Magazine* in 1834. The letter describes a construction like "to fully understand" as a "fault"—and notably a fault without a name, as the term *split infinitive* does not take off until the late 1800s. The letter's author doesn't like the split infinitive because it is used—or so this author perceives—by uneducated writers. It is a quintessential shibboleth (a practice or bit of knowledge that allows us to distinguish groups of people from each other), dividing those who know the rule and "know better" than to split an infinitive from those who don't.

John Horne Tooke mentions split infinitives in 1840 in *The Diversions of Purley;* he compares the history of English with German and criticizes the split infinitive on the grounds that it is not true to English's Teutonic roots. So the rationale for the rule may be that the infinitive is one word in another language, but that language appears to be German (or Old English), not (or perhaps in addition to) Latin.

For all the public criticism of split infinitives, it is hard now to find a usage guide that takes a super hard line on these constructions. H. W. Fowler, writing a hundred years ago, categorized split infinitives under "fetishes" and "superstitions," mocking those who follow the prescription doggedly. Bryan Garner creates the category of "justified splits."

Do we split infinitives? Yes, and some sound idiomatic, such as *to better serve* or *to better understand, to not only say but also . . . ,* or *to just leave.* As speakers and writers, we often like to place the adverb right next to the verb itself, as opposed to before the *to* that comes before the verb. We can sometimes put the adverb after the verb (e.g., *to understand better*), but sometimes that is not possible (e.g., *to leave just, to say not*). Linguist David Crystal points out that there may be prosodic factors (that is, patterns of word stress) that encourage us to split some infinitives, in particular to maintain the rhythm of weak-strong-weak-strong stress: *to boldly go* maintains that pattern, whereas *boldly to go* (strong-weak-weak-strong) or *to go boldly* (weak-strong-strong-weak) do not. This wording from *Star Trek* is not bold in breaking any new grammatical territory; the only way in which it might be bold is in flouting grammatical sticklers.

If we accept that there is nothing fundamentally wrong with split infinitives, then it makes sense to ask whether all split infinitives are equally okay. Here the territory gets a bit less clear-cut. Some split infinitives work better than others. Or, to put it differently, some split infinitives are not stylistically ideal, specifically when writers put a lot of material (that is, an especially long adverbial phrase) between *to* and the verb. Consider this sentence:

> This rubric-based grading helps writing instructors to effectively and consistently, if not necessarily quickly, grade students' essays.

A seven-word split! It is a stretch to say the sentence is confusing, but the writer has created a lot of real estate between the two parts of the infinitive: *to* and *grade.* It's not wrong, but the sentence could probably be improved by putting *to grade* together, first: "to grade effectively and consistently, if not necessarily quickly." This revision also nicely avoids having commas in the adverbial that is splitting the infinitive—an audacious split, to say the least.

Some ardent sticklers about splitting infinitives cast the net widely and argue that adverbs should not come between auxiliary verbs and the main verb either, a so-called *split verb* (e.g., *can better understand*). This notion became a national issue in the United States in 2008 when U.S. Chief Justice John Roberts changed the oath of office when he swore in President Obama. Linguist Steven Pinker speculated in *The New York Times* that Chief Justice Roberts was trying to avoid an auxiliary verb–adverb–main verb construction. The oath goes as follows:

> I do solemnly swear that I will faithfully execute the office of the President of the United States.

The adverb *faithfully* boldly, and very colloquially, comes between the auxiliary verb *will* and the main verb *execute*. Justice Roberts's version was:

> I do solemnly swear that I will execute the office of the President of the United States faithfully.

That *faithfully* has moved ten words away from where President Obama expected it to be, and the unexpected change in the oath caused him to stumble. (The oath ceremony was repeated the next day to make sure no one contested whether or not President Obama had taken the oath.)

Both versions are clear and unambiguous. Any concern about the split verb is not a concern about clarity or even euphony, given that "will faithfully execute" is colloquial. With this chapter's context about the history of split infinitives, I hope everyone feels comfortable leaving the oath of office as is.

the bottom line

Don't be a stickler here. Most of the time, you do not have good grounds for going grammando on other writers' split infinitives. And if you choose to listen to your inner grammando on this, much of the time you probably will make the prose sound more stilted rather than more stylish.

Here's better advice: It is fine to split infinitives with an adverb, even in formal writing. For clarity, though, you might want to avoid splitting an infinitive with a long adverbial phrase. Given that the two parts of the infinitive (*to* and the main verb) are closely related grammatically, it can be more stylistically effective not to separate them by more than one to four words. Once you create a longer separation than that, you're asking your reader to hold on to that *to* and wait, wait, wait to learn what the verb is. But oftentimes the result of waiting a word or two, so that the adverb can be right next to the verb, is well worth it for your reader.

prepositions not to end a sentence with

There's a joke about prepositions out there that people tell me every few months, given that they know I appreciate a good grammar joke. It goes like this:

> A first-year student is on Harvard's campus and asks a senior, "Excuse me, can you tell me where the library is at?" The senior replies haughtily, "At Harvard, we do not end a sentence with a preposition." The first-year student tries again, "Can you tell me where the library is at, jerk [or fill in the insult of your choosing]?"

The rule about not ending a sentence with a preposition is widely known—it comes up whenever I ask students about rules they learned in high school. I have devoted this entire chapter to the rule because it is so well-known and widely enforced, and yet there is confusion about when it should apply and whether it is a worthwhile rule to follow at all.

Let's start with what is going on in the joke. The question "Where is the library at?" ends in a preposition, but I think the concern in this case is about redundancy: At least in theory, once you have the interrogative pronoun *where*, you don't need the preposition *at* too. In this question, the preposition *at* is redundant but not stranded.*

We could reword the question to get a stranded preposition: "Which library are we meeting at?"

So what happens to strand a preposition at the end of a sentence? A preposition is typically followed by a noun phrase. The preposition gets "stranded" when its linked noun phrase moves up to the front of the clause, as it does in the question "Which library are we meeting at?" What makes a noun phrase pop up to the front of the clause? There are two kinds of grammatical constructions where this happens: *wh*- questions and relative clauses. Of course, you do this all the time without thinking about it, and this is your chance to look at the mechanics of the grammar.

One of the ways we ask questions in English is with a set of *wh*- words (more formally known as interrogative pronouns): *who, what, where, when, why,* and *how.* (Okay, clearly *how* does not start with *wh*-, but you can see why the class of words got its nickname.) No matter what function the interrogative pronoun plays in the question, it typically zips up to the front of the question. For example:

You said what to your mother?

What did you say to your mother?

---

* The phrase "where we're at (now)" seems to work a bit differently. Bryan Garner calls it uneducated. It certainly feels informal. But linguist Mark Liberman, in a very interesting post on the blog *Language Log,* shows how it appears on NPR and CNN—lots of highly educated speech—as well as in writing. For example, here's someone talking about China: "And that's where we're at right now, this very fluid and precarious situation." Why does this happen? We see two phenomena interacting here. First, we like to contract, especially in speech, so *we are* becomes *we're.* But once we contract to *we're,* we need something else after it. We can't say or write "that's where we're." Hence the redundant *at.* I'm not recommending scattering this phrase throughout your formal writing, but I am saying that it sometimes appears in more formal places and we may not notice. It's not uneducated, and we can explain why the redundancy happens.

You could certainly ask the first version of the question, but it would be marked (that is, not neutral). Most of us would need to put some serious emphasis on *what*: "You said WHAT to your mother?"

Given this general rule about how we make *wh-* questions, we know that the interrogative pronoun will bump up to the beginning of the question even when it is the object of a preposition. Then the question becomes whether the preposition will follow it or stay put. Let's look at an example, first with the question in a form where the interrogative pronoun is still positioned as the object of the preposition, and then with the interrogative pronoun first:

You sent your boss an email about what?

What did you send your boss an email about?

Once the interrogative pronoun *what* gets fronted, the preposition *about* is left stranded at the end of the question. But it doesn't have to be. We could front the preposition too, in which case we get the fairly formal, maybe even stilted:

About what did you send your boss an email?

Both versions of the question are grammatical in the descriptive sense. The real question is which one we find more pleasing or appropriate in context. I will admit that I find the "about what" question awkward, and in a formal context, were I to avoid a stranded preposition to appease any potential grammandos, I would probably reword the question to something like "What was the content of the email you sent to your boss?"

There is a delightful phrase in linguistics to describe what happens to the preposition in the "about what" version of the question: It gets "pied-piped." Imagine the interrogative pronoun as the Pied Piper from the German legend, with his magic pipe that seduces the town's rats (and then the town's children) to follow him. The preposition follows the (magic pipe-playing) interrogative pronoun up to the front of the sentence/question just like the rats.

The same kind of fronting happens in relative clauses with *that* and *which*. Let's imagine we're in a coffee shop and I'm telling you about this amazing cookie I had for lunch—a cookie you must try if you ever get a chance. Suddenly I spot the same cookie in the case in the coffee shop. I blurt out: "There it is! That's the cookie that I was telling you about." That version sounds very colloquial, appropriately casual for the occasion. The relative pronoun *that* got fronted, but the preposition *about* was stranded at the end. Were we to pied-pipe the preposition, we would get: "There it is! That's the cookie about which I was telling you." If the formality of that utterance doesn't make it feel very spontaneous to you, you wouldn't be alone.*

So what's right? There clearly isn't one answer to this question, even though the rule "Don't strand a preposition at the end of a sentence" gets bandied about as if there were no doubts. It depends in part on how formal you want your speech or prose to sound. It also depends on how stranded the preposition feels. So how did we get to the point where people think you can never, ever strand a preposition?

We need to talk about John Dryden. John Dryden was a celebrated seventeenth-century English playwright, poet, and literary critic, who cared deeply about the details of language—and about who was regulating the language. In the 1660s he chaired a committee that met to propose a language academy, modeled after the Académie Française. The proposal came to naught (first there was the Great Plague, and then the Great Fire, in London), but Dryden may be responsible for first noticing (at least publicly) and disparaging the stranded preposition. His sense that Latin grammar was superior to English grammar may have had a hand here, as Latin does not allow stranded prepositions.

In 1672, Dryden picked out for critique the writing of the de-

---

* It is fair to wonder here why *that* ("that I was telling you about") turns into *which* ("about which I was telling you") as soon as we pied-pipe the preposition. This is one of those idiosyncrasies of English grammar.

ceased Ben Jonson. Here's the relevant line from Jonson: "The bodies that those souls were frighted from." Dryden commented: "The Preposition in the end of the sentence; a common fault with him, and which I have but lately observ'd in my own writings." The confession that he himself falls prey to this "common fault" is a nice human touch—but Dryden doesn't seem to have cut himself any slack after he noticed the problem. From what we can tell, he subsequently not only avoided stranded prepositions in his own prose but also went back and revised earlier work that contained stranded prepositions.

In the 1600s and 1700s, grammarians pointed out that English grammar sometimes naturally and even elegantly strands prepositions. But Bishop Lowth's opinion on the construction, written down and disseminated in the enormously influential *English Grammar* of 1762, ended up overriding these more descriptive approaches. It is worth quoting the passage:

> The Preposition is often separated from the Relative which it governs, and joined to the Verb at the end of the Sentence, or of some member of it: as, "Horace is an author, *whom* I am much delighted *with*." . . . This is an Idiom, which our language is strongly inclined to; it prevails in common conversation, and suits very well with the familiar style in writing; but the placing of a Preposition before the Relative is more graceful, as well as more perspicuous, and agrees much better with the solemn and elevated Style.

Notice that when Lowth wrote it, it was not yet a rule per se. Lowth first playfully strands a preposition in the sentence "This is an Idiom, which our language is strongly inclined to." I love this! It's reassuring to know these early grammarians had a sense of humor. Lowth then opines that it is more graceful, solemn, and elevated to pied-pipe the preposition—probably in formal writing, given the contrast that Lowth sets up with "common conversation" and "familiar style in writing."

Lowth's opinion seems to start influencing the usage of authors, even as some grammarians argued that sometimes the language was better served by stranding the preposition at the end of the sentence. The final nail that secured this rule in the English grammatical tradition is Lindley Murray's best-selling American English grammar of 1795. Murray copied many of Lowth's words in his influential grammar (plagiarism was not policed the way it is today), except that he unstranded Lowth's preposition in "which our language is strongly inclined to" and wrote "this is an Idiom to which our language is inclined." Yes, he really did. What a shame that Murray seems to have lost any sense of humor about this construction.

Over time, the prescription became less about what is elegant and more about what is "bad usage." In fact there is even evidence of grammarians arguing that the natural construction in English is to pied-pipe the pronoun ("to which," "about whom"). In that scenario, the stranded preposition somehow becomes unnatural to the English language. Clearly that is not where this "rule" started—and the idea that pied-piped prepositions are more natural strikes me, at least, as counterintuitive.

By end of the eighteenth century, some grammar books state the rule as starkly as "Never close a sentence with a preposition," and many people still believe this or have been taught it in school. But if you look at more recent style guides, the tide has turned.

You might be surprised to learn that as far back as the 1920s, H. W. Fowler, in *A Dictionary of Modern English Usage*, tried to make the conversation again about elegance rather than about hard-and-fast rules (or "a cherished superstition" as he called this rule). In later editions of Strunk and White's *The Elements of Style*, they advise that we must have a good ear for what we're trying to accomplish as writers. I recognize that this advice may be frustrating if you worry that you don't have a good ear, perhaps especially as a formal writer, but know that they are easing up the restrictions here, so you have less to worry about. (That stranded preposition sounds good to my ear.) Here are Strunk and White in the fourth edition:

Years ago, students were warned not to end a sentence with a preposition; time, of course, has softened that rigid decree. Not only is the preposition acceptable at the end, sometimes it is more effective in that spot than anywhere else. "A claw hammer, not an ax, was the tool he murdered her with." This is preferable to "A claw hammer, not an ax, was the tool with which he murdered her." Why? Because it sounds more violent, more like murder. A matter of ear.

Sadly, the Microsoft Word grammar checker can't be as flexible as some of these usage guides. It doesn't have an ear, and so it identifies every stranded preposition as a potential problem. When the box pops up, it states: "Although a preposition at the end of a sentence may be used informally, consider deleting or repositioning the preposition for a more formal or traditional tone." Certainly the explanation allows some flexibility (if writers pull up the explanation rather than just changing the construction to make the green squiggly line go away), but it suggests that the stranded preposition is somehow always wrong in formal writing. Which it is not. (Nor is the well-placed sentence fragment, for that matter.)

PUTTING UP WITH AND UP WITH PUTTING

Before I end this chapter, I need to bust a myth out there about Winston Churchill and the rule that one should never end a sentence with a preposition. The story maintains that Churchill said to someone who had copyedited his prose in a way that he found ludicrous and inappropriate: "That is a silly rule up with which I will not put."

Or he said, "That is the sort of bloody nonsense up with which I will not put."

Or "This is the type of arrant pedantry" or "the sort of English up with which I will not put." Or he scrawled some version of that across the top of the memo.

Ben Zimmer, executive editor of Vocabulary.com and language

columnist for *The Wall Street Journal,* has done some digging, though, and we don't have evidence that Churchill said this. Or wrote this. Ever. The first instance of the quote is in *The Strand Magazine* in 1942. Churchill contributed to *The Strand,* but here's the quote, which is quoting *The Wall Street Journal,* not Winston Churchill:

> *The Wall Street Journal,* 30 Sep 1942 ("Pepper and Salt"): When a memorandum passed round a certain Government department, one young pedant scribbled a postscript drawing attention to the fact that the sentence ended with a preposition, which caused the original writer to circulate another memorandum complaining that the anonymous postscript was "offensive impertinence, up with which I will not put."

Just six years later, in 1948, Sir Ernest Gowers wrote in *Plain Words*: "It is said that Mr. Winston Churchill once made this marginal comment against a sentence that clumsily avoided a prepositional ending: 'This is the sort of English up with which I will not put.'" In other words, very quickly it was being said that Churchill said this about the rule that we should never end a sentence with a preposition.

What makes the supposed Churchill quote funny is that he is playing with a phrasal verb, not a prepositional phrase. If Churchill (supposedly) had said, "That is the sort of English on which I heap scorn," it wouldn't be nearly as funny. Then he would just have been pied-piping a preposition. Instead, the purported quote plays with the phrasal verb *put up with*. Phrasal verbs are two- or three-part verbs composed of a main verb and a particle or two (e.g., *call up, ask out, flip out, mess around, put up with*). These verbs don't like to have the particle fronted because the particle doesn't work like a preposition; it is instead part of the verb. So we wouldn't typically produce any of these as grammatical utterances (in the descriptive sense):

Up I called him and out I asked him.

Out I flipped when he said yes because I thought around we might mess.

The lesson here: Remember that some of the words that look like prepositions at the end of sentences are not functioning as prepositions, and follow your judgment about when it works well—even elegantly—to strand a preposition.

the bottom line

The description "stranded" to capture the preposition left at the end of the clause by itself can make it sound like it is a problem. Perhaps it helps to think about it as an independent, freestanding preposition. English grammar lets prepositions be freestanding at the end of a clause or sentence, and we should think twice before deciding it's the right thing to take away that preposition's independence. It's kind and it allows you to make good stylistic decisions. It's what your inner wordie can now recommend, having read this history of the "rule." As I have tried to capture in this chapter, preposition stranding can be very idiomatic, often elegant, and worth advocating for.

30

··················

when *and* can start a sentence

When I poll audiences of all ages about usage rules they have learned in school, at or near the top of the list—almost every time!—is the rule "Don't start a sentence with *and* or *but*." Never mind how many published articles, books, papers, pamphlets, official websites, instruction manuals for how to assemble the bookshelf we just bought, and other documents we have encountered that start sentences with *and* and *but*. This "rule" has been tenacious in the conventional wisdom about what is proper in formal writing. I learned it as a student from my teachers and from my mother, when she edited my high school papers at the kitchen table. And (!) I carefully never started my sentences that way—until graduate school, when I looked into the history of the "rule."

Yes, I do keep putting scare quotes around "rule" because it is hard even to call this one a rule. It's more of a myth. When you check standard usage guides, you can't find it. In the 1920s, H. W. Fowler, who was not known for his live-and-let-live grammar attitudes, does address the idea that you can't start a sentence with *and,* and he calls it a "faintly lingering superstition."

I'm not sure it's fair to say it is only faintly lingering, though. It is a superstition perpetuated by many a language gatekeeper and thousands of English teachers, including my own many years ago. The *Merriam-Webster Concise Dictionary of English Usage* nicely summarizes the situation this way: "Everybody agrees that it's all right to begin a sentence with *and,* and nearly everybody admits to having been taught at some past time that the practice was wrong. Most of us think the prohibition goes back to our early school days. . . . [T]he prohibition is probably meant to correct the tendency of children to string together independent clauses or simple declarative sentences with *and*s."

Why do children tend to string together independent clauses with *and*? Because that is how we talk. Here's a nice example of what more formal yet unscripted speech often looks like from a 1993 interview with David Letterman on an ABC special:

When CBS started promoting the show, promoting myself, I couldn't leave my yard. They just ran promotional announcements, you know, twenty-four hours a day, two or three times a minute, it seemed like. **And** we were shooting some videotape down in Chinatown this summer, **and** a very nice group of elderly Chinese people came up to me on the street, **and** they must have been eighty years old, at least, a man and a woman and some other people, **and** they looked at me **and** looked at me **and** looked at me. **And** finally they said, "You go to Channel 2?"

Think this exceptional? It's just David Letterman being David Letterman? It's not. Here's an excerpt from a 2014 interview with Edie Falco on NPR's *Fresh Air.* The host Terry Gross is asking about Falco's breast cancer diagnosis, and Falco responds:

I found out in the morning, **and** then I had to go to work, **and** I said—I told very few people, but I told the producer—one of the producers. **And** I said, I have an opportunity to meet this doctor in an hour, can I go and do that and then come back and shoot? **And** that's what I did. I met this one doctor, who talked me through the next step or whatever, **and** then I went and shot a couple of scenes after that, **and** that was pretty surreal.

This pattern is one of the many reasons why you should not believe the advice "Just write it like you would say it." Um, don't do that for more formal prose. In addition to all the *um*'s and *uh*'s almost all of us would then be writing down, we would often be writing *and*-laden run-on sentences.

The expectations for more formal prose promote structures with subordinators like *while, when, although, because,* and *since,* with maybe even a non-legal *whereas* every once in a while. And written prose often benefits from variety in how we connect sentences of different lengths, rather than lots of *and*'s in a row.

It is worth noting that this subordinated style hasn't always characterized more formal English writing. In the Old English period (up through the eleventh century), when most people were not literate, and written texts were often meant to be read out loud, the grammar of written texts often mirrored the grammar of speech more closely. Look at this passage from the Parker version of the *Anglo-Saxon Chronicle,* which documented the history of medieval England year by year. I recognize that the Old English will look unfamiliar (one hint: The runic letter þ represents the sound we now spell *th*). At the same time, how amazing is it that this is what English looked and sounded like a thousand years ago? How much the language has changed. This passage is from the year 893 and describes one of the many, many Viking raids plaguing England:

> þā hīe gefēngon micle herehyð ond þā woldon ferian norþweardes ofer Temese, in on Eastseaxe ongēan þā scipu, þā forrad sio fierd hīe foran ond him wið gefeaht æt Fearnhamme, ond þone here geflīemde ond þā herehyþa āhreddon, ond hīe flugon ofer Temese būton ælcum forda, þā ūp be Colne on ānne iggað.

"Where are the *and*'s?" you might be asking. "What is going on here?" Here is a modern translation:

> When they [Vikings] seized great plunder **and** wanted to carry it northward over the Thames, into Essex toward the ships, then the army intercepted them in front **and** fought against them in Farn-

ham, **and** the enemy army put (them) to flight **and** rescued the plun-
der, **and** they fled over the Thames without any fords, then up
along the Colne [River] onto an islet.

Many English teachers would now write "run-on sentence" next to
this passage and ask for more sentence variety. Fair enough!

So, back to the advice about not starting a sentence with *and* or
but. You can see why teachers might say this to young writers to
encourage them not to rely too much on *and* as a coordinator.
Teachers are trying to help students start to write in less colloquial
ways, in ways that are valued in academic and professional contexts. But advice for young writers is, of course, different from a
hard-and-fast rule.

We need to tell that to the Microsoft Word grammar checker.
For years the Microsoft grammar checker (when I turned it on,
which I did only when I was carrying out research on it) put a green
squiggly line under any *and* or *but* that appeared at the beginning
of one of my sentences. That squiggly line sure makes it seem like
there is something wrong with those initial *and*'s and *but*'s. If you
pull up the pop-up box in Microsoft Word 2010 for an explanation, it says that it is informal to start a sentence that way and then
notes: "Although sentences beginning with 'and,' 'but,' 'or,' or
'plus' may be used informally, use the suggested replacement for a
more formal or traditional tone." The program suggests replacing
but with words like *nevertheless* or *however*.

After years of teaching, I'm not sure everyone makes a distinction between informal and "wrong." And I'm fairly sure most writers are not pulling up the pop-up box when the grammar checker
puts a green squiggly line under a word. More importantly, I'm not
at all convinced that starting a sentence with *and* or *but* is informal:
You can find sentence-initial *and* and *but* all over academic writing,
in literature, and in the Bible ("And God said, 'Let there be light'").

By contrast, the word *plus* to start a sentence remains somewhat
informal. Maybe. There's nothing wrong with it, and right now it
appears to be on the rise in written English, which means it may

lose that informal ring to it over time. I was expecting the *American Heritage Dictionary* Usage Panel to be critical of it, given its up-and-coming status, and I was surprised to see that the majority of the panel voted with me to accept it. In our 2009 survey, 67 percent of the panel accepted the example "He has a lot of personal charm. Plus, he knows what he's doing." And 63 percent accepted an example expressing negative judgment: "We were a terrible team. Plus, we had bad uniforms." Look at the panel endorsing another useful sentence-initial coordinator!

So, in the end, not only is there nothing wrong with starting a sentence with *and* or *but* or *plus*, but it also isn't inherently informal.

SO . . .

How did you feel about that initial *so* to start the previous sentence? Many of you likely didn't notice, and there's no reason you would or should. It's only the second time I used a sentence-initial *so* in the chapter, which doesn't seem excessive in that distracting, now-I-can't-notice-anything-else kind of way. But I hear from a lot of people who are noticing a lot of sentence-initial *so* in speech right now. And they're right. What's up with that?

In speech, *so* can function not only as a coordinating conjunction or coordinator (like *and, but, or, nor, for, yet*), but also as a discourse marker. Discourse markers are those little words and phrases that don't carry "content" in terms of the literal meaning of the utterance but instead do interpersonal work. We often think of them as empty words, just filling up space. And sometimes they do just that! For example, if we're trying to remember something or we're not ready to give up the floor and want to indicate that we're not finished, we may say, "uh, uh . . ." That's a way to signal to others that they should not jump in yet. And *like* can certainly act like a filler, if we say something like "Like, um, you may not want to say that." (*Like* can do many other things, including serve as a preposition as it did in the previous sentence to introduce that bit of speech—see chapter 9.)

Discourse markers can help position the speaker and the listener in different ways. If I add a *you know* in my sentence, I may be seeking to create connection with you as a listener. If I say "I mean, that's my perspective," I may be using (unconsciously) *I mean* to minimize my authority, to create more room for your thoughts. And linguist Galina Bolden at Rutgers University has argued that the discourse marker *so* is a "lean in" way to start an utterance. It suggests that I'm eager to tell you what I'm about to say or that I see what I'm saying as directly following up on your statement or question. By contrast, *well* can work in more of a "lean back" way to start an utterance.

Discourse markers also function like traffic signals, indicating to a listener what is about to happen. One of my favorite examples is the use of *well* or *um* to signal a "dispreferred response." What does that mean? Let's imagine that I need to tell you something I think you don't want to hear. You ask me, "Are you still going to be able to come to dinner tonight?" And I say, "Well . . ." or "Um . . ." I probably don't even have to continue. I have already prepared you that I'm about to say no. This is why it can lead to miscommunication if I then say yes. You might fairly respond, "Are you sure? It doesn't sound like you want to come." I have sent mixed signals with my discourse marker! New work on what is being called "backstory *so*" suggests that *so* is also preparing a listener for a response that may be longer than they were expecting— and this is rapidly on the rise.

So can direct conversational traffic in a couple of other ways. It is a way we start stories. When I hear you start with "So, as I was driving to work this morning . . . ," I may settle in to hear a story. *So* can also signal the equivalent of paragraph breaks in a spoken narrative or explanation.

When it starts a paragraph or a sentence in writing, should *so* have a comma? Totally your call stylistically. (See chapter 23 for more details.)

the bottom line
. . . .

Enjoy having sentence-initial *and* and *but* in your sentence-building toolbox. Any grammando saying otherwise is steering you wrong. Effective writing draws on a diversity of sentence structures, which includes switching up how you begin and connect sentences to each other. Balance long sentences with short ones. Juxtapose simple, coordinated, and subordinated sentence structures. This kind of variation can nicely engage readers and help you as a writer package related information together and expertly link the ideas within and across sentences.

31

·················

the perceived danger of danglers

don't remember that many grammar lessons from junior high school, but for whatever reason, one sentence from the lesson about dangling and misplaced modifiers has stuck with me. Here's the sentence: "Clinging to the side of the aquarium, Mary saw a starfish." Poor Mary! It is exhausting to have to cling to the side of an aquarium that way.

Now, of course, if we heard this sentence, we would probably assume it was the starfish clinging to the side of the aquarium. We know what's what in the world. But if you look closely at the structure of the sentence, the participial phrase *clinging to the side of the aquarium* modifies Mary. Why? We're working from the assumption that participles and other modifiers grammatically abut what they modify. So if we wanted to rewrite the sentence without a dangling participle, it would be "Clinging to the side of the aquarium, the starfish transfixed Mary," or "Mary saw the starfish clinging to the side of the aquarium."

The issue seems straightforward enough: Put the modifier next to the noun phrase it modifies. Except for when you don't have to. Seriously? Sometimes you can dangle the modifier? Yes. At this point in the book, I doubt you're surprised to learn that another "straightforward" rule turns out not to be so straightforward.

What exactly are you dangling, or not dangling? The "modifier" is often a participle or participial phrase, which is why you may have heard about "dangling participles" as well as "dangling modifiers." A participle is an *-ing* form or an *-ed/-en* form of a verb that in this case acts like an adjective: *clinging to the side of the aquarium* in the opening sentence, or *transfixed by the starfish* in the sentence "Transfixed by the starfish, Mary contemplated becoming a marine biologist."* A modifier can also be a prepositional phrase, as in "*As a teacher,* I hear from students about their grammar phobias." That modifier could become misplaced if we phrased the sentence this way: "As a teacher, students tell me about their grammar phobias." Now *as a teacher* is modifying *students,* but they are not the teacher in this scenario.

You've undoubtedly noticed that I keep shifting between the term "dangling modifier" and "misplaced modifier." Some books use these terms synonymously, but there is a useful distinction—and the "acceptable" instances are mostly dangling modifiers.

DANGLING VS. MISPLACED MODIFIERS

"Misplaced" modifiers are sometimes also called "wrongly attached" modifiers, and that latter description captures nicely what is happening. The modifier is next to the wrong noun or noun phrase. The noun or noun phrase it is supposed to modify is present in the sentence, just not next to the modifier. It's Mary and the starfish. And these sentences can sometimes give you a good laugh. For example:

> Kicking over the log, hundreds of spiders scurried out and scared the bejeebers out of me.

---

* I know someone who claims that you can't say you know English grammar unless you can identify a gerund. And I want you to be able to say you know English grammar, whatever criteria someone is using! A gerund is an *-ing* form of a verb that functions like a noun or noun phrase. Here's a straightforward example: "Morgan dislikes running." In this sentence, *running* is acting as the direct object of the verb *dislikes.* You can also get a full gerund phrase (let's go back to clinging): "*Clinging to the side of an aquarium* is exhausting."

Those are some strong spiders! Even if there are hundreds of them, they don't usually have the wherewithal to kick over logs. We have to assume the speaker kicked over the log—and in speech we would. In this case, we would call the modifier "misplaced" because the speaker is in the sentence; they are just not positioned as the subject, next to the modifier *kicking over the log*.

A dangling modifier has no noun or noun phrase in the sentence to attach to. Often the modifier is referring to the speaker or writer, who is understood as an actor in the sentence even though they do not explicitly appear. Here's an example:

Glancing through the document, the typos jumped off the page.

Typos might metaphorically jump off the page, but they are definitely not the person or thing glancing through the document here. You knew just how to read the sentence: You inserted the speaker as the glancer—but technically the modifier *glancing through the document* is dangling.

Sometimes these dangling modifiers that refer to an understood narrator seem very natural, perhaps especially if we have an existential *it*. Here's a sentence about something that happens to me more often than I would like at parties and work events:

Without knowing his name, it was difficult to introduce him.

You can see that technically *without knowing his name* is dangling out there, waiting for something to attach to—and that something is definitely not *it*. *It* in this sentence is an empty placeholder in the grammar of the sentence. But you know what I mean when I say this sentence! And it is very colloquial—something we can imagine saying or hearing every day. This is why I'm struck when grammarians call sentences like this "ungrammatical." It's fundamentally not ungrammatical. You and I both know exactly what it means, and it follows an established pattern in the language, which is that modifiers can modify an understood narrator.

Now, that doesn't mean that leaving your modifier out there dangling in the syntactic wind is always preferable or a good stylistic choice, especially in writing where you can't be there to clear up any resulting ambiguity. One of the real problems with misplaced and dangling modifiers is that they can create ambiguity. We know that Mary isn't clinging to the side of the aquarium, but we can't be so sure who or what is slithering here:

> Slithering across the floor, Mary tried to coax the snake into the box.

Maybe Mary has gotten down on the floor to get eye to eye with the escaped snake; maybe she is leaving the slithering to the snake. Or let's think about this sentence with a dangling modifier (the situation every student is hoping for):

> Reviewing the grades at the end of the term, it became clear that the curve needed to be adjusted up.

Without enough context, we as readers could be left wondering who did the reviewing here. The instructor? The chair of the instructor's department? Some enterprising students who are about to complain about low grades for everyone in the course?

In real life, though, we usually have enough context to interpret this kind of ambiguity—to the point that we often don't notice the sentence was ambiguous at all. This gets us to the dangling modifiers that have come to be accepted as stylistically unproblematic.

PERMISSION TO DANGLE

Some participles have been dangled so often that they have come to be understood as something else entirely. Considering the way they work in a sentence, these participles are often categorized as prepositions or as "disguised conjunctions." And did you see what I just did there? I used one of these disguised conjunctions: *considering.* Here's the sentence again:

> Considering the way they work in a sentence, these participles are often categorized as prepositions or as "disguised conjunctions."

The participles themselves aren't considering anything. They are being considered by . . . By whom? By people. The relevant people, of course. The relevant people have considered how these participles work, and as a result the participles have come to be recategorized. We use *considering* this way all the time: "It's amazing we're only thirty minutes late, considering the traffic," or "Considering the danger, she is lucky to have gotten out alive."

Given how *considering* works in sentences like these (oh, by the way, *given* is also a participle that has come to work as a preposition or disguised conjunction), you can see why some might call it a preposition: It is followed by a noun phrase like a preposition would be in a phrase like *considering the danger.* It's called a disguised conjunction sometimes because, it is argued, it is doing the equivalent of introducing a clause the way a conjunction would: "When we consider the danger . . ." as opposed to "Considering the danger . . ."

And these disguised conjunctions or participial prepositions, when they dangle (which they often do), are deemed okay. Some of the most common culprits: *according, assuming, concerning, considering, given, judging, regarding, owing to, speaking (of).* When we start a sentence with *Roughly speaking,* that participial phrase is understood to function adverbially, the same way a one-word sentence adverb would, like *honestly* or *frankly* or *hopefully.* You might avoid some of these disguised conjunctions in formal writing because they sound too colloquial. For example, it is unlikely that you would cleverly transition from one topic to another in a formal essay with "Speaking of interest rates . . ." Instead you might write "In terms of interest rates" or "Regarding interest rates" (a more formal disguised conjunction).

WHO DECIDES?

Now is a good moment to ask when a dangling participle gets to become a disguised conjunction or a preposition. Who makes the call? H. W. Fowler raised this question almost a hundred years ago. The example sentence he used started this way:

> Referring to your letter, you do not state . . .

Clearly the person writing the sentence is referring to the letter and then telling the listener/reader something about the letter. If we were to deem this a dangling participle in need of correction, we would need to rewrite the sentence to start this way:

> Referring to your letter, I find that you do not state . . .

But, if we let *referring to* be a disguised conjunction, then we can leave the sentence the way it is. Which seems clear and concise.

So, is it okay to let *referring to* work like *owing to* and be a disguised conjunction? Right now, you're not going to find the answer in most usage guides. There is no usage note in the *American Heritage Dictionary*. One option would be to play it safe and not let a *referring* modifier dangle. I decided to pursue another option and see what is happening in published writing. Are editors allowing *referring to* to dangle?

The answer: Sometimes, but most of the time *referring to* sits next to the person doing the referring. In a large database of academic writing, I found a lot of sentences like "Referring to X, the author argues . . ." Nothing dangling there. But I also found sentences like this one: "Referring to Figure 2, the presence of the safety provisions shifts the demand curve up." That sure looks like a disguised conjunction.

So if we take formal, edited usage as our guide, it looks like *referring to* remains a modifier for most authors and editors, and they are not letting it dangle. But it is also safe to say that there is nothing confusing about a sentence like "Referring to Figure 2, the data suggests . . ." (Please return to chapter 13 if your inner grammando balks at singular *data*.) If I were asked on the usage ballot to rate the acceptability of that sentence, I would not say it was unacceptable. Based on the evidence, I would probably vote somewhat acceptable—and feel bad about the "somewhat," knowing that it probably won't be that long before it becomes completely acceptable.

the bottom line

The first and most important thing with danglers is to remember the different demands of speech and writing. Dangling and misplaced modifiers are generally not a big deal in speech or written forms such as texting. Context usually resolves any ambiguity, and if by some chance it doesn't, someone can ask, for example: "Wait, who was reviewing the grades?" With formal writing, we have to be more careful, and the dangling or misplaced modifier presents more danger for misunderstanding. As a general rule, when you edit more formal writing, let your inner grammando check the modifiers that start sentences to see what comes after them, remembering that some *-ing* modifiers like *considering* and *regarding* are now considered exceptions.

At the same time, as a reader, please be generous when you see a dangling or misplaced modifier in writing. Rather than letting your inner grammando scream "Wrong!" when a dangling or misplaced modifier appears in a piece of writing, see whether there really is ambiguity that you cannot resolve based on the context. And be open-minded about letting participles become prepositions or disguised conjunctions, which allows them to dangle as they will.

32

. . . .

passives were corrected

n 2009, *The Chronicle of Higher Education* published an essay called "50 Years of Stupid Grammar Advice," written by Geoff Pullum, a linguist at the University of Edinburgh and an active blogger for *Language Log* and, for years, *Lingua Franca*. Pullum is not known for pulling his punches, especially when it comes to Strunk and White's *The Elements of Style*, which he has called "one of the worst things to have happened to English language education in America in the past century." The essay was published a day after the fiftieth anniversary of the 1959 edition, and as the title of the essay makes clear, it was far from celebratory.

Pullum concedes that some of the style advice is fine, if not especially revolutionary: Be clear; omit needless words. His concern is what he considers bad grammar advice (grammar and style get all mixed up in the book), and central to his case is the treatment of the passive voice in Strunk and White. Given how many people continue to use Strunk and White and given this chapter's focus on the passive voice, the confusion that this guide sows about the passive seems like a good place to begin.

The relevant section in *Elements of Style* is called "Use active voice," and it is important to note that it is about using the active voice, not about not using the passive voice. Strunk and White give us the following advice:

> The active voice is usually more direct and vigorous than the pas-
> sive. . . . This rule does not, of course, mean that the writer should
> entirely discard the passive voice, which is frequently convenient
> and sometimes necessary. . . . The habitual use of the active voice,
> however, makes for forcible writing.

The leeway in this advice is important: The passive is sometimes both convenient and necessary; and as we'll return to, the passive is also highly conventionalized in scientific writing and other kinds of academic prose.

Where Strunk and White run into trouble is that their examples potentially could confuse readers about what is passive and what is not. They provide four example sentences, and only one of them is actually passive. Yes, one. Now, to be fair, the book introduces the sentences by saying they show "how a <u>transitive</u> in the <u>active</u> voice" can be more effective. In other words, two different pieces of advice (both not entirely accurate) have gotten smushed in here together: Use transitive verbs and use the active voice to "improve" the sentence. But given that the whole section is about active voice, the transitive verb part can get lost.

Here are the four sentences, and you can test yourself on which one is in the passive voice:

1. There were a great number of dead leaves lying on the ground.

2. At dawn the crowing of a rooster could be heard.

3. The reason that he left college was that his health became impaired.

4. It was not long before she was very sorry that she had said what she had.

As I'm sure many of you caught, only Sentence 2 is passive: "At dawn the crowing of the rooster could be heard." And this sentence doesn't sing stylistically. It is perfectly grammatical, but it runs right into one of the ways the passive can create stylistic stumbles: The sentence oddly introduces an unknown agent who is hearing the rooster. The crowing of a rooster could be heard by who(m)? We could rewrite the sentence as "The rooster crowed at dawn," and now whoever heard it heard it! For the record, this rewritten sentence, which is perfectly effective, does not use a transitive verb (the verb *crow* has no object in the sentence); this is part of why I noted above that Strunk and White's advice about transitive verbs, like their advice about the passive, is not entirely accurate.

This seems like an apt moment to pause and make sure we're all on the same page about what the passive is. To create the passive, we need a verb that is being used transitively: a verb that has a direct object and perhaps an indirect object too. In the active version of a sentence, it will occur in this order: subject (agent)—verb—object (thing/person acted upon). For example:

Calvin tickled Hobbes.

In the passive version, the object gets fronted to become the grammatical subject, and the former subject (the agent) gets moved to the end of the sentence into a prepositional phrase with *by* (and this phrase becomes optional).* For example:

Hobbes was tickled by Calvin.
Hobbes was tickled.

You'll notice that the verb changed too. To make the passive, we need to add the auxiliary verb *be* (in the appropriate tense and aspect), and the main verb (e.g., *tickle* in the sentence above) appears

---

* You may have noticed that both clauses in this sentence are passive too. I told you the passive could be useful! I'll come back to the *get* passive.

in the past participle. *Aspect?* Did I just say *aspect?* Aspect includes something like the progressive. So we could transform the active and passive sentences above this way (and I have put them in the present tense this time, just for giggles):

> Calvin is tickling Hobbes.
>
> Hobbes is being tickled by Calvin.

The point is that the recipient of the action becomes the subject, and the agent moves to the end and becomes optional. That's right: We no longer have to say who or what carried out the action.

The optionality of agent is helpful in a couple of circumstances. First, sometimes we as agents don't want to take responsibility for the things we have done. Let's imagine that you didn't realize what could happen if you threw a red shirt into the washing machine with a load of whites, and now all the formerly white socks, undies, shirts, and shorts are a not-so-lovely shade of pink. It was a mistake, and you want to avoid people making fun of you for not knowing. You might say, "A red shirt was put in with the whites." No agent, no teasing (or maybe less teasing!).

One very famous agentless passive is "Mistakes were made." President Richard Nixon and his press secretary Ron Ziegler both used this phrasing about corruption in the administration, but they are far from the only ones—both in the White House and outside it—who have used this sentence to admit there are real problems and simultaneously avoid taking responsibility for serious errors that led to the problems.

The passive is also helpful—almost to the point of feeling necessary—when we don't know who is responsible for an action; in other words, the agent is unknown. Maybe your car "was sideswiped in the parking lot" and no one left a note, so you don't know who did it. So annoying! (I know this firsthand.) You could say, "Someone sideswiped my car in the parking lot," but the passive allows you to put the focus on the dinged-up car: "My car was sideswiped." You'll often see the passive used in describing crimes where the perpetrator has not yet been identified or confirmed (which is only responsible): "He was murdered," or "The home was burglarized." Or you may see the passive when the agent is obvious: "I got fired."

Let's now return to the non-passive sentences in Strunk and White, which are not working well—but we can't blame passive voice. All three sentences feature a form of *be,* a verb without a lot of action-related clout. But it's important not to equate all instances of *be* with the passive (as I have seen instructors do in writing classes—and I had to suppress my desire to leap from my seat to correct the misunderstanding).

Let's review each sentence in turn.

Sentence 1: There were a great number of dead leaves lying on the ground.

A form of *be* (in this case, *were*) became necessary in this sentence when we added the introductory *there*: "There were a great number of dead leaves . . ." Linguists call this *there* "existential *there*"; it functions grammatically as a placeholder in subject position and bumps the focal material (in this case, all those dead leaves) to the second half of the sentence, where new information tends to occur. (For more on this, see chapter 33.) African American English uses existential *it* instead: "It was a great number of dead leaves . . ." In these examples, *there* and *it* are performing the same function.

Back to the sentence: Now we have two verbs, *were* and *lying.* These kinds of *there* constructions are quite frequent in speech, but in writing they are worth watching: While the opening *there was/ were* focuses our attention on what is to come, the phrasing is also adding verbiage. In this case, the question for the writer: Can you replace *lying* with another descriptive verb that could serve as the main verb? One possible rewrite: "Dead leaves covered the ground." You'll notice that I managed to get rid of *a great number* too, because the verb *cover* usefully suggests there must be a lot of dead leaves. We also went from twelve words to five!

Sentence 3: The reason that he left college was that his health became impaired.

This sentence presents a similar issue to Sentence 1. "The reason that X is Y" introduces a *be* verb, and it is worth looking at whether, in context, we can use a *because* construction instead: "He left college because his health became impaired." Context matters here, as there is arguably a shift in emphasis. My rewrite puts more focus on his (whoever he is!) leaving college, whereas the original sentence stresses why he left college. Imagine, for instance, that I am talking to someone who thinks this person just quit college, and I want to emphasize there was a different reason: "The reason that he left college . . ."

Sentence 4: It was not long before she was very sorry that she had said what she had.

Okay, yikes. There's a lot going on in this sentence—more than needed, I think. It's just not a great sentence. The two *be* verbs (in this case, both *was*) are the least of its problems! "It was not long before" could become "soon" or "quickly"—depending on what the writer means. Then "she was very sorry" could become "she regretted" (really a word choice issue that involves verbs). And "she had said what she had"—which is perhaps the most awkward wording in the sentence—could become "she said what she did" or even "she regretted her words." We need a little more context to be able to rewrite this one.

In any case, you can see why putting all four of these sentences under the advice "Use active voice" becomes potentially confusing, particularly in terms of equating all uses of *be* as a main verb with the passive voice. All these sentences could benefit from some revision—but in only one case because it is an awkward passive.

What is better advice about the passive? Consider whether a passive construction is the most rhetorically effective choice. I'm not just being wishy-washy here to get out of providing a clear-cut answer: There are several reasons why the passive might be the best choice rhetorically, and I'll outline them here.

Before I do, let's look at some of the passives you probably should rewrite because they are not rhetorically effective. The first is from a student essay that I received a few years ago:

> The exam began, and the shuffling of paper was heard in the room.

Like that crowing rooster that was being heard, this sentence also introduces an unspecified presence with the power to hear the shuffling. We could easily change the second clause to "the shuffling of paper filled the room." Here's another example, this time from a memo that made its way to me:

> A more streamlined process was envisioned by the committee.

The context provided no convincing reason not to let the committee do the envisioning in the grammar of the sentence (i.e., "The committee envisioned . . .").

What do I mean that the context might make the passive construction effective? There are times when to maintain continuity between sentences, the passive helps us. To provide one example, I distinctly remember writing this opening of a blog post a few years ago:

> I have a new favorite mug. It was given to me by graduate students in the English and Education program.

Why do I remember it? Because given what I do, commenters on the blog made it something of a sport to point out grammatical or stylistic "mistakes" in my writing. So I remember thinking, "What might the commenters say about this passive?" I left it, and here's why. I could have written:

> I have a new favorite mug. Graduate students gave it to me.

But when I write the two sentences that way, there is a jump: The first sentence introduces the mug, and then the second sentence starts with graduate students, who I haven't mentioned before (and yes, I know that technically should be *whom*, but as we talked about in chapter 19, it just doesn't sound great there). The way I wrote the two sentences, the second sentence picks up with the mug to create more continuity. That's what I mean when I say the passive may be more rhetorically effective in some contexts.

Then there is scientific writing. As anyone who has written or read a scientific article—or even a lab report in school—can tell you, scientific writing tends to follow a set of unique conventions in terms of how articles are structured overall (e.g., methods sections, results, then discussion); and the passive has become more conventionalized in this register than in many others. Think about the description of an experiment. In fact, researchers are doing all the actions: for example, taking the sample, putting it in a test tube, adding whatever they're adding, etc. If we described the experiment like a story (which at some fundamental level it is), there would be people involved: "We took the sample and put it in the test tube. Then we added . . ." But that narrative style no longer sounds all that scientific to us. It sounds like a story.

Instead, scientific writing tends to favor something more along these lines: "Four mLs of distilled water were placed in the test tube. Two drops of the unknown sample were then added." In this version, the human agents are invisible—or at least marginalized. The unknown sample takes center stage, and the presentation sounds more objective, more scientific. This more passive style can also hide the very human decisions involved in science, along with unavoidable bias and uncertainty. (I say this with the utmost respect for good science. Uncertainty and bias are part of all academic inquiry.)

Here is a great example of a string of passive constructions in the *Journal of Experimental Biology,* from an article called "Biomechanical Control of Vocal Plasticity in the Echolocating Bat." Yes, bats! Who can echolocate (how cool would that be?). Here is the passage:

> Six individuals of adult *Phyllostomus discolor* (3 males and 3 females) were tested in an echo- and sound-attenuated acoustic chamber. During the experiment, two bats were tested simultaneously, with bats held individually in pyramidal mesh cages. . . . Bats were assigned to the same pairs throughout the experiment. . . . Sound recording and noise playback were synchronized through an audio interface. . . . Bat vocalizations were continuously sampled at 192 kHz . . . [and specific data] were saved to hard disc.

This kind of scientific writing is in every way unremarkable now. After all, bats were assigned to the same pairs, vocalizations were continuously sampled, and data were saved. All the focus is on the bats and the data gathered from the bats, which makes sense. Clearly there were humans involved in selecting the bats, assigning the bats to pairs, putting them in their pyramidal cages, synchronizing the sound recording and noise playback, sampling the bat vocalizations, and saving the data. But those human hands are absent from the description.

You may be thinking, "Well, of course the human hands are absent! This is scientific writing, after all." But scientific writing hasn't always been this way. Here is a passage from physiologist John Hunter (1775), borrowed from Dwight Atkinson's work on the history of scientific writing. Early in the passage, Hunter is using some passive, object-centered language, but then the language shifts:

> The first experiment was made on two carp. They were put into a glass vessel with common river water, and the vessel put into the freezing mixture; the water did not freeze fast enough; and therefore, to make it freeze sooner, we put in as much cooled snow as to make the whole thick. The snow round the carp melted; we put in more fresh snow, which melted also; and this was repeated several times, till we grew tired.

The second half of this passage is delightful in its humanness. While at the beginning things seem to just happen to the carp and the glass vessel, suddenly Hunter and his colleagues appear, putting snow into the water to make it freeze faster. We can almost imagine the conversation about what to do to speed up the freezing, when someone lights on the idea of adding cooled snow—and then putting in more as it continued to melt in proximity to the warmth of the carp. Until, of course, they grew weary.

Given current scientific style, students are no longer taught—or even allowed—to describe their experiments this way in a lab report. But there is a scientific reality captured in Hunter's description.

A few other passive constructions routinely pop up in academic writing that don't typically get edited out as ineffective passives—e.g., "It could be argued" or "Other relevant factors must be considered." The phrasing "It could be argued" is one way writers introduce counterarguments as part of defending claims. These counterarguments may have been argued by others or they may be hypothetical—in context, the argument, not the arguer, is the focus.

The phrasing "X must be considered" can provide a neat solution to the abstract *we* in academic writing. If I write, "We must consider other relevant factors," it raises the question: Who is we? The author(s)? The author and the readers? All researchers in the field? All researchers in the field and the readers? In some ways, we as writers have to pick our poison: the passive and its absent agent, or the abstract *we*. Both present stylistic issues.

While we're talking about the passive, let's talk about a variant that doesn't use a form of *be* as the auxiliary but instead uses *get*. Here are a couple of examples:

My car got sideswiped in the parking lot.
My friend got fired.

Without a doubt, *get* passives feel more colloquial. Right now, they rarely appear in formal writing (in the bat experiment, the write-up did not say that the data "got saved"). In addition to being more colloquial, *get* passives may also carry two other differences in connotation. The use of *get* may suggest more responsibility of the grammatical subject, which in the passive is the recipient of the action. Consider:

My friend was fired.
My friend got fired.

Is your friend more culpable for the firing in the second sentence? Is there a sense that she did something that got her fired? In addition, the *get* passive may suggest that the speaker is conveying adversity ("My car got hit") or sympathy ("She got cheated").

In the history of English, *get* passives are relative newcomers—although they may be older than you expect. They are not a twentieth-century occurrence. *Get* passives are first attested in the mid to late seventeenth century, although they appear only sporadically until the late eighteenth century. As they become more long-lived in the language, they may come to feel less colloquial.

ARCHAIC CONCERNS ABOUT THE PASSIVE

Today we hear concerns about the passive more generally, but I want to end this chapter with a concern of yesteryear about the passive that now seems downright weird. The nineteenth century witnessed the rise of a construction we now call the passive progressive, and when it came into usage, people hated it. I mean, *hated* it. So what is the passive progressive? It is a passive that is in progress, so something like: "The house is being built." Obviously, this construction is now completely unremarkable. And in fact, you are probably wondering how you would say that the house is being built if you couldn't say that the house is being built? Hang on and you'll see.

Here is George P. Marsh criticizing the passive progressive in *Lectures on the English Language* (1863):

> the clumsy and unidiomatic continuing present of the passive voice, which, originating not in the sound common sense of the people, but in the brain of some grammatical pretender, has widely spread, and threatens to establish itself as another solecism in addition to the many which our syntax already presents. The phrase "the house *is being built*," for "the house *is building*," is an awkward neologism, . . . an attempt at the artificial improvement of the language in a point which needed no amendment.

Yes, speakers and writers really would have used "The house is building" to capture that the house is being built. Here is an example with trunks (suitcases) from Jane Austen's *Northanger Abbey*: "The clock struck ten while the trunks were carrying down."

Marsh had many allies in this war against the passive progressive. David Booth wrote in *An Analytical Dictionary of the English Language* (1830): "For some time past, 'the bridge is *being built*,' 'the tunnel is *being excavated*,' and other expressions of a like kind, have pained the eye and stunned the ear." (He added this bit in the 1830 edition; it did not appear in the 1805 edition.) Richard Grant White, in 1870, described the passive progressive as the worst of "those intruders in language . . . which, about seventy or eighty years ago, began to affront the eye, torment the ear, and assault the common sense of the speaker of plain and idiomatic English." But by that time he had to admit that it "seem[s] to many persons [to be] of established respectability."

The passive progressive, and the hatred it engendered, provide a useful reminder of how grammar changes over time as well as how what is considered standard and what is "abominable," an assault to the eye and ear, also can change over time. A construction like "The house was building" now sounds funny to us, while "The house is being built" sounded funny to people in the nineteenth century. The sensibilities of our eyes and ears shift with time.

the bottom line
....

As a reader or editor or teacher, please do not disseminate the unjustified, grammando-fueled guidance never to use the passive. It's not good advice. Instead, focus on the passives that aren't working well stylistically.

As a writer, be a savvy user of the passive. Think about the genre of writing. Think about whether you want to express agency overtly or whether there are good reasons not to. Think about the continuity between sentences.

Another piece of good advice: Look at each time you use a form of *be* as a main verb in your writing and see if you could employ a more dynamic, evocative verb instead (which may simultaneously change the syntax of the sentence). There is (note the existential *there*!) nothing "grammatically wrong" with *be* as a main verb, but stylistically you may be able to do better, at least some of the time (e.g., to avoid repetition, to increase concision). Diversity of verbs spices up your writing just like diversity of sentence structures.

33

....

why writing doesn't "flow"

A colleague of mine at the University of Michigan, who is an award-winning writing instructor, has no patience for describing "flow" in writing. "Flow?" he asks in aggravated disbelief. "Rivers flow. Writing does not flow." And he's absolutely right. This flowy metaphor has some serious limits.

Here's one of them. When students ask us as instructors how to make their writing flow better (an understandable response if we tell them it is not flowing yet!), we are often left with few specifics beyond "Make the transitions better." That's not very fair, especially if we're going to be grading the essay later. Then there is the opposite of flow, which is choppiness. I will admit that early in my career I was guilty of telling students and others that a paragraph was "choppy," without then providing specifics about what that meant or how to fix it.

This final chapter is designed to help you navigate some of the choppy waters of more formal writing—so to speak! There are some specific features of writing that can make it feel disjointed from sentence to sentence (or "choppy"), and the good news is that there are some concrete ways to diagnose and resolve some of these issues. To do so, we're going to apply information about subjects, predicates, conjunctive adverbs, and relative clauses that I've covered in earlier chapters—and you'll see some of the real payoff of having more grammatical knowledge under your swim cap. So put on your bathing suit and here we go. (Okay, okay, I promise to stop the water analogy. At least for a few paragraphs.)

When we say a piece of writing—or even just a paragraph—is "choppy," we're usually saying that we're struggling to see connections between sentences. Somehow, our expectations as readers are not being met. We're reading along and expecting one thing, and then we get something else, and so our head metaphorically jerks up. "What? Why is that right there? Where is this passage going?" This raises the key question: How can you know what your readers are expecting? And how can you help them navigate your prose? You can't entirely know your readers' expectations, but let me share some patterns that can help.

To think in more concrete ways about metaphorical choppiness in writing, we need to talk about metaphorical weight. With sentences, we can think in two ways about where we place the weight in a sentence: weight in the sense of content (where we are introducing a lot of new information) and weight in the sense of sheer number of words in different elements of a sentence. Content weight is especially important in terms of how we transition between sentences and signal to readers what is coming next.

We sometimes think transitions are only about conjunctive adverbials such as *therefore, nonetheless,* and *consequently* and phrases like *in addition* or *in sum.* These adverbials help us understand how one sentence is connected to the next. They help our readers prepare for what is coming and see how new information is related to old information.

That said (just to use a conjunctive adverbial! You now know I'm about to provide a counter or caveat), there is a more fundamental principle at work in terms of how we can present information sentence to sentence in a way that will be familiar to readers. It is often called the "known-new contract" or "given-new contract." What I love about this concept is that it's not rocket science; it is actually very intuitive. And it can be completely revelatory about what is not working in a passage of writing.

Here's the fundamental idea: As readers, we typically expect information we know to precede new information. We tend to work from where we are and what we know toward what we don't know, what is new. This plays out visually in terms of how we present information. Because in English we read from left to right, timelines tend to be structured from left to right, with the past (the known) to the left and the future (the new) to the right. This fact can help you make sure any tables you create are easily readable. When we confront a table for the first time, we expect context or information we know to the left and new information to the right. So I recommend putting context/old/given information in lefthand columns and then information to pay attention to in righthand columns.

How does this play out grammatically? Often, known information will be in subject position and new information in the predicate. Or known information will be an introductory phrase—for example, an adverbial like "Given that the study demonstrated X." The weight of new information often comes in the predicate, which is generally seen as the stressed position in the sentence.

Let's look at how the known-new contract plays out in prose. Examples from real writing will help here. Here is a straightforward example from *The Boys in the Boat* by Daniel James Brown, a book about the American rowing team at the 1936 Berlin Olympics. (Why did I pick this book? Honestly, because it was within easy reach on my bookshelf.) This excerpt is just two sentences, to get us started:

> Since early in the eighteenth century, the London watermen had also made a sport of racing their dories in impromptu competitions. They were rough-and-tumble events.

The first sentence introduces the impromptu competitions in the predicate. The second sentence then takes those competitions as given information, places the competitions in subject position in the sentence (*They*), and provides additional, new information about their rough-and-tumble nature. I know this seems almost painfully obvious, but it's helpful to see how writing "reads well" when it meets our expectations as readers.

Now let's look at a longer passage, this one from *The Immortal Life of Henrietta Lacks* by Rebecca Skloot (also on my bookshelf, quite near *The Boys in the Boat*—I don't have a great ordering system!). As context for this passage, HeLa cells are the cells that were derived from cervical cancer cells extracted from Henrietta Lacks in 1951; they were the first human cells grown in a lab that were "immortal." Here is the passage, which comprises five sentences:

> Researchers had long believed that human cells contained forty-eight chromosomes, the threads of DNA inside cells that contain all of our genetic information. But chromosomes clumped together, making it impossible to get an accurate count. Then, in 1953, a geneticist in Texas accidentally mixed the wrong liquid with HeLa and a few other cells, and it turned out to be a fortunate mistake. The chromosomes inside the cells swelled and spread out, and for the first time, scientists could see each of them clearly. The accidental discovery was the first of several developments that would allow two researchers from Spain and Sweden to discover that normal human cells have forty-six chromosomes.

The passage presents a good amount of information but in a way that is relatively easy to follow. Let's unpack or "map" how the information is presented in these five sentences in terms of the given-new contract. The first sentence tells us that researchers believed there were forty-eight chromosomes in human cells. We now may well expect that the next sentence will either focus on the researchers or the chromosomes, as both are now given information. Sure enough: The second sentence puts chromosomes in subject position and tells us about how they clump together and impede accurate counting.

The third sentence does something interesting: It breaks the contract, but it warns us that it is going to do that. The sentence starts with "Then, in 1953." That *Then* prepares us as readers for the introduction of new information right there, in the subject position; and that is what we get: a geneticist in Texas who appears out of nowhere, but we were prepped for that, so we're likely not surprised to see this geneticist, who accidentally mixes the wrong liquid in with some cells. The fourth sentence returns to the given-new contract by returning to the chromosomes as the subject, and we're prepared to learn something new about them: They swelled and spread out. The fifth sentence takes all that we have been talking about in the paragraph so far as given and sums it up with the subject *The accidental discovery* and then tells us the implications of that accidental discovery: that two researchers from Spain and Sweden discovered that normal human cells have only forty-six chromosomes.

All in all, the passage is easy to follow, in part because given-new expectations are met as we go in terms of how information is presented to us. We don't have to work too hard as readers in terms of how the information is structured, so we can focus on the story the sentences are telling.

One key point to think about as a writer is that each sentence creates expectations for what is going to come next. As readers, we don't read in a completely open-minded way, equally happy to see whatever the author is going to talk about next. We make predictions as we read, and we can be thrown when our predictions or expectations are not met. As writers, we should keep in mind the experience and expectations of future readers.

Let me show you what I mean about what happens if we don't take seriously enough readers' expectations about what is going to come next. Let's take these sentences from a May 2014 article in *The Atlantic* called "To Remember a Lecture Better, Take Notes by Hand." I chose this article because I often ask students to take notes by hand in my own classes, and so I shared this article with them. Here is a four-sentence passage:

A new study—conducted by Mueller and Oppenheimer—finds that people remember lectures better when they've taken handwritten notes, rather than typed ones. Adolescents these days suffer from short attention spans. The educational system must respond to new technologies. Perhaps it is time to bring back the pencil.

As I sometimes say, yikes. This excerpt is jumping around. Definitely something we could describe as "choppy." The first sentence introduces handwritten notes and then the second sentence leaps to adolescents and short attention spans. But forget those short attention spans, let's jump to educational reform due to new technologies in the third sentence. And then, just to round things out, the final sentence comes back to the pencil and, by implication, handwritten notes.

Now I need to be honest. This passage is choppy because I rewrote the passage to make it choppy. Let's look at what I did and then what the real article does—to give full credit to the authors for their non-choppy prose in the original.

The first sentence is real: "A new study—conducted by Mueller and Oppenheimer—finds that people remember lectures better when they've taken handwritten notes, rather than typed ones." Let's now think about your expectations as a reader: Where do you expect to go in the next sentence? Three logical possibilities are handwriting, typing, or additional details about the study. But in my adulterated version, I introduced adolescents and their attention spans—which are related, but nothing in my second sentence directly picks up information in the first sentence to make it given information. The second sentence—"Adolescents these days suffer from short attention spans"—could lead us to expect that the next sentence will be about these short attention spans or the effects of them. Instead what follows is "The educational system must respond to new technologies." We're smart readers and we'll try to connect dots: Let's see, we were just talking about short attention spans, so maybe that is linked to the new technologies, but the sentence starts with the educational system needing to respond to new technologies, which is not linked to attention spans explicitly. . . . What I'm trying to capture here is that readers are having to do a lot of work, which is not ideal. The passage introduces information and then seems not to follow through because things don't get clearly picked up in the next sentence. As a result, the passage likely feels "choppy" and not fully satisfying.

What does the actual article do? Here's the passage as it stands, not butchered by me:

> A new study—conducted by Mueller and Oppenheimer—finds that people remember lectures better when they've taken handwritten notes, rather than typed ones. What's more, knowing how and why typed notes can be bad doesn't seem to improve their quality. Even if you warn laptop-notetakers ahead of time, it doesn't make a difference. For some tasks, it seems, handwriting's just better.

The second sentence picks up the idea of typed notes, which was introduced in the predicate of the first sentence. The third sentence is still on this topic, this time picking up typed notes by talking about laptop-notetakers.

What we're doing in this chapter is mapping how information is presented in terms of the structure or grammar of the sentences. It is a usefully concrete way to understand how our written content is being "packaged" and how that might or might not work well for our readers. Here's more good news: There are some basic templates for what readers often find helpful. I'm going to introduce three useful patterns for adhering to the known-new contract. These will seem basic, but that is because it is a boiled-down map or template; these three templates actually can underlie long, complex, and beautiful sentences. And it's not that we always have to map out information across sentences in this way, but it is helpful to think about if you're wrestling with your own writing—or trying to help someone else with their writing that feels "choppy."

Here are three general methods for following the known-new contract:

1. Constant (i.e., we're keeping the subject constant): A → B, A → C, A → D

Here is an example where the subject is literally repeated: "The study shows that taking notes by hand helps students retain more information. The study further suggests that even when you tell laptop-notetakers not to take notes verbatim, they still struggle to take effective notes."

This second example is a bit more sophisticated in how it holds the subject constant: "Richard Grant White held strong opinions about what constituted correct language. The nineteenth-century grammarian singled out for critiques verbs liked *donate, leave,* and *state.*"

2. Derived (i.e., the subject of the next sentence is derived from the subject of the first): A → B, subset of A → C

Here's an example where the second sentence picks up with an example of the time demands introduced in the first sentence: "The time demands on student-athletes can be intense. For example, voluntary practices may not always feel voluntary."

3. Chained (i.e., the new information introduced in the first sentence is picked up as the subject or known information in the second sentence): A → B, B → C, C→ D

Let's return to the *Boys in the Boat* example, and I'm going to add my own third sentence (Daniel James Brown is not responsible for it!): "Since early in the eighteenth century, the London watermen had also made a sport of racing their dories in impromptu competitions. They were rough-and-tumble events. This informal exuberance could lead to heated debates about cheating and who had actually won." Here the third sentence captures the rough-and-tumbleness in the subject ("this informal exuberance") and tells us more about it. Chaining can work well, but be careful because it means your paragraph can end fairly far away from where it started.

Of course, what happens in most actual prose is a combination of all these methods, with conjunctive adverbials as connectors thrown in. For example, two sentences in a row may be chained and then the next sentence may hold the subject constant, etc.

The known-new contract can also help us think about when a sentence is too long. A sentence may have become overly long when there are too many pieces of new information that need stress or emphasis; it is more than one sentence can handle. In other words, look at whether you're trying to introduce a lot of new information in one sentence. If you are, revise. Readers can find new information more easily if it is in its own sentence, in "new information" position. And you want readers to be able to identify and pay attention to the new information you are presenting, rather than try to make sense of it all squashed together in one sentence.

Let's talk about one more way a sentence can trip over itself in a way that doesn't "flow." It involves the equivalent of inserting grammatical hurdles into a sentence. This piece of advice comes from an article called "The Science of Scientific Writing" by George Gopen and Judith Swan. You can see how they are building on what we've just been talking about in their subtitle: "If the reader is to grasp what the writer means, the writer must understand what the reader needs." Now it's not that all readers need exactly the same thing—I want to be careful about generalizations. But as writers we can unintentionally insert hurdles that will trip a lot of readers.

Here is a tip from the article that we have not covered: Beware of putting too much information in between the subject and the verb. You think: "I would never do that!" Well, I wouldn't be so sure. This happens when we want to tell readers more about the subject noun phrase while keeping it all in one sentence. Here's an example:

> The study, which looked at what happens when people take notes with laptops (with or without access to the internet) versus when they take notes by hand, found that people with pencils retained more of the information.

Our brains, which have processed *the study* as the subject, are now looking for the verb—which is twenty-five words away! Our brains, it turns out, can struggle to hold the sentence open and process all the new information in the subject noun phrase while also waiting for the verb. In other words, in this sentence, we're learning new information about the study all in the subject position (as part of the *which*-relative clause), and part of our brain is holding out, waiting for the verb, expecting that it may learn new information in the predicate too. This is a good way to overload your readers' brains.

the bottom line

In terms of how to proceed, let me share one of my favorite quotes from the Gopen and Swan article: "Complexity of thought need not lead to impenetrability of expression." I think all of us should frame this advice on our walls or post it above our computer screen: "Complexity of thought need not lead to impenetrability of expression." We have the power to shape our sentences in ways that can convey complex ideas with readable, accessible grammar.

EPILOGUE

····················

navigating grammandos and good sense

You have read this book and made it all the way to the epilogue because you care about words. Language matters to you. As you can tell, I care a lot about language too. The question for each of us is what we do with all that caring.

Sometimes deep care about language can take the form of policing other people's language—or going grammando. The policing of other people's language can be celebrated as a way to protect the language, an understandable impulse. And we can find community in this kind of protective impulse (e.g., the T-shirt, meme, postcard, and poster that proudly assert, "I'm silently correcting your grammar"). The idea is: The people who really care about the details of language are strict about their own and others' usage.

But as you have seen, some of the rules you learned about what is correct in language are not well-founded or inclusive of the change and variation that make a living language vibrant. And judging people's language is a powerful move. The languages/language varieties that we speak are core parts of our identities and the identities of our communities. And there are lots of ways to use language effectively, far beyond what we may have learned as "right" and "wrong" in school.

I hope that this book has given you a different perspective on what it can mean to care deeply about language and be kind to others, all at the same time. To feed your inner wordie is to care about the details of language with curiosity and openness about how language works, where usage rules come from and how justified they are, and how we can be the most effective and inclusive speakers, writers, and audiences (be that as a teacher, an editor, a reader, or a listener). Your inner wordie should be allowed to ask, "Says who?"

In your daily life as a speaker and writer, you will continue to confront usage questions not covered in this book. It happens to me all the time, including as I was finishing this book.

An English professor friend, who generously volunteered to read the final draft of this book, flagged a sentence in chapter 15:

> There are also a few adjectives that have that *-ly* ending (e.g., *homely, comely, manly, friendly*), and this is for historical reasons.

He suggested adding the noun *idiosyncrasy* after *this*: "this **idiosyncrasy** is for historical reasons." I smiled because I spent most of my adult writing life also concerned about unattended *this*: the pronoun *this* standing alone to refer back to an object, concept, situation, or other antecedent.* I'd been "corrected" before, and a few years ago I wrote a post for *The Chronicle of Higher Education*'s blog *Lingua Franca* about what helped my inner grammando get over it.

At some point it was drummed into me that "good writers" do not leave the pronoun *this* unattended, and I never asked, "Says who?" I would always add a noun to clarify the referent: this *idea,* this *assertion,* this *whole complex web of arguments I've been describing for the past three paragraphs* (sometimes it is hard to identify the referent!). And as a teacher, I would underline every

---

* Did you wince when you read *refer back to*? There are style guides that recommend avoiding this redundancy, arguing that the verb *refer* already implies backness. I'm not convinced. We can refer back, but we can also refer forward or outside the text entirely. And in this case, I want to be clear that the unattended *this* is referring back to previous text—so the potential redundancy feels clarifying, not extraneous.

unattended *this* I came across, sometimes suggesting a possible noun.

Then in 2009, when I was teaching an upper-level course called Grammar Boot Camp, the students and I read an article called "Attended and Unattended 'This' in Academic Writing: A Long and Unfinished Story" by John M. Swales. It forever changed me as a writer and editor.

In a study of 240 academic articles, Swales shows that anaphoric *this* is frequent in academic prose, and about half of those *this*'s occur in subject position (as mine does above). Of these subject-position *this*'s, about one-third are "unattended." In other words, published writers are regularly using unattended *this*, and editors are regularly letting published writers keep unattended *this*. So why was I being so strict with myself and with students?

Once you lift the across-the-board prohibition on unattended *this*, you can ask a more nuanced question: Is it clear from context what I am referring back to with this *this*? If so, leave it. If not, add a noun to make the prose clearer—or rewrite the sentence for clarity. This is where many standard usage guides now land, although I had not checked them because I was so secure in what had been drilled into me in, I don't know, high school.

I tell this story to humanize my own position. While I have a well-informed and vocal inner wordie, my inner grammando is still in my head talking to me. I find myself occasionally adhering to long-ago-learned rules I cannot justify once I look into them. The key is that I am then open to talking the usage issue through with my inner grammando so that I can either get over it or come to a better informed understanding of it—and usually make my writing more nuanced, given more stylistic choices.

I also have become very careful as a writing teacher and a copy editor about how I mark prose that I think is worth revisiting. Sure, if it's a typo, I correct it. But for all the grammatical and stylistic choices I run across where I might recommend something different based on my own sense of the audience, I underline rather than cross out, and then I write a suggestion in the margin, sometimes with a question mark to indicate that I offer it as a possibility to consider. I know it may seem subtle: underlining versus crossing out. But the message is very different. Crossing out says: This usage doesn't belong here. Underlining says: This usage struck me as a reader and I want to make sure it is exactly what you meant to do and want to do as a writer. It respects the writer as someone who is making choices to achieve their writerly goals, based on their understanding of their audience.

I ask you to remember that many of you are or will be the gatekeepers who can use language to keep people out or invite them in to new opportunities. This book has shown you how you can care deeply about the details of language and open the gates to invite in more linguistic diversity and celebrate language change.

One of the biggest challenges of writing this book has been picking among the hundreds of usage issues I could cover. Every usage issue is my favorite child when I'm writing about it—and there are so many I couldn't squeeze into these pages. But I hope I have given you a frame to think through new usage issues as they arise, helping your inner wordie and your inner grammando hash it out, and supporting you as you navigate a world where grammandos lurk.

We don't want to be caught wearing our linguistic pajamas to a job interview—although we might choose to defy expectations in some of our language choices in the same way that we might want to push the boundaries on the clothes or hairstyles typically worn in that workplace. Pushing those boundaries can be what makes a workplace more inclusive. We also don't want to show up for a backyard barbecue in a verbal tux, asking "To whom shall I pass the ketchup?" It's not that the to-whom question is grammatically "wrong," but it may not be the best choice for the context.

We are gauging audiences all the time. And part of that gauging is figuring out where the grammandos may be out in full force and where the grammandos are going to lead us far astray. I sometimes refer to it as gauging the "crankiness meter." And that could be crankiness about usage that historically has been labeled as incorrect or ungrammatical, or about language that is seen as too hifalutin or, I'm going to say it, "snobby" for the context.

In that way, I've tried to provide clear, nuanced guidance that goes beyond "right" and "wrong" to empower you to make informed language choices. I've showed you how linguists use the term *grammatical* to capture the systems that govern all varieties of English. I've pulled back the curtain to reveal where many of the grammar rules we learned in school actually come from and to unmask the forces that drive dictionary editors—or the *American Heritage Dictionary* Usage Panel—to label certain words *slang* or *unacceptable*. I've showed you resources like the Google Book Ngram Viewer and other online databases where you can explore what speakers and writers actually do and have done over the decades and centuries.

As you've seen, *right* and *wrong* are usually not the best terms to use. Sometimes we're witnessing a change in progress, which doesn't make the new form "wrong" even if it might not be familiar. Sometimes it is a stylistic question of formality. Sometimes it is a rule that never made sense. Sometimes it is guidance that actually usefully helps us minimize ambiguity. And sometimes variation reflects diversity in how we speak—which is core to the diversity of who we are as a community of English speakers and writers.

Wordies take the time to figure out what they're hearing or seeing on the page. They appreciate clarity and precision in language and recognize that there are many ways to attain it. They also know that occasionally, ambiguity is our friend! Wordies, as part of caring deeply about language, appreciate diversity in language usage as part of the diversity of speakers and see creative play with language—a surprising grammatical construction or a new way of using a word they haven't seen before—as a reflection of human creativity. And like the trained bird-watcher, they study the new usage bird, to understand what it is and how it works and where it came from, rather than immediately trying to kill it.

What I hope you will discover is that this approach to language is joyful, and it allows you to be kind to your fellow speakers and writers. Your curiosity about language will inspire curiosity in others. Your well-informed care with language will include others. And if your experience is anything like mine, you'll find new usage questions to explore around every corner, allowing you to become an ever-savvier speaker and writer of the language yourself.

acknowledgments

This book is a passion project, one I have been preparing to write for much of my career—and have been working on for more years than I am going to share! "Magic time" is what I have come to call the hours carved out for writing, as I have juggled university administration, teaching, and other commitments. And the magic is both in finding the time and in losing track of time—as happens when you're working on material you love and find endlessly fascinating. With a long-standing project like this, there are so many people to thank, people who helped this book come into being—and I am grateful for the opportunity to acknowledge so many of them here. Any remaining faults in the book are entirely my own.

One of the greatest joys and privileges of teaching at a university is spending time with undergraduates, and I want to start by thanking the thousands of students I've worked with over the past thirty-plus years. They have taught me about the changes happening in the English language all around us (from the rise of *on accident* to new slang like *extra*) and helped me hone an engaging, linguistically informed approach to talking about English usage. I have also had the pleasure of working with dozens of wonderful graduate students, who have pushed my thinking about language change and language attitudes.

My former Ph.D. advisor Richard W. Bailey showed me how

linguistics matters for real people in real time, which inspired me to pursue a career in the field. And in graduate school I started reading the brilliant work of linguist Geneva Smitherman, whose career has since been a benchmark for me of meaningful impact beyond the academy. Her voice is a clarion call for using linguistic knowledge to create more inclusive education and a more just world, and specifically to combat prejudice and discrimination against speakers of African American English.

Many friends and colleagues have contributed to this book over many years. I want to thank my writing group, who read many chapter drafts along this journey and provided invaluable feedback (even when the drafts were rough!): Anne Ruggles Gere, Mary Schleppegrell, and Meg Sweeney. Lisa Damour has been a co-author and collaborator since graduate school; her inspiration made this book possible and her edits made it better. I also want to thank Michael Adams, who agreed to co-author a textbook with me some twenty years ago and who has enriched my thinking about the history of English throughout our partnership. I have worked with remarkable graduate research assistants at the University of Michigan, who have helped with the book at different stages: Sofia Bento, Steven Cullinane, Hayley Heaton, Casey Otemuyiwa, Kendon Smith, and Kristin VanEyk. I am grateful for the many other people who have generously read parts or all of the book and provided comments, including Susan Garrett, Kate Gjaja, and Robin Queen. My colleagues in English, Linguistics, and Education at the University of Michigan have been brain-stretching thought partners for twenty-one years. I have felt extremely lucky to call the University of Michigan my academic home for most of my academic career.

The idea for this book first took shape when I created the course English Grammar Boot Camp for The Great Courses (now Wondrium), and I want to thank Jessica Darago and James Blandford for their detailed commentary when we were putting together that course. Creating an audio/video course about grammar taught me key lessons about how to present the material in ways that are accessible and digestible; it has shaped me as an author and academic ever since. The radio show *That's What They Say,* which I have co-hosted with Rebecca Kruth and Rina Miller for twelve years, has been a truly joyful part of my career, and our listeners consistently bring new usage issues to my attention, which is irreplaceable.

Gail Ross, my agent extraordinaire, has believed in this book since she first heard about it, and I am grateful for her patience, enthusiasm, wisdom, and guidance at every stage of the process. It's also been a pleasure to work with Madhulika Sikka, my editor at Crown Books, who understood from the beginning the balance of play and rigor that I was striving to bring to this book and partnered with me to bring that to the page.

My mother, Mary Curzan, inspired in me from an early age an abiding interest in language and ensured that I knew all the copy-editing symbols. She was my partner in editing the first two books I wrote, and I wish she could have read this book too. I am grateful to both my parents for their unwavering belief that their daughters could do anything they set their mind to. (It seemed only appropriate to strand a preposition in a paragraph about my mother!) My sisters and their families have been cheerleaders and pillars in my support system. And finally, I want to express my deepest gratitude to Pierre Theodore, who has asked thought-provoking questions about language from the moment I met him, provided foundational joy and support in my life, read every chapter, and helped me find the magic time to finish the book.

notes

Throughout this book, I reference some well-known style guides as barometers for prescriptive advice over the twentieth century into the twenty-first. The ones appearing most frequently: H. W. Fowler and F. G. Fowler's *The King's English,* 2nd ed. (London: Clarendon Press, 1908) and H. W. Fowler's *A Dictionary of Modern English Usage* (Oxford: Clarendon Press, 1926); various editions of William Strunk, Jr., and E. B. White's *The Elements of Style,* in addition to William Strunk's original *Elements of Style* (1918); and Bryan Garner's *Garner's Modern English Usage,* 5th ed. (New York: Oxford University Press, 2022).

One of the most helpful descriptive resources available is *Merriam-Webster's Dictionary of English Usage* (Springfield, Mass.: Merriam-Webster, 1994), edited by E. Ward Gilman, and its companion *Merriam-Webster's Concise Dictionary of English Usage* (Springfield, Mass.: Merriam-Webster, 2002). Organized alphabetically, these volumes provide detailed histories of common usage issues.

If you're looking for more technical, linguistic information about English grammar, I recommend two comprehensive descriptive grammars: Rodney Huddleston and Geoffrey K. Pullum, *The Cambridge Grammar of the English Language* (Cambridge: Cambridge University Press, 2005); and Douglas Biber, Stig Johansson, Geoffrey Leech, Susan Conrad, and Edward Finegan, *Longman*

Grammar of Spoken and Written English (New York: Longman, 1999).

When I tell word histories, I am relying extensively on the *Oxford English Dictionary,* published originally in twelve volumes, with the in-progress third edition now available online. Much has been written on this magnificent scholarly achievement, including Simon Winchester's *The Professor and the Madman: A Tale of Murder, Insanity, and the Making of the Oxford English Dictionary* (New York: HarperCollins, 1998); Lynda Mugglestone's *Lost for Words: The Hidden History of the Oxford English Dictionary* (New Haven, Conn.: Yale University Press, 2005); Charlotte Brewer's *Treasure-House of the Language: The Living OED* (New Haven, Conn.: Yale University Press, 2014); and Peter Gilliver's *The Making of the Oxford English Dictionary* (Oxford: Oxford University Press, 2016).

We now have access to remarkable online databases of language where we can search actual spoken and written usage. I frequently refer to the Google Books Ngram Viewer, which searches millions of online books; and the Corpus of Contemporary American English, which includes spoken language and several genres of writing (part of a valuable set of corpora created by Mark Davies, available through Brigham Young University at www.english-corpora.org/).

INTRODUCTION

x **regional variation in American dialects**   If you're interested in learning more about regional features such as positive *anymore,* the most comprehensive resource is the *Dictionary of American Regional English* (Cambridge, Mass.: Belknap Press of Harvard University Press, 1985–2013). *DARE* is available in six printed volumes as well as a digital version. For an authoritative textbook on American dialects, see Walt Wolfram and Natalie Schilling, *American English: Dialects and Variation,* 3rd ed. (Malden, Mass.: Wiley Blackwell, 2015).

CHAPTER 1. INNER GRAMMANDO VS. INNER WORDIE SHOWDOWN

3 **what "careful" writers do**   Bryan A. Garner, *Garner's Modern English Usage,* 5th ed. (New York: Oxford University Press, 2022), 575.

6 ***The New Yorker* reported**   Mark Singer, "Usage," *The New Yorker,* July 4, 1977, 20.

7 **The Usage Panel was discontinued**   For a poignant reflection on the Usage Panel and its disbanding, see David Skinner, "The Dictionary and Us," *The Weekly Standard*, December 2, 2018, www.washington examiner.com/weekly-standard/the-american-heritage-dictionary -usage-panel-defining-characteristic-the-dictionary-and-us.

9 **originating in jargon**   Garner, *Garner's Modern English Usage*, 575.

10 **Benjamin Franklin didn't like**   Benjamin Franklin to David Hume, September 27, 1760, available at the National Archives, Founders Online, founders.archives.gov/documents/Franklin/01-09-02-0066.

10 **despaired over the newish word**   Henry Alford, *The Queen's English: Stray Notes on Speaking and Spelling* (London: Strahan, 1864).

CHAPTER 2. *AIN'T:* WHAT GETS INTO DICTIONARIES, AND HOW

12 *Irregardless* **taps into some** For an excellent discussion of the history of *irregardless,* including its emphatic use, and dictionary readers' strong responses to the word, see Kory Stamper, *Word by Word: The Secret Life of Dictionaries* (New York: Vintage Books, 2017), 53–60.

13 **When people say**   In 2014, I gave a talk for TEDxUofM on the topic of what makes a word "real": www.ted.com/talks/anne_curzan_what _makes_a_word_real.

13 **As if dictionaries are unauthored**   But, of course, dictionaries have editors. And for the record, this means that dictionaries should appear in our references when we cite dictionaries in published work! For an interesting history of notions of "proper" English with a specific focus on dictionaries, see Jack Lynch, *The Lexicographer's Dilemma: The Evolution of "Proper" English, from Shakespeare to "South Park"* (New York: Walker and Company, 2009).

15 **meaning of** *suck*   For a lively, smart treatment of slang, including the history of *suck,* see Michael Adams, *Slang: The People's Poetry* (New York: Oxford University Press, 2009), 11.

17 **former University of Michigan football coach Rich Rodriguez**   Austin Murphy, "Ain't No Doubt About It," *Sports Illustrated*, September 21, 2009, vault.si.com/vault/2009/09/21/aint-no-doubt-about-it.

18 **David Skinner's book**   David Skinner, *The Story of Ain't: America, Its Language, and the Most Controversial Dictionary Ever Published* (New York: HarperCollins, 2012).

18 **a descriptive usage note**   Merriam-Webster, *Webster's Third New International Dictionary of the English Language* (Springfield, Mass.: Merriam-Webster, 1961).

19 **"vulgar abbreviations"**   Quoted in E. Ward Gilman, ed., *Merriam-*

Webster's Dictionary of English Usage (Springfield, Mass.: Merriam-Webster, 1994), 61.

CHAPTER 3. DOUBLE NEGATIVES: HOW RULES BECOME RULES

23   *"þe erthe ne bar"*   A digital edition of the *Peterborough Chronicle* can be found at the Bodleian Library, digital.bodleian.ox.ac.uk/objects/87d8c5b2-28de-4fe5-944c-67f0849b8fdb/.

23   *"He nevere yet"*   Geoffrey Chaucer, *The Canterbury Tales,* line 70.

23   *"I cannot go"*   William Shakespeare, *As You Like It,* act 2, scene 4.

24   **includes a great quote**   Fitzedward Hall, *Modern English* (New York, 1873), 279.

25   **Bishop Lowth published**   Robert Lowth, *A Short Introduction to English Grammar,* 2nd ed. (London, 1763), 139. For readers interested in the legacy of Robert Lowth, I recommend Ingrid Tieken-Boon Van Ostade, *The Bishop's Grammar: Robert Lowth and the Rise of Prescriptivism* (Oxford: Oxford University Press, 2011).

25   **This statement got picked up**   Lindley Murray, *English Grammar* (York: Wilson, Spence and Mawman, 1795), 121.

27   **A dialect like African American English**   There are many valuable books on African American English (AAE). For a book written for a general audience, see John R. Rickford and Russell J. Rickford, *Spoken Soul: The Story of Black English* (New York: Wiley, 2000). For a more technical description of the syntax of AAE, see Lisa J. Green, *African American English: A Linguistic Introduction* (New York: Cambridge University Press, 2002). For a powerful discussion of what it can mean to delegitimize AAE in classrooms, see Geneva Smitherman, "Ebonics, *King,* and Oakland," *Journal of English Linguistics* 26, no. 2 (1998): 97–107.

27   **held on to the final -s**   Peter Trudgill, "Standard English: What It Isn't," in *Standard English: The Widening Debate,* ed. T. Bex and R. J. Watts (London: Routledge, 1999), 117–28.

27   **Standardized English is not the parent**   John McWhorter, *Word on the Street: Debunking the Myth of a "Pure" Standard English* (Cambridge, Mass.: Perseus, 1998), 29.

CHAPTER 4. "PC" LANGUAGE: WHY EMOTIONS RUN HIGH

31   **defines *political correctness* as**   Kareem Abdul-Jabbar, "Every GOP Candidate Is Wrong About Political Correctness," *The Washington Post,* February 22, 2016, www.washingtonpost.com/posteverything/wp/2016/02/22/kareem-abdul-jabbar-in-defense-of-political-correctness/.

32 **a column in 2021**   Anne Curzan, " 'They' Has Been a Singular Pronoun for Centuries. Don't Let Anyone Tell You It's Wrong," *The Washington Post,* October 21, 2021, www.washingtonpost.com /opinions/2021/10/21/they-has-been-singular-pronoun-forever-dont -let-anyone-tell-you-its-wrong/.

32 **Debates about language are almost always**   Deborah Cameron, *Verbal Hygiene* (London: Routledge, 1995), 116–65; Rosina Lippi-Green, *English with an Accent: Language, Ideology, and Discrimination in the United States,* 2nd ed. (London: Routledge, 2012).

34 **it's usually not "just words"**   Cameron, *Verbal Hygiene,* 140–43.

35 **studies show it is not preferred**   Luis Noe-Bustamante, Lauren Mora, and Mark Hugo Lopez, "About One-in-Four U.S. Hispanics Have Heard of Latinx, but Just 3% Use It," Pew Research Center, August 11, 2020, www.pewresearch.org/hispanic/2020/08/11/about -one-in-four-u-s-hispanics-have-heard-of-latinx-but-just-3-use-it/.

36 **The *chief* in CEO**   John McWhorter, "San Francisco Schools Are Retiring 'Chief.' That's Not as Frivolous as It Seems," *The New York Times,* June 7, 2022, www.nytimes.com/2022/06/07/opinion /san-francisco-chief.html.

37 **I argued, in print**   Anne Curzan, *Gender Shifts in the History of English* (Cambridge: Cambridge University Press), 172–76.

37 **an op-ed for *The Michigan Daily***   Jason Dean, "Moving On from 'You Guys,' " *The Michigan Daily,* February 5, 2019, www.michigan daily.com/viewpoints/op-ed-moving-you-guys/.

CHAPTER 5. THE FUNNEST CHAPTER

45 **had this to say about *fun***   Allan M. Siegal and William Connolly, eds., *The New York Times Manual of Style and Usage* (New York: Three Rivers Press, 1999).

45 **as a "casualism"**   Garner, *Garner's Modern English Usage,* 487.

47 **lay down the line**   H. W. Fowler and F. G. Fowler, *The King's English,* 2nd ed. (London: Clarendon Press, 1908), 58.

48 **takes on *unique***   William Zinsser, *On Writing Well,* 30th anniversary ed. (New York: Harper Perennial, 2012), 40.

48 **picks up Fowler's language**   Garner, *Garner's Modern English Usage,* 1127.

48 **changes in word meaning**   If you enjoy word histories, I recommend two volumes from the editors of American Heritage dictionaries: *Word Histories and Mysteries: From Abracadabra to Zeus* (Boston: Houghton Mifflin, 2004); and *More Word Histories and Mysteries: From*

Aardvark to Zombie (Boston: Houghton Mifflin, 2006). I also recommend David Crystal, *The Story of English in 100 Words* (New York: St. Martin's Press, 2011).

49   **a compelling defense**   Patricia O'Conner and Stewart Kellerman, "A Justifiable Usage," *Grammarphobia,* www.grammarphobia.com/blog /2008/01/justifiable-usage.html.

CHAPTER 6. VERBING

51   **Franklin's letter**   Benjamin Franklin to Noah Webster, December 26, 1789, franklinpapers.org/framedVolumes.jsp?vol=46&page=378.

54   **in a 1760 letter to David Hume**   Benjamin Franklin to David Hume, September 27, 1760, National Archives, Founders Online, founders .archives.gov/documents/Franklin/01-09-02-0066.

55   **notes that *utilize***   Eric Partridge, *Usage and Abusage* (New York: Harper, 1942), 343.

55   **"boorish bureaucratic misspeak"**   Edward Rothstein, "Is a Word's Definition in the Mind of the User?" *The New York Times,* November 25, 2000, www.nytimes.com/2000/11/25/books/shelf-life-is-a -word-s-definition-in-the-mind-of-the-user.html; Benjamin Dreyer, *Dreyer's English: An Utterly Correct Guide to Clarity and Style* (New York: Random House, 2019).

CHAPTER 7. FEELING HOPEFUL ABOUT *HOPEFULLY*

61   **The graph below from *Time* magazine**   From the Time Magazine Corpus, www.english-corpora.org/time.

63   ***The Associated Press Stylebook***   AP Stylebook Online, www.apstyle book.com/.

63   **This change made headlines**   Monica Hesse, "AP's Approval of 'Hopefully' Symbolizes Larger Debate About Language," *The Washington Post,* April 17, 2012, www.washingtonpost.com/lifestyle/style /aps-approval-of-hopefully-symbolizes-larger-debate-over-language /2012/04/17/gIQAti4zOT_story.html; Geoff Nunberg, "The Word 'Hopefully' Is Here to Stay, Hopefully," *Fresh Air,* May 30, 2012, www.npr.org/2012/05/30/153709651/the-word-hopefully-is-here-to -stay-hopefully.

CHAPTER 8. QUITE LITERALLY

69   **expressed deep disapproval**   H. W. Fowler, *A Dictionary of Modern English Usage* (Oxford: Clarendon Press, 1926), 328.

69   **the echoes of Ambrose Bierce**   Ambrose Bierce, *Write It Right: A Little Blacklist of Literary Fault* (New York: Neale Publishing,

1909). For a concise summary of the historical criticism of *literally*, see Jesse Sheidlower, "The Word We Love to Hate: Literally," *Slate*, November 1, 2005, slate.com/human-interest/2005/11/the-trouble -with-literally.html.

71 **a 2017 interview with Steve Bannon** Eric Shawn, "Blaming GOP Establishment, Bannon Speech Warns of 'Brutal' 2018 Race," Fox News, November 13, 2017, www.foxnews.com/politics/blaming-gop -establishment-bannon-speech-warns-of-brutal-2018-race.

71 **an example from *The Daily Beast*** Lizzie Crocker, "Crystals, Feathers, and Spanx: Secrets of the Oscar Red Carpet Stylists," *The Daily Beast*, April 11, 2017, www.thedailybeast.com/crystals-feathers-and -spanx-secrets-of-the-oscar-red-carpet-stylists.

72 **Some argue** Steven Pinker, *The Language Instinct: How the Mind Creates Language* (New York: William Morrow, 1994), 377.

CHAPTER 9. BECAUSE *LIKE*

75 **had thoughts about *like*** Noah Webster, *Rudiments of English Grammar* (Hartford, Conn.: Elisha Babcock, 1790), 47. He lists other peeves addressed in this book, including *lay* for *lie, the reason is because,* and *him and me went.* He also corrects "You will write him often" to "write to him," which likely does not resonate with today's reader.

77 **Linguists have been fascinated** The most comprehensive treatment of *like* is Alexandra D'Arcy, *Discourse-Pragmatic Variation in Context: Eight Hundred Years of Like* (Amsterdam: John Benjamins Publishing, 2017). For an accessible summary of the research and defense of *like,* see Valerie Friedland, *Like, Literally, Dude* (New York: Viking, 2023), 99–123.

77 **the use of *like* has been increasing** Sali A. Tagliamonte and Alexandra D'Arcy, "Frequency and Variation in the Community Grammar: Tracking a New Change Through the Generations," *Language Variation and Change* 19, no. 2 (2007): 199–217; Sali A. Tagliamonte, Alexandra D'Arcy, and Celeste R. Louro, "Outliers, Impact, and Rationalization in Linguistic Change," *Language* 92, no. 4 (2016): 824–49.

78 ***"reason* implies *because"*** Garner, *Garner's Modern English Usage,* 926.

79 ***because* + noun phrase** *Because* in this construction is functioning as a preposition and this has been described as a new use, contrasted with the use of *because* as a subordinating conjunction. But Rodney Huddleston and Geoffrey Pullum, in their remarkable *Cambridge Gram-*

mar of the English Language (Cambridge: Cambridge University Press, 2005), argue that *because* is always a preposition. For a nice summary of their position in the context of *because* + noun phrase, see Neal Whitman, "Why Is the Word of the Year 'Because'? Because . . . ," January 8, 2014, www.vocabulary.com/articles/dictionary/why-is-the -word-of-the-year-because-because/.

CHAPTER 10. GENDER-NEUTRAL CHAIRS

82 **The speed with which gender-neutral language** Anne Pauwels, *Women Changing Language* (London: Longman, 1998). In the foundational book *Language and Woman's Place*, published in 1975, linguist Robin Lakoff couldn't imagine that generic *he* could be replaced, noting that an attempt to change pronominal usage "will be futile" (71).

84 **changing policies about smoking in public** Cameron, *Verbal Hygiene*, 143.

CHAPTER 11. ASK, AKS, AND ASTERISK

92 **nothing wrong with the pronunciation "aks"** For a smart, accessible, concise discussion of the history and attitudes toward "aks," check out this short podcast: Shereen Marisol Meraji, "Why Chaucer Said 'Ax' Instead of 'Ask,' and Why Some Still Do," *Code Switch*, December 3, 2013, www.npr.org/sections/codeswitch/2013/12/03/248515217/why -chaucer-said-ax-instead-of-ask-and-why-some-still-do.

93 **the pronunciation was common in New England** Noah Webster, *Dissertations on the English Language* (Boston: Isaiah Thomas and Company, 1789).

96 **pronunciation of *nuclear* as "nucular"** For a more nuanced discussion of this issue, see Stamper, *Word by Word*, 210–15.

96 **enough to make him sick** Alexander Dyce, ed., *Recollections of the Table-Talk of Samuel Rogers* (New York: D. Appleton, 1856), 248.

CHAPTER 12. COUNTING LESS/FEWER THINGS

99 **this headline from Reuters** "Fist Bumps Relay 90 Percent Less Germs Than Handshakes," Reuters, July 28, 2014, www.reuters.com /article/us-usa-fistbump/fist-bumps-relay-90-percent-less-germs-than -handshakes-study-idUSKBN0FX1Q820140728.

99 **committed to paper in 1770** Quoted in *Merriam-Webster's Dictionary of English Usage*, 592–93.

99 **no longer framed as a personal preference** William Strunk, Jr., *Elements of Style* (New York: Harcourt, Brace, 1918), 41.

100 questions for *The Chicago Manual of Style Online* "Less or Fewer,"
     Style Q&A, *The Chicago Manual of Style Online,* www.chicago
     manualofstyle.org/qanda/data/faq/topics/LessorFewer/faq0001.html.

CHAPTER 13. *DATA* AND OTHER DISPUTED PLURALS

103 *data* is plural   *Publication Manual of the American Psychological
     Association,* 7th ed. (Washington, D.C.: American Psychological As-
     sociation, 2020).

104 this one from the sports section   Michelle Kessler and Erik Brady,
     "Tension Mounts with Fans," *USA Today,* September 15, 2004 (re-
     trieved from the Corpus of Contemporary American English).

CHAPTER 14. DIFFERENT FROM/THAN *BETWEEN* AND *AMONG*

109 a "monstrous barbarism"   Thomas De Quincey, *Miscellaneous Es-
     says* (Boston: Ticknor, Reed, and Fields, 1851), 13.

110 younger speakers use *on accident*   Leslie Barratt, "What Speakers
     Don't Notice: Language Changes Can Sneak In," TRANS Internet-
     Zeitschrift für Kulturwissenschaften 16 (2005), www.inst.at/trans
     /16Nr/01_4/barratt16.htm.

113 old-fashioned and even pretentious   Garner, *Garner's Modern En-
     glish Usage,* 57.

CHAPTER 15. DRIVING SAFE OR SAFELY

119 "perhaps the most frequently misplaced"   Garner, *Garner's Modern
     English Usage,* 779.

119 went after the phrasing   Lowth, *Short Introduction to English
     Grammar,* 139.

119 defends "misplaced" *only*   Fowler, *Dictionary of Modern English
     Usage,* 405–6.

121 "how slow This old Moone wauns"   Shakespeare, *A Midsummer
     Night's Dream,* act 1, scene 1.

122 *firstly* a pedantic neologism   Cited in *Merriam-Webster's Concise
     Dictionary of English Usage,* 341.

122 dismissed it in his influential   Fowler, *Dictionary of Modern English
     Usage,* 181.

122 It's a fast-moving set of words   Sali Tagliamonte and Chris Roberts,
     "So Weird; So Cool; So Innovative: The Use of Intensifiers in the Tele-
     vision Series *Friends,*" *American Speech* 80, no. 3 (2005): 280–300.

CHAPTER 16. WELL, I'M GOOD

125 **Greetings have a routine to them**   To read more about the coopera-
tion involved in conversation, see N. J. Enfield, *How We Talk: The
Inner Workings of Conversation* (New York: Basic Books, 2017).

CHAPTER 17. HAVING PROVED OR PROVEN IT

132 **English had two kinds of regular verbs**   For a very good technical
textbook on the history of English, see C. M. Millward and Mary
Hayes, *A Biography of the English Language,* 3rd ed. (Boston: Wads-
worth, 2011). For an accessible, concise summary of verb classes in
the history of English, see Arika Okrent, *Highly Irregular: Why
Tough, Through, and Dough Don't Rhyme and Other Oddities of
the English Language* (New York: Oxford University Press, 2021),
59–65.

133 **dramatic increase in this form**   Garner, *Garner's Modern English
Usage,* 1013.

136 **Here is Richard Grant White**   Richard Grant White, *Words and
Their Uses, Past and Present* (New York: Sheldon, 1870), 220.

136 **only recently removed**   Garner, *Garner's Modern English Usage,* 892.

136 **Consider this sentence**   Iva Savic, "The Russian Soldier Today,"
Journal of International Affairs, April 18, 2010, jia.sipa.columbia
.edu/russian-soldier-today.

CHAPTER 18. THE SINGULARITY OF *THEY*

141 **As the website Grammar Girl**   Now captured in Mignon Fogarty,
Grammar Girl's 101 Troublesome Words You'll Master in No Time
(New York: St. Martin's Griffin, 2012), 116.

142 **Studies show that *they***   Michael Newman, *Epicene Pronouns: The
Linguistics of a Prescriptive Problem* (New York: Garland, 1997).

142 **It made headlines in 2015**   Bill Walsh, "The Post Drops the 'Mike'—
and the Hyphen in 'E-mail,'" *The Washington Post,* December 4,
2015, www.washingtonpost.com/opinions/the-post-drops-the-mike
--and-the-hyphen-in-e-mail/2015/12/04/ccd6e33a-98fa-11e5
-8917-653b65c809eb_story.html; John E. McIntyre, "There They Go
Again," *The Baltimore Sun,* December 7, 2015, www.baltimoresun
.com/opinion/columnists/mcintyre/bal-there-they-go-again
-20151207-story.html; Arika Okrent, "The Washington Post Style
Guide Now Accepts Singular They," *Mental Floss,* December 9, 2015,
www.mentalfloss.com/article/72262/washington-post-style-guide
-now-accepts-singular-they.

145 **recent historical research**   Mark Balhorn, "The Rise of Epicene *They*," *Journal of English Linguistics* 32, no. 2 (2004): 79–104; Curzan, *Gender Shifts in the History of English*, 58–82.

145 **contemporary grammar by a woman**   Ann Fisher, *A New Grammar*, 2nd ed. (Newcastle upon Tyne, 1750).

145 **Murray presents a sentence**   Murray, *English Grammar*, 96.

145 **had become such common sense**   William Strunk, Jr., and E. B. White, *Elements of Style*, 3rd ed. (Boston: Pearson, 1979), 60. This was revised by the fourth edition, published in 2000, which reads, "The use of *he* as a pronoun for nouns embracing both genders is a simple, practical convention rooted in the beginnings of the English language. Currently, however, many writers find the use of the generic *he* or *his* to rename indefinite antecedents limiting or offensive" (60).

146 **in their widely used book**   Andrea Lunsford and Robert Connors, *The Everyday Writer* (Boston: St. Martin's Press, 1997), 141.

146 **many new generic pronouns suggested**   Dennis Baron has done pioneering work on the history of invented pronouns and the singular generic pronoun question in general. His most recent book-length treatment: Dennis E. Baron, *What's Your Pronoun?: Beyond He and She* (New York: W. W. Norton, 2020). See also Dennis E. Baron, "The Epicene Pronoun: The Word That Failed," *American Speech* 56, no. 2 (1981): 83–97.

CHAPTER 19. FOR WHO(M) THE BELL TOLLS

154 **notes how common it is to hear phrasing**   Joseph Priestley, *The Rudiments of English Grammar, Adapted to the Use of Schools; With Notes and Observations for the Use of Those Who Have Made Some Proficiency in the Language* (London: T. Becket and P. A.De Hondt, 1768), 107.

CHAPTER 20. BETWEEN YOU AND ME/I/MYSELF

157 **"All debts are clear'd"**   Shakespeare, *The Merchant of Venice*, act 3, scene 2.

157 **"you haue seene *Cassio*"**   Shakespeare, *Othello*, act 4, scene 2.

158 **"Are ye fantasticall"**   Shakespeare, *Macbeth*, act 1, scene 3.

158 **"I do beseech yee"**   Shakespeare, *Julius Caesar*, act 3, scene 1.

160 **a notably descriptive approach**   Priestley, *Rudiments of English Grammar*, 102–3.

160 **material from a 2003 study**   Philipp S. Angermeyer and John Victor Singler, "The Case for Politeness: Pronoun Variation in Co-Ordinate

NPs in Object Position in English," *Language Variation and Change* 15, no. 2 (2003): 171–209.

CHAPTER 21. NONE IS/ARE CONFUSING

167 **highly prescriptive, best-selling grammar book**   Murray, *English Grammar*, 35.

168 **others were pushing back**   J. Lesslie Hall, *English Usage: Studies in the History and Uses of English Words and Phrases* (Chicago: Scott, Foresman, 1917), 179; Thomas Lounsbury, *The Standard of English Usage* (New York: Harper and Brothers, 1908), 162.

168 **distinguishes between *none***   Garner, *Garner's Modern English Usage*, 749.

171 **showed that existential *there* constructions**   William J. Crawford, "Verb Agreement and Disagreement: A Corpus Investigation of Concord Variation in Existential *There + Be* Constructions," *Journal of English Linguistics* 33, no. 1 (2005): 35–61.

CHAPTER 22. *WHICH*-HUNTING

178 **We can trace the prescription back**   Fowler and Fowler, *King's English* (1908), 80.

179 **what would be best usage**   Fowler, *Dictionary of Modern English Usage*, 634–35.

180 **version of the "rule"**   Strunk and White, *Elements of Style*, 3rd ed., 59.

180 **makes no exceptions**   Darrell Christian, David Minthorn, and Sally A. Jacobsen, eds., *The Associated Press Stylebook 2012*, 47th ed. (New York: Associated Press, 2012), 259.

180 **strong stance on this historical jumble**   Garner, *Garner's Modern English Usage*, 1086.

CHAPTER 23. COMMAS, COMMAS, AND COMMAS

185 **according to a study in 1987**   Charles Meyer, *A Linguistic Study of American Punctuation* (New York: P. Lang, 1987).

186 **let's turn to early Roman antiquity**   For an excellent history of punctuation, see M. B. Parkes, *Pause and Effect: An Introduction to the History of Punctuation in the West* (Berkeley: University of California Press, 1993). See also David Crystal, *Making a Point: The Persnickety Story of English Punctuation* (New York: St. Martin's Press, 2015).

187 **a watershed moment for punctuation**   The landmark history of the printing press is Elizabeth L. Eisenstein, *The Printing Press as an Agent of Change* (Cambridge: Cambridge University Press, 1980).

196 **Bishop Lowth's wise words**   Lowth, *Short Introduction to English Grammar*, 169.

CHAPTER 24. ROLLING STOPS WITH SEMICOLONS

198 **writes evocatively about the semicolon**   Lewis Thomas, "Notes on Punctuation," in *The Medusa and the Snail: More Notes of a Biology Watcher* (1979), available at www-personal.umich.edu/~jlawler /punctuation.html.

199 **divided a compound sentence**   Murray, *English Grammar*, 166.

202 **wrote an article about it with Lizzie Hutton**   Lizzie Hutton and Anne Curzan, "The Grammatical Status of *However*," *Journal of English Linguistics* 47, no. 1 (2019): 29–54.

203 **the now-classic 1959 first edition**   William Strunk, Jr., and E. B. White, *The Elements of Style*, 1st ed. (New York: Macmillan, 1959), 39.

203 **more recently has called**   Garner, *Garner's Modern English Usage*, 554.

CHAPTER 25. THE WILD WEST OF DASHES AND HYPHENS

207 **"He had done nothing"** George Eliot, *Middlemarch* (Edinburgh: William Blackwood and Sons, 1872).

208 **delightful description of a semicolon**   Richard Hodges, *The English Primrose* (1644; Menston, England: Scolar Press, 1969), N3.

208 **"the most unpredictable of marks"**   Crystal, *Making a Point*, 260.

210fn **The construction *try and***   Charlotte Hommerberg and Gunnel Tottie, "*Try to* or *Try and*? Verb Complementation in British and American English," *ICAME Journal* 31 (2007): 45–64.

CHAPTER 26. WHEN IT'S *ITS* AND OTHER APOSTROPHE CONUNDRUMS

216 **the possessive of singular nouns**   Strunk and White, *Elements of Style*, 4th ed., 1.

216 **defers to this tradition**   Garner, *Garner's Modern English Usage*, 854.

217 **Apostrophe Protection Society**   www.apostrophe.org.uk/.

218 **Kill the Apostrophe website**   www.killtheapostrophe.com/.

218 **famously and eloquently disliked the apostrophe**   George Bernard Shaw, "Notes on the Clarendon Press Rules for Compositors and Readers," *The Author* 12 (April 1902): 171–72.

CHAPTER 27. BEQUEATHING CAPITAL LETTERS

225 **points out the contradiction**   Garner, *Garner's Modern English Usage,* 179.

CHAPTER 28. TO BOLDLY SPLIT INFINITIVES

231 **the original catchphrase**   The catchphrase was later revised to "To boldly go where no one has gone before."

233 **the first published criticism of the split infinitive**   "To Boldly Go: *Star Trek* and the Split Infinitive," Merriam-Webster Usage Notes, www.merriam-webster.com/words-at-play/to-boldly-split-infinitives.

233 **an anonymous letter to the editor**   Richard W. Bailey, "Talking About Split Infinitives," *Michigan Today,* June 2006, deepblue.lib .umich.edu/bitstream/handle/2027.42/62004/words.html.

233 **the rationale for the rule**   Moisés D. Perales-Escudero, "To Split or to Not Split: The Split Infinitive Past and Present," *Journal of English Linguistics* 39, no. 4 (2011): 313–34.

233 **categorized split infinitives**   Fowler, *Dictionary of Modern English Usage,* 177, 586.

233 **creates the category**   Garner, *Garner's Modern English Usage,* 1030.

234 **there may be prosodic factors**   David Crystal, *The Fight for English: How Language Pundits Ate, Shot, and Left* (Oxford: Oxford University Press, 2007), 126.

235 **Linguist Steven Pinker speculated**   Steven Pinker, "Oaf of Office," *The New York Times,* January 21, 2009, www.nytimes.com/2009/01 /22/opinion/22pinker.html.

CHAPTER 29. PREPOSITIONS NOT TO END A SENTENCE WITH

238fn **interesting post on the blog *Language Log***   Mark Liberman, "Where We're At," *Language Log,* April 12, 2012, languagelog.ldc .upenn.edu/nll/?p=4125.

240 **Dryden picked out for critique**   Quoted in *Merriam-Webster's Concise Dictionary of English Usage,* 609.

241 **Bishop Lowth's opinion on the construction**   Lowth, *Short Introduction to English Grammar,* 127–28.

242 **unstranded Lowth's preposition**   Murray, *English Grammar,* 122.

242 **we must have a good ear**   Strunk and White, *Elements of Style,* 4th ed., 77–78.

244 **we don't have evidence**   Ben Zimmer, "A Misattribution No Longer to Be Put Up With," *Language Log,* December 12, 2004, itre.cis.upenn

.edu/~myl/languagelog/archives/001715.html (originally posted on alt
.usage.english).

CHAPTER 30. WHEN *AND* CAN START A SENTENCE

247 **1993 interview with David Letterman**   Retrieved from the Corpus of
Contemporary American English.

247 **2014 interview with Edie Falco**   Ibid.

248 **This passage is from the year 893**   Punctuation is modern; quoted in
Millward and Hayes, *Biography of the English Language,* 117–18.

250 **Discourse markers are those little words**   For more discussion of the
dynamics of conversation, including discourse markers and pauses,
see Enfield, *How We Talk.* Readers might also enjoy Michael Erard,
Um: Slips, Stumbles, and Verbal Blunders, and What They Mean
(New York: Pantheon Books, 2007).

251 **what is being called "backstory *so*"**   Syelle Graves, *New Use of an
Old Discourse Marker: The Interface of Implicit Attitudes, Explicit
Attitudes, and Rapid Language Change of "So"* (Ph.D. diss., Gradu-
ate Center, City University of New York, September 2018).

CHAPTER 32. PASSIVES WERE CORRECTED

261 **it was far from celebratory**   Geoff Pullum, "50 Years of Stupid Grammar Advice," *The Chronicle of Higher Education,* April 17, 2009,
www.chronicle.com/article/50-years-of-stupid-grammar-advice/.

261 **The relevant section**   Strunk and White, *Elements of Style,* 4th ed.,
18–19. This advice remains largely unchanged edition to edition.

269 **Here is the passage**   Jinhong Luo and Lutz Wiegrebe, "Biomechanical Control of Vocal Plasticity in the Echolocating Bat," *Journal of
Experimental Biology* 219, no. 6 (2016): 878–86.

269 **the history of scientific writing**   Dwight Atkinson, *Scientific Discourse in Sociohistorical Context: The Philosophical Transactions of
the Royal Society of London, 1675–1975* (Mahwah, N.J.: Lawrence
Erlbaum, 1999).

272 **criticizing the passive progressive**   George P. Marsh, *Lectures on the
English Language* (London: John Murray, 1863), 461.

272 **many allies in this war**   David Booth, *An Analytical Dictionary of
the English Language* (London: J. and C. Adlard, 1830); White,
Words and Their Uses.

CHAPTER 33. WHY WRITING DOESN'T "FLOW"

279   **"A new study—conducted by Mueller and Oppenheimer"**   Robinson Meyer, "To Remember a Lecture Better, Take Notes by Hand," *The Atlantic,* May 2014, www.theatlantic.com/technology/archive/2014/05/to-remember-a-lecture-better-take-notes-by-hand/361478/.

280   **three general methods**   For more on the known-new contract, see Martha Kolln and Loretta Gray, *Rhetorical Grammar: Grammatical Choices, Rhetorical Effects,* 7th ed. (Boston: Pearson, 2013), 86–90. For a pedagogically oriented presentation of the methods for creating cohesion between sentences, see David Brown, *In Other Words: Lessons on Grammar, Code-Switching, and Academic Writing* (Portsmouth, N.H.: Heinemann, 2009), 91–93.

282   **This piece of advice**   George Gopen and Judith Swan, "The Science of Scientific Writing," *American Scientist* 78 (1990): 550–58.

EPILOGUE. NAVIGATING GRAMMANDOS AND GOOD SENSE

285   **a few years ago I wrote a post**   Anne Curzan, "This Rule I Learned and Then Unlearned," *The Chronicle of Higher Education,* September 5, 2016, www.chronicle.com/blogs/linguafranca/this-rule-i-learned-and-then-unlearned.

286   **the students and I read an article**   John M. Swales, "Attended and Unattended 'this' in Academic Writing: A Long and Unfinished Story," *ESP Malaysia* 11 (2005): 1–15.

286   **if it's a typo**   For an interesting study on how readers respond to typos and grammos, see Julie E. Boland and Robin Queen, "If You're House Is Still Available, Send Me an Email: Personality Influences Reactions to Written Errors in Email Message," PLoS ONE 11, no. 3 (2016): e0149885, doi.org/10.1371/journal.pone.0149885.

index

about the author

ANNE CURZAN is the Geneva Smitherman Collegiate Professor of English, Linguistics, and Education and an Arthur F. Thurnau Professor at the University of Michigan, where she also currently serves as the dean of the College of Literature, Science, and the Arts.